ISR 37

Interdisciplinary Systems Research
Interdisziplinäre Systemforschung

Hartmut Bossel
(editor)

Concepts and Tools of Computer-assisted Policy Analysis

Vol. 2 Causal Systems Analysis

1977 Birkhäuser Verlag, Basel und Stuttgart

CIP-Kurztitelaufnahme der Deutschen Bibliothek

Concepts and tools of computer-assisted policy analysis/
Hartmut Bossel (ed.). – Basel, Stuttgart:
Birkhäuser.
Vol. 2. Causal systems analysis. – 1. Aufl. – 1977.
(Interdisciplinary systems research; 37)
ISBN 3-7643-0922-9

NE: Bossel, Hartmut [Hrsg.]

CONTENTS

Vol.2 Computer Tools for the Analysis of Material Systems

CONSTRUCTION OF DYNAMIC SYSTEM MODELS USING INTERACTIVE COMPUTER GRAPHICS

Walter Hudetz

SURVEY

The construction of system models and their simulation on digital computers has been an important part of systems analysis in the physical sciences for several years now. More recently this method is also being used in the social and life sciences. To simplify and accelerate the simulation process, dynamic simulation programs were developed. Improvements and price reductions in computer peripheral hardware now enable widespread use of interactive graphic terminals. This in turn has initiated work on a new generation of simulation software which takes advantage of the improved man-machine communication made possible through the use of interactive graphic man-machine interfaces.

The following article describes such a new simulation method GRIPS (Graphic Interactive Programming System). GRIPS enables the user to construct a block diagram of his model on an interactive video-terminal with the help of a light pen. The program then requests interactively all necessary information such as model parameters and initial conditions. After the system responses have been computed by the program, the user may choose among several forms of output. If requested, GRIPS will provide the user with a complete FORTRAN program of the simulation model, which can be compiled and executed on any computer with a FORTRAN IV compiler. GRIPS is a structured-data program, written entirely in FORTRAN IV and thus portable. It is highly modular and can be changed to accommodate additional features. GRIPS has been developed on a minicomputer with 28K words memory, magnetic disk, and an interactive graphic video display with light pen. Segmented into several overlays it requires only about 18K words of actual memory.

1. INTRODUCTION: CONSTRUCTION OF SIMULATION MODELS

To develop a computer model of a dynamic system, the model builder commonly goes through the following steps:

1 - Definition of the problem
2 - Construction of a block diagram of the model
3 - Mathematical description of the model

4 - Programming the mathematical model
5 - Testing and validation of the model
6 - Execution of simulation runs and analysis of results.

Step 4 involves the development of a computer program. In the early days of digital computers this meant the coding of the model equations in machine or assembly language, which proved to be very time-consuming and in general required a skillful programmer. With the development of higher level computer languages such as FORTRAN the coding task was simplified and many model builders now could do their own programming. To further reduce and simplify the programming effort, problem-oriented languages were created. These languages aim at helping the user in solving a limited class of problems, in particular the simulation of dynamic systems on a digital computer. The most widely used continuous dynamic system simulation languages are CSMP[1] (IBM Computers), DYNAMO[2] (implemented on several computer makes), and CSSL[3] (CDC computers). Some of the better known simulation languages for discrete systems are GPSS[4] , SIMSCRIPT[5], and SIMULA[6].

Initially written for batch processing, some of these languages have been expanded for interactive use. The above languages were almost exclusively developed for large general purpose computers and require a considerable amount of core memory. The steady increase in computing power together with improvements in software of minicomputers has made them more attractive for simulation use. A small number of continuous system simulation languages have lately been written for minis such as ISL-8[7] and DARE II[8].

Dynamic system languages were originally developed for the simulation of analog computers on a digital computer. The analog computer was then used quite extensively for the simulation of continuous dynamic physical systems. Programming in many simulation languages still resembles the way analog computers are programmed. There are five basic steps involved in preparing a simulation using such a language:

1 - A block diagram of the model is developed using the describing equations as a basis. Blocks for various functions and system elements are used, e.g. integrators, adders, function generators, etc.

2 - Depending on the language, the block diagram is coded for the computer using either tabular form or descriptive statements similar to FORTRAN notation.

3 - Parameters and initial conditions are input in a specified format.

4 - Run-time information such as integration interval, total run-time, and, if implemented, error bounds and integration method are specified.

5 - Output variables, form, and medium are fixed.

Usi ng a batch oriented language, coding is commonly done on paper cards and output is received on a printer or plotter. Batch processing implies that the user will have to wait some time until the results of his simulation will be available. This can seriously slow down the model construction stage. With the increasing popularity of time-sharing, interactive versions of problem-oriented languages were developed. These languages allow the user to input his model structure, data, etc. directly to the computer using either a teletype or an alphanumeric video terminal. Output from the simulation run is now sent immediately to the teletype printer or screen as it becomes available from the computer. Turn-around time is thus cut significantly and model development speeded up considerably.

With increasing availability of graphic terminals, the use of simulation languages can be further simplified and the man-machine interaction improved. A few simulation languages were developed that make use of special graphic terminals (see BIOMOD[9]) to allow the user great flexibility in specifying the model structure at the expense of special terminal hardware and large computer memory requirements. The following pages describe a new continuous dynamic simulation language which makes extensive use of a standard, commercially available graphic video terminal with light pen. The light pen is used to construct the model structure on the screen and the simulation results are also shown graphically on the refresh type screen. Part two gives a brief outline of the structure of GRIPS and the logical flow of information through the program. Next a more detailed description of how a model is developed using GRIPS is presented. In appendix A the use of GRIPS is illustrated with an example. A summary of GRIPS elements as well as restrictions currently in effect are enumerated in appendix B.

2. GRIPS STRUCTURE AND LOGICAL FLOW OF INFORMATION

Structure

GRIPS was developed to provide the model builder with an easy-to-use tool to simulate continuous dynamic systems. The program is coded entirely in FORTRAN IV and implemented on a PDP 11/40 minicomputer. Running under the RT-11 operating system in several overlays,GRIPS needs about 18K words of core memory and as back-up memory a disk cartridge. Total size of GRIPS is about 42K words. The man-machine communication is carried out using a standard teletype or DEC writer and an interactive graphic screen with light pen (DEC-GT/44). The program is data-structure oriented, i.e. data arrays are manipulated when carrying out various simulations. No translation or linking is necessary.

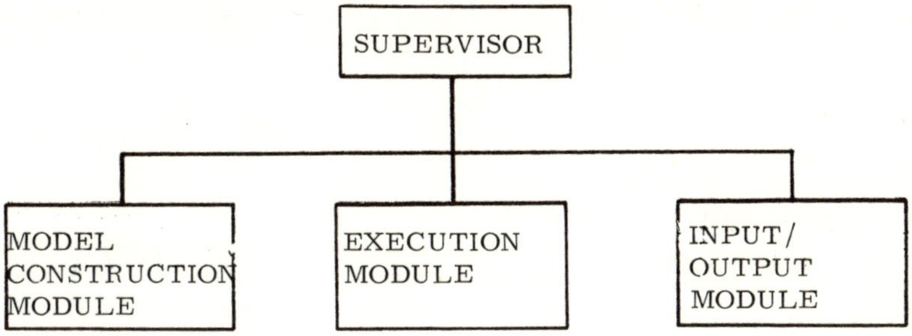

Fig. 1 - GRIPS Structure

As can be seen in Fig. 1, GRIPS consists of three basic modules and a supervisory program.

I. The supervisor controls and sequences the execution of GRIPS by coordinating between the other modules and subprograms.

II. The model construction module contains the necessary routines to interactively define the model structure and specify its parameters.

III. The execution module carries out the actual simulation.

IV. The input/output module processes the simulation results for output on the screen (graphical form) or printer and handles additional input or output required by the supervisor.

Being modular in design GRIPS allows easy adaptation of special integration routines or additional output forms. A number of display files are used by the program for presenting information on the screen. For each simulation GRIPS will create on disk three files for future use:

1 - A display file of the block diagram drawn by the user.

2 - A sequential file containing structural connections and parameters of the model represented by the block diagram.

3 - A random access file with the results of the simulation run as requested by the user for the above model.

Logical Flow of Information

The logical flow through the program is shown in Fig. 2 below. The supervisor module controls the sequence of events. However, the user has the possibility to influence this sequence at certain points in the program. After starting GRIPS the user may choose among several alternatives such as constructing a new model or running a previously developed one (block 1 in Fig. 2). Once the construction of the block diagram is finished, the program requests the model parameters and initial conditions, as well as the specification of the exogenous variables (system inputs),if any (blocks 3, 4, 5 in Fig. 2). The structure of the block diagram can now be stored on disk together with the chosen parameters, initial conditions and exogenous variables for future use.

The computational part is initiated by first specifying the run time information such as the integration interval (block 8 in Fig. 2). As there is no need for compilation or linking, the actual simulation is only dependent on the computational time required by the program. The user should choose the variables he wishes to observe after the simulation run so that only a selected number of the computed variables are stored on disk for output after the run.

After the simulation run the output form and the variables to be output are selected by the user (part 11 in Fig. 2). Only up to five variables can be observed at one time. However, this process can be repeated as often as desired. Previous model runs with perhaps different parameters can be displayed together with the current results. If there is no more output desired, the user may select to stop the program or he can choose among several alternatives such as changing parameters or structure of the model.

3. MODEL CONSTRUCTION PHILOSOPHY

Models can be of many kinds. We shall limit our discussion to continuous dynamic models. The development of the model of a given system can be divided broadly into two subtasks: obtaining the model structure and supplying the data. These two tasks are closely interwoven, one depending on the other. The structure of a dynamic model consists of three components:

1. Indicators which can be measured and reveal the state of the system - called state variables.

2. Relationships or interconnections between the indicators.

3. The environment, acting on the initial state of a system and its exogenous quantities.

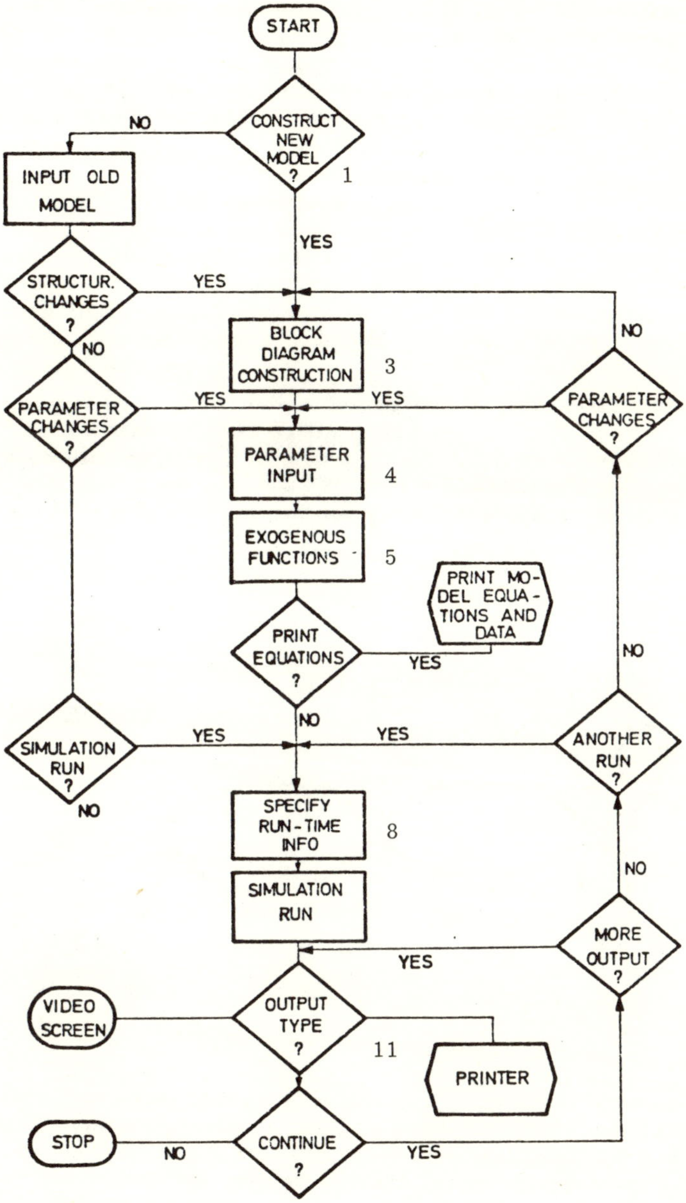

Fig. 2: Logical flow diagram of GRIPS

State variables can be considered to represent some sort of levels or reservoirs. These levels can be people, goods or information, for example. To obtain the model structure it is convenient to start with the conceptual framework which can be best described by a causal-diagram representing graphically the components of the system and their causal interdependence.

Consider a predator-prey system, for example moose and wolves. The more moose exist (their number is limited by the carrying capacity of the piece of land they occupy), the more food is available for the wolves, and their population will increase. But as the wolf population increases, more moose will be eaten, thus negatively influencing the moose population, with the corresponding effect on the wolf population. This description of the wolf/moose system is first translated into the causal loop diagram of Fig. 3.

This diagram presents the conceptual model of the two species prey-predator relationship. The arrows with positive sign indicate a positive (i. e. increasing) influence on the respective quantity, arrows with negative sign have a negative (decreasing) effect. We see that the moose contribute to the wolves' population (biomass) whereas the opposite is true in the reverse case.

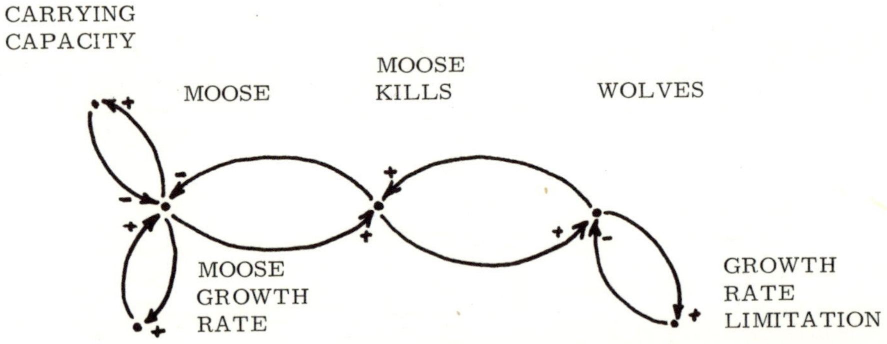

Fig. 3: Causal diagram of a predator-prey model

From the causal diagram of a model it is a relatively small step to produce a block diagram which will show in a more systematic way the structure of a model and the functional relationships. The block diagram should clearly distinguish between the model state variables, the exogenous quantities, and the functional connections. Employing the symbols of GRIPS, the predator-prey model of Fig. 3 can be described in a block diagram form as shown in Fig. 4. The blocks labelled S represent the state variables of the system. We need two of these blocks, one for the moose and the other for the wolves.

The functional relationships are shown partly as elements with the F labels and partly as connecting paths or feedback loops. Thus the growth rate effects of the two species are represented by the two feedback loops (No. 1 and No. 8). The moose kills on the other hand are given by the F_1 block. For an analysis of the model a mathematical description is in most cases necessary.

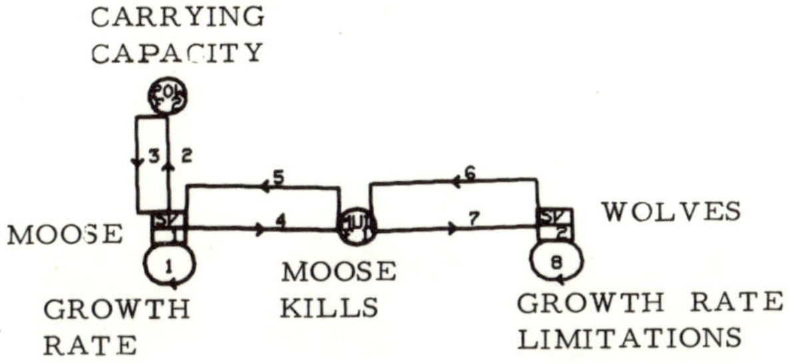

Fig. 4: Block diagram of predator-prey model

The block diagram forms the basis for developing the set of equations describing the model. For continuous dynamic systems these equations can always be represented as a set of (generally nonlinear) first order differential equations of the form:

$$\frac{dx_1}{dt} = f_1 (x_1, x_2, \ldots x_n, p_1, p_2, \ldots p_m, u_1, u_2, \ldots u_l, t)$$

$$\frac{dx_2}{dt} = f_2 (x_1, x_2, \ldots x_n, p_1, p_2, \ldots p_m, u_1, u_2, \ldots u_l, t) \qquad (1)$$

$$\frac{dx_n}{dt} = f_n (x_1, x_2, \ldots x_n, p_1, p_2, \ldots p_m, u_1, u_2, \ldots u_l, t)$$

Here x_i are the state variables, p_i are the system parameters, u_i are the inputs to the system (exogenous variables), t is the independent variable time, and f_i are functions representing the structural interconnections. The left side of Eqs. 1 represents the rate of change of the state variables.

Associated with the state variable blocks in Fig. 4 is integration w. r. t. time. If we assume that at the input of an S-block we have the rate of change of a state variable, then the output will be the value of the state variable as a function of time. If we furthermore associate with each branch in Fig. 4 a constant coefficient multiplier we can write the system equation of the predator-prey model directly from the block diagram as:

$$\frac{dS_1}{dt} = p_1 S_1 + p_3 F_2 + p_5 F_1$$

$$\frac{dS_2}{dt} = p_8 S_2 + p_7 F_1 \qquad (2)$$

with

$$F_1 = f_1 (p_4 S_1, p_6 S_2)$$
$$F_2 = f_2 (p_2 S_1) \qquad (3)$$

Substituting Eqs.3 into Eqs.2 we get

$$\frac{dS_1}{dt} = p_1 S_1 + p_3 f_2 (p_2 S_1) + p_5 f_1 (p_4 S_1, p_6 S_2) \qquad (4)$$

$$\frac{dS_2}{dt} = p_8 S_2 + p_7 f_1 (p_4 S_1, p_6 S_2)$$

The functions f_1 and f_2 are still to be specified by the model builder.

The solution to Eq. 4 represents the system behavior or response. In all but the most simple cases, the system equations cannot be solved analytically and computer methods have to be employed. There exist a number of algorithms for solving ordinary differential equations on a digital computer[10]. They all involve a discretization of the time axis into a number of usually evenly spaced increments (see Fig. 5). To illustrate a simple method of obtaining an approximate solution of a differential equation, let us consider the following equation

$$\frac{dx}{dt} = f(x, t) \qquad (5)$$

The curve x(t) in Fig. 5 represents the true solution of Eq. 5, i.e. it describes the behavior of the state variable x as a function of time. If we start at t = o with a known value (initial condition) of x, we can get the value of x at $t = \Delta t$ using the equation

$$x/_{t = \Delta t} = x/_{t = o} + \Delta t \cdot \frac{dx}{dt}/_{t = o} \qquad (6)$$

We can generalize Eq. 6 for the computation of x at some time t and also using Eq. 5 we get

$$x/_{t} = x/_{t - \Delta t} + \Delta t \cdot f(x, t)/_{t - \Delta t} \qquad (7)$$

Eq. 7 represents a simple recursive algorithm for obtaining the solution to a first order differential equation. This method,also called Euler's method can be used repeatedly to solve numerically a set of differential equations.

One should realize by looking at Fig. 5, that the values of x thus calculated are only approximate, i.e. an error ϵ (called the truncation error) is introduced at each step. This error can accumulate to produce a possibly false solution. It can be shown[11] that the truncation error ϵ in above method is proportional to the step size Δt. There is another error inherent in computations using digital computers. Due to the finite word size of computers, a fixed number of digits are used in mathematical operations. The round-off error introduced during multiplication, for example, can be compounded and with many operations (required if Δt is small) this error can become significant. Selecting a small Δt will reduce the truncation error but may produce a non-negligible round-off. Thus the choice of Δt is important and not always easy to make. There exist a number of more complex algorithms[11] which provide a more accurate solution at the expense of additional memory requirements and computational speed. GRIPS currently uses Euler's method, however, more sophisticated algorithms can be added, if desired.

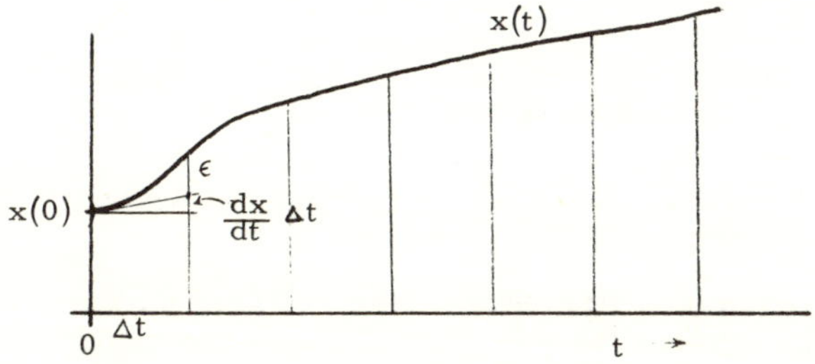

Fig. 5: Integration interval and truncation error

The program GRIPS is designed to assist the model builder in the development of his model and subsequent simulation on the digital computer. The GRIPS concept of model construction follows the procedure outlined above, whereby the model builder first develops his conceptual model in form of a causal-diagram and then uses GRIPS to continue from there. The discussion of a detailed example of model construction and simulation with GRIPS given in the next section should help to clarify this technique.

4. MODEL CONSTRUCTION PROCEDURE: AN EXAMPLE

Let us consider again the predator-prey ecosystem mentioned in the previous section. The prey species are taken to be moose, the predators are wolves. To model this system we have to determine the interaction of these two populations. The interaction between the moose and the wolves is of course that of predation - moose are killed and eaten by wolves. The biomass of the wolves will increase if more prey are killed which in turn will decrease the moose population and reduce their biomass. But the reduction of the moose population will decrease the potential food source of the wolves, and with less food available the wolves population will also tend to decrease. This in turn will initiate an increase in the moose population ... and so on.

Besides being effected by the predation of the wolves, the moose population will also depend on the availability of food or the carrying capacity of the niche they occupy, and of course, their own intrinsic growth rate. The wolves biomass will be controlled by their predation rate, the availability of prey, and their intrinsic growth rate. The conceptual model of the predator-prey behavior has already been described by the causal diagram in Fig. 3. It should be pointed out that this model is a rather simplified abstraction of the real system.

Utilizing above system description the predator-prey model can be developed and run on the computer by following the six steps described below.

(1) Block diagram construction
(2) Specification of parameters and initial conditions
(3) Specification of exogenous variables
(4) Setting the integration interval, total run-time, and output increment
(5) Specification of computed variables to be observed
(6) Output of results

Block Diagram Construction

To develop a block diagram one first selects the required blocks from the menu displayed on the screen (see Fig. 6) and places them on the screen using the light pen. One best starts with the state variables of the system which are represented by the S-block. For the predator-prey model we need two S-blocks. The output of S1 represents the prey (moose) population whereas the output of S2 stands for the predator (wolves) population. It should be pointed out that S1 and S2 are measured as biomass of the respective species.

From the causal diagram we see that the model contains a number of auxiliary quantities which depend on and influence the two state variables. Two of these, the intrinsic growth rates, are represented by direct feedback loops. The moose kills and the predation rate can be combined and represented by a functional block (F-block). The moose carrying capacity enters the model in a nonlinear form and is thus also represented by an F-block. The blocks so required are positioned on the screen as shown in Fig. 6.

To indicate the structural connection of the system variables, the blocks are joined by directed paths (lines). To improve the pictorial representation three path types are available for interconnection (see Fig. 7).

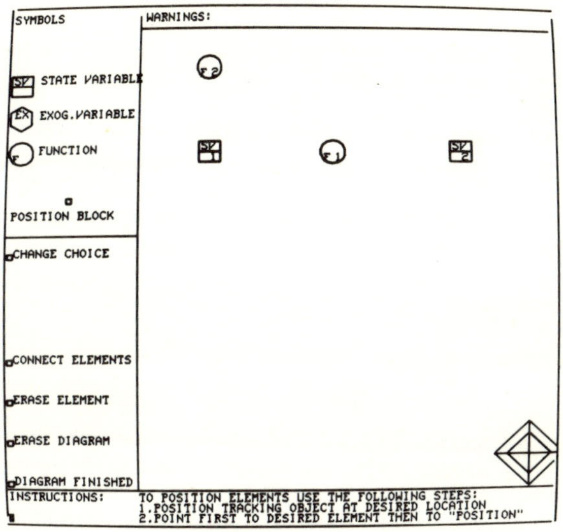

Fig. 6: Selection of the model elements

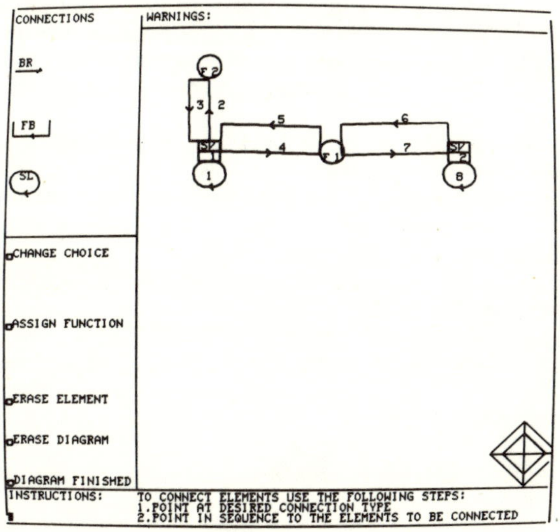

Fig. 7: Connection of the elements

(I) Direct path - this type is used to provide a straight connection between two blocks (variables).

(II) Feedback path - it is employed to accentuate a feedback connection between two blocks.

(III) Self-loop path - as implied by its name it provides a means to indicate a connection from the output of a block to its own input.

With each of the above paths there is associated a constant multiplier. All three paths have the same functional significance

$x \longrightarrow y$ implies $y = px$

where p is a constant which can represent a model parameter to be specified by the user.

The intrinsic growth rates, that is their time constants, are assigned to feedback loops (self-loops) as already mentioned. The values of these time constants are specified by the p multiplier of the respective self-loops. The connections between the model elements are made according to the functional dependence illustrated in the causal diagram. Care has to be exercised to choose the correct direction of each path as this indicates the causal flow direction of the quantities involved.

Once the blocks have been connected, the operators of the functional blocks are choosen (see Fig. 8). A list of the built-in functions or operations is given in appendix B. Some of these operations such as division require an additional specification (in this case the dividend). This is accomplished by pointing with the light pen at the incoming branch representing the dividend.

The amount of moose killed by the wolves and consequently eaten is a function of prey availability (moose population) and the wolves population itself. Following Volterra's equation [12] we assume this function to be related to the product of the two populations. That is the amount of moose lost to the wolves will be given as

$$\text{moose biomass lost} = c \cdot S1 \cdot S2 \qquad (8)$$

Similarly the gain in wolves biomass due to predation will be assumed as

$$\text{wolves biomass gained} = c' \cdot S1 \cdot S2 \qquad (9)$$

The constants c and c' are coefficients specific to the predation and consumption habits of the wolves.

The F1-block will thus serve as a multiplier, the coefficients c and c' will be assigned to the paths originating at F1 and terminating at the respective S-blocks. The carrying capacity limits ultimately the moose population.

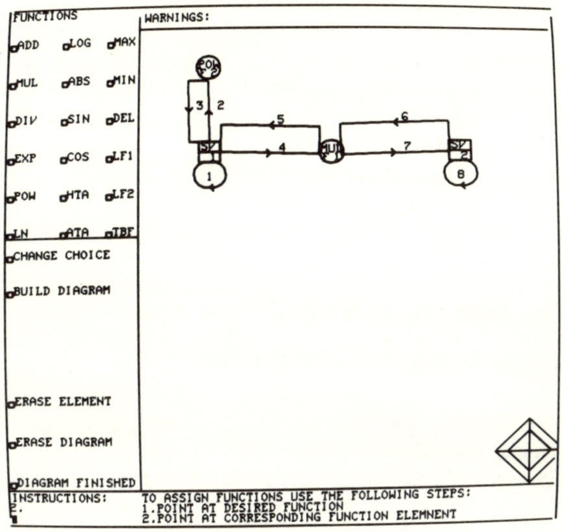

Fig. 8: Specification of the function elements

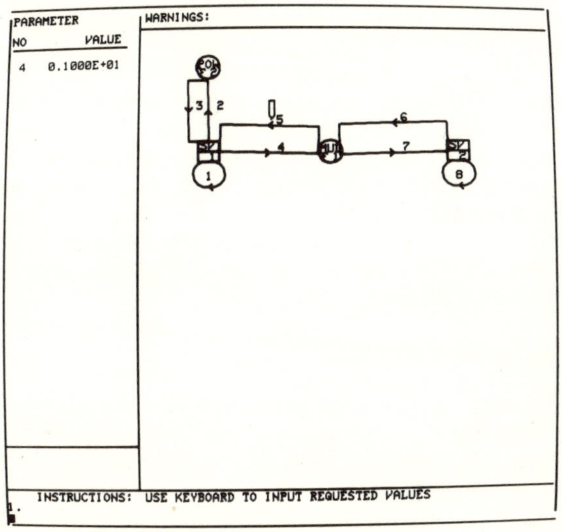

Fig. 9: Input of parameters

It is assumed that as soon as the carrying capacity is reached the moose population will stabilize at that level, i. e. we get zero growth rate in the moose biomass. This of course assumes that decimation of the moose by the wolves will not be a limiting factor. The reduction of the moose growth rate can be modelled as a quadratic term in the moose biomass with a coefficient b related to the carrying capacity, i. e. we get

$$\text{carrying capacity limitation} = b \cdot (S1)^2 \qquad (10)$$

We, therefore, select the square function for the F2-block.

At this point, the structure of the model has been specified and can be stored in the computer. Next the model data have to be furnished by the user.

Specification of Parameters and Initial Conditions

In addition to the system parameters, the initial state of the system to be modelled has to be specified. Quite often the parameters and the initial conditions are only vaguely known. However, for a computer program concrete values have to be supplied by the model builder. The program interactively requests all initial conditions and parameters from the user (see Fig. 9). Constant parameters are usually associated with the multipliers of the paths. Time-dependent parameters have to be specified using exogenous variables. In addition to the parameters and initial conditions the program at this point also requests specification of any table functions required and the delay times if delays are used. Table functions can be described using either the ordinate values of the break points or sketching the function using the light pen (see Fig. 10).

For the predator-prey model we input initial values of the moose and wolves biomass. When specifying the model parameters we have to be careful to assign unity (1.0) to all branches used but not associated with a specific model parameter. For example branch 1 represents the parameter c but branch 4 has no parameter assigned to it and its coefficient should be set to 1.0. Any mistakes made in above input to the program can be corrected right away as the program repeats all specifications and provides a means for selective changes (see Fig. 11).

Specification of Exogenous Variables

At this point the only unspecified quantities for the model description are the exogenous variables or functions. For each exogenous variable block used,the program requests the user to specify the type of function needed and the parameter required by the function selected. A list of exogenous functions available is given in appendix B (see also Fig. 12). There are no exogenous variables needed in the predator-prey model thus the program will skip this part.

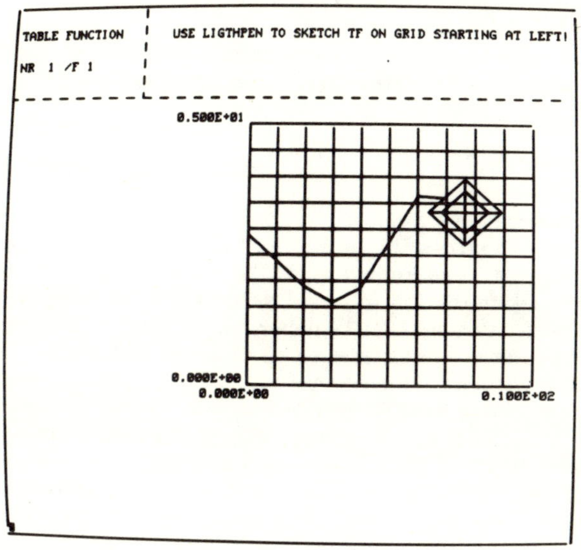

Fig. 10: Sketching of table function

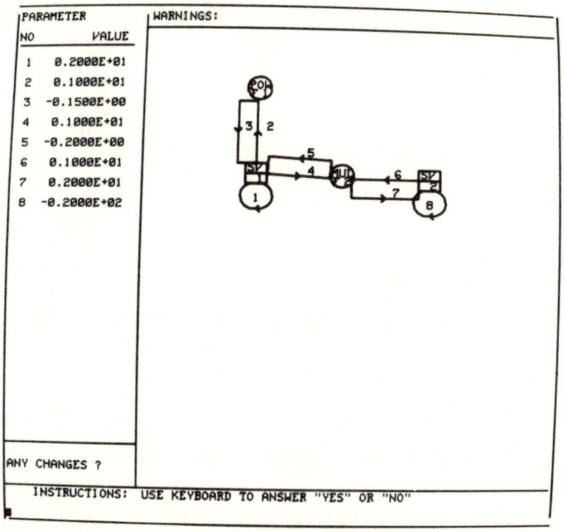

Fig. 11: Changing parameter values

With the model completely specified the user now has the option to print on the teletype the model equations (in a form given by equation 1 above), or he can just list the model parameters and initial conditions, or both. Fig. 13 contains a listing of the predator-prey equations and model data as provided by GRIPS.

Setting the Integration Interval, Total Run-time, and Output Increment

As pointed out before (see Section 3), the simulation of a dynamic system on a digital computer requires the use of numerical methods for solving the differential equations. The accuracy of the solution depends largely on the time increment or integration interval selected. The integration interval is selected as default value by GRIPS depending on the total solution time (the time span over which the user wishes to observe his model behavior). This total run-time has to be specified by the model builder. To obtain a good accuracy GRIPS chooses a small integration interval which implies that a large number of solution steps will be computed. In fact this number will be much higher than the number of points needed for actual output on either the screen or the printer. GRIPS limits the number of output points by assuming a corresponding output increment. The user may override the default conditions and specify his own choice of integration interval and/or output increment.

Specification of Computed Variables to be Observed

The program will save by default all variables computed (up to a maximum of 50) on disk for further output to the user. However, for large models the user has the option of selecting a limited number of the computed variables to be saved.

This is the last step prior to the start of computations. GRIPS now has all necessary information to carry out the simulation. The length of the simulation varies depending on the structure of the model, the integration interval, and the total model run-time. No compilation or linking has to be done prior to the simulation run.

Output of Results

After the simulation is completed the user may choose the variables to be output and the form in which the output should be presented. Output can be produced on either the screen or the printer (teletype). The output forms available are listed in Fig. 14.

Output is limited at any time to at most 5 variables, however, additional output can be requested as often as necessary. For comparison of results, output of previous simulation runs can be obtained together with the current results.

```
THE FOLLOWING TYPES OF EXOG.FUNCTIONS ARE AVAILABLE

1   DELTA FUNCTION : δ (T)

2   STEP :  U(T)

3   RAMP : U(T)*T

4   SINE WAVE : SIN(W*T+α )

5   RECTANGULAR WAVE

6   RANDOM NUMBER GENERATOR(EVEN.DISTR. BETW. 0.-1.)

7   TABLE FUNCTION (UP TO 11 BREAK OR CORNER POINTS)

8   EXPONENTIAL IN TIME (C**T)
- - - - - - - - - - - - - - - - - - - - - - - - - - - - -


CHOOSE EXOGENEOUS VARIABLE NO 1


INSTRUCTIONS:FOR EACH EXOG.VARIABLE CHOOSE THE DESIRED FUNCTION
    THEN INPUT SPECIFIED QUANTITIES (USE THE KEYBOARD) - FORMAT F1.F2.F3
```

Fig. 12: Exogeneous functions available

```
SYSTEM EQUATIONS FOR THE MODEL:PREDT      22-OCT-76
------------------------------------------------------


STATE EQUATIONS
---------------

DS 1 =   P 1*S 1 + P 3*F 1 + P 5*F 2

DS 2 =   P 7*F 2 + P 8*S 2

AUXILIARY EQUATIONS
-------------------

                       2.00
F 1 = ( P 2*S 1)

F 2 =  P 4* S 1   *   P 6* S 2

INPUTS (EXOGENOUS VARIABLES)
- -----

E 1 = T(T--0.0000)
```

Fig. 13a: Predator-prey equations produced by GRIPS

```
PARAMETERS FOR THE MODEL:PREDT       22-OCT-76
----------------------------------------------------------

 P #          VALUE

   1       0.2000E+01
   2       0.1000E+01
   3      -0.1500E+00
   4       0.1000E+01
   5      -0.2000E+00
   6       0.1000E+01
   7       0.2000E+01
   8      -0.2000E+02

INITIAL CONDITIONS
------------------

 S #          VALUE

   1       0.1000E+02
   2       0.1000E+02
```

Fig. 13b: Model parameters and initial conditions

```
   COMPUTATION TIME:      16.54 SECONDS
  YOU MAY NOW:
OUTPUT SELECTED VARIABLES:

   1. ON PRINTER (TABULAR FORM)

   2. AS TIME PLOTS ON SCREEN

   3. AS TIME PLOTS ON PRINTER

   4. AS X-Y PLOT ON SCREEN(2 VARIABLES ONLY!)

   5. NONE OF THE ABOVE

INSTRUCTIONS: INPUT NUMBER OF YOUR CHOICE
```

Fig. 14: Output options available in GRIPS

The behavior of the predator and prey biomasses is shown as a time series plot in Fig. 15. With the parameters as given in Fig. 12, the populations will settle after some initial oscillations, caused by the choice of the initial conditions, to a steady state level. If we change P1 (representing the intrinsic growth rate of the moose) from 2.0 to 1.5 we obtain an oscillating system as depicted in Fig. 16.

The response of a system can also be analysed by observing the trajectories of some of its state variables in a so-called phase plane. This involves a plot of one state variable against another as they develop in time. This type of plot is particularly useful for stability analysis. A stable system exhibiting damped oscillations for example appears as a decreasing spiral (compare Fig. 15 and Fig. 17). A phase plane plot of the moose and the wolves biomasses is shown in Fig. 17 for the original data and in Fig. 18 with the changed value of P1.

After having observed and/or recorded all desired output, the user can repeat any of the steps above. Structural or parameter changes are easily accomplished and as there is no compilation of the program, the results of any changes can be obtained in a relatively short time span. If the user decides to stop the program, all of his files will be saved for future use. This includes the output which was stored on disk.

As an additional feature, GRIPS will prepare for the user - if requested - a complete FORTRAN IV program of his model with the data supplied by the user. This FORTRAN program can be compiled and executed on a different computer or it could be combined with other programs if desired.

Making Changes

To illustrate the ease with which structural changes can be made consider the following addition to the predator-prey model. Let us assume that the availability of food for the moose is not, as initially proposed, a constant but varies according to some time-dependent patterns. We could approximate, for example, the seasonal availability of food by a sinewave with a minimum in winter and a maximum in summer. To include such a change in our model we would alter the structure of the block diagram as shown in Fig. 19. The variation of the food supply is simulated by the E1-block which is choosen to be a sinewave (Fig. 20). This change is quickly done and a simulation run of the new model results in the output shown in Fig. 21. We can see that the variation in food supply is reflected in the biomass of the moose as well as the wolves, as would be expected.

5. CONCLUSION

The development of models for the simulation of dynamic systems is a complex and time-consuming process. Simulation languages have done a great deal to reduce the programming effort. With the spread of simulation from the phy-

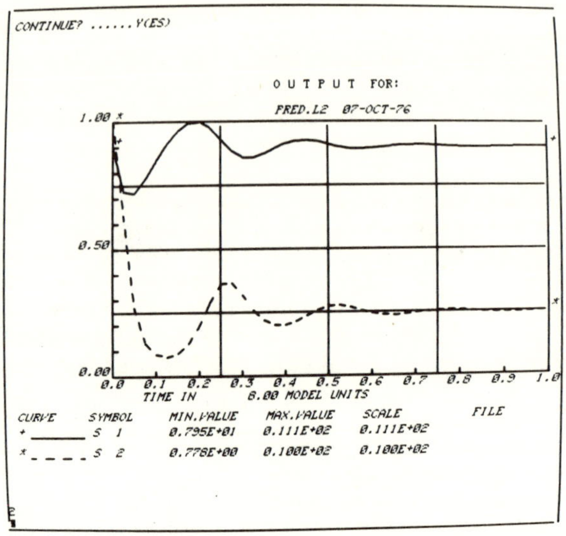

Fig. 15: Predator (S2) and prey (S1) behavior with the parameters of Fig. 13b

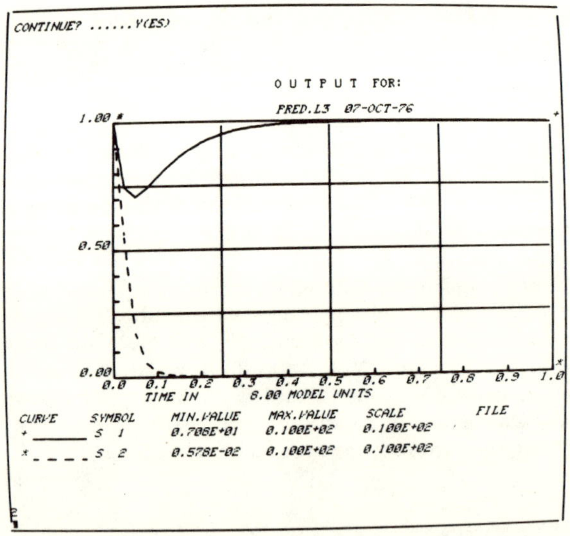

Fig. 16: Predator (S2) and prey (S1) behavior with $p_1 = 1.5$

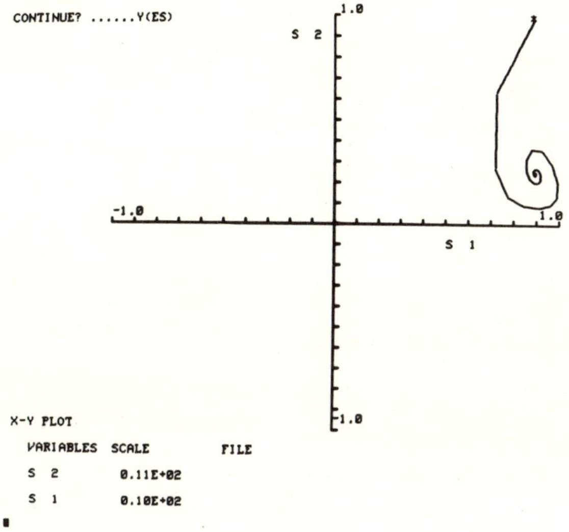

Fig. 17: Phase plane behavior of model with original parameters

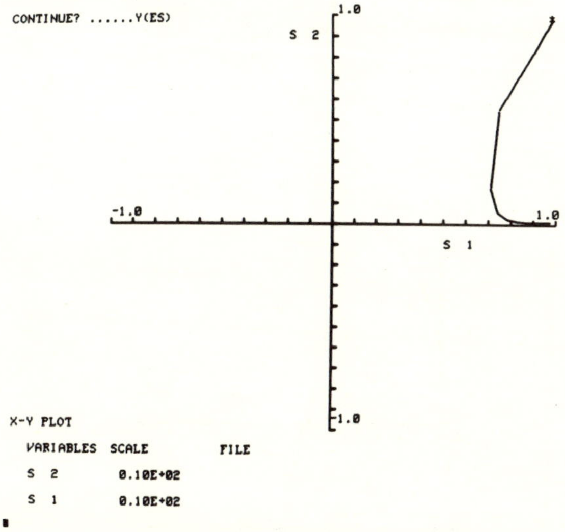

Fig. 18: Phase plane behavior of model with $p_1 = 1.5$

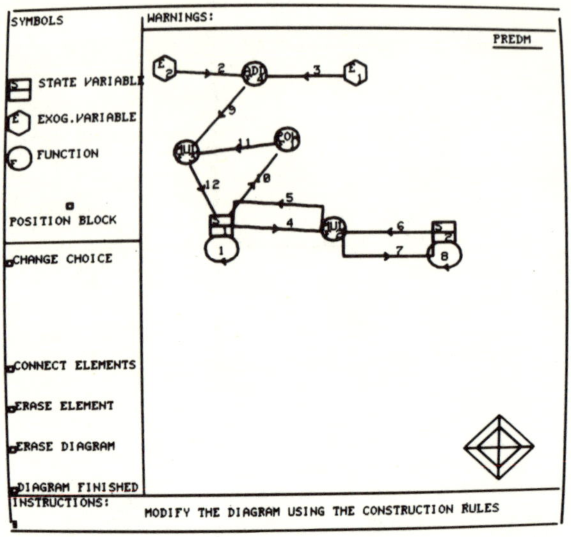

Fig. 19: Block diagram of predator-prey model with non-constant carrying capacity

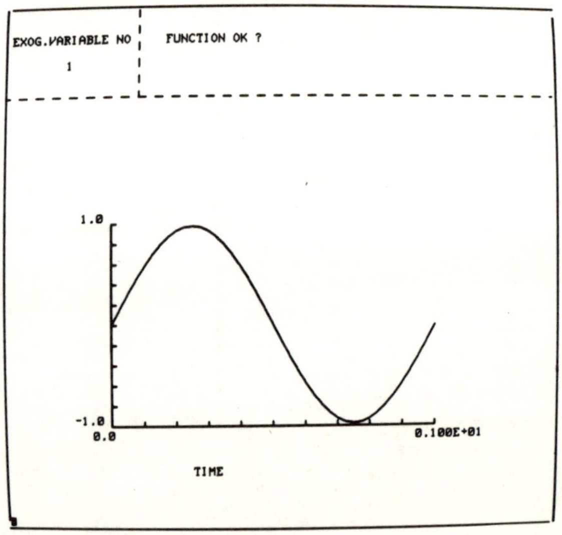

Fig. 20: Seasonal change in moose food supply

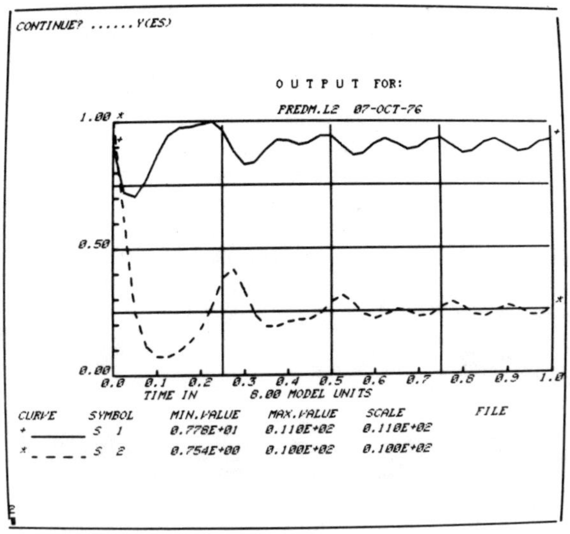

Fig. 21: Model behavior with varying moose carrying capacity

sical sciences to the social and life sciences additional demands are placed on the simulation languages. The ease of use is now a prime criterion for selection of a language. As more persons with little or no background in computer science become involved in modelling and simulation, easier to learn and less technical simulation software should be developed. The process of developing the formal model should also be simplified with the aid of computers. With interactive graphic peripheral equipment readily available now, a greater part of the model development could be done on the computer. GRIPS is a first step in the direction of computer aided model building. More research needs to be done in this area to produce computer software which could provide the model builder with tools equivalent to the computer aided design programs[13] widely used in the development of technical models.

REFERENCES

1. System / 360 Continuous System Modeling Program User's Manual, IBM Manual H 20-0367-3, 4th Edition, 1969

2. DYNAMO User's Manual, Pugh, A.L., 2nd Edition MIT Press, 1963

3. "The SCI Continuous System Simulation Language (CSSL)" Simulation Vol. 9, No. 6, Dec. 1967

4. GPSS / 360 User's Manual, IBM Manual H 20-0326

5. Markowitz, H.M. et al. SIMSCRIPT a Simulation Programming Language, Prentice Hall, Englewood Cliffs, N.J., 1963

6. Birtwistle, G.M. et al. SIMULA Begin, Auerbach Publ. Philadelphia, Pa., 1973

7. Benham, R.D. "Interactive Simulation Language - 8" Simulation Vol. 16, No. 3, March 1971

8. Liebert, T.A. "The DARE II Simulation System" Proceedings SCSC Denver, Colorado 1970

9. Groner, G.F. et al., "BIOMOD - An Interactive Computer Graphics System for Modeling", FJCC, Vol. 39, 1971

10. Mc Calla, T.R., Introduction to Numerical Methods and FORTRAN Programming, J. Wiley and sons, New York 1967

11. Ralston, A., A First Course in Numerical Analysis, McGraw-Hill, New York 1965

12. Smith, J. M., Models in Ecology, Cambridge University Press, 1974

13. Narahara, R. M. "Computer Aided Design" Space/Aeronautics Dec. 1969

14. Schäfer, G., Klaczko, S., and Georgieff, P., Working Paper, Institut für Systemtechnik und Innovationsforschung, Karlsruhe, 1976.

APPENDIX A: AN ECONOMETRIC MODEL

Although GRIPS was designed to handle models of continuous dynamic systems, it can also be used for other purposes such as curve-fitting or, as described below, to perform econometric type computations.

As part of a study to determine the long-term effect of intervention by state institutions on the investment activities of city governments in Germany[14] a sensitivity analysis was carried out using GRIPS. In particular it was desired to determine a correlation between the investment activities and the tax allotments given to the cities by the state institutions. A number of cities were to be studied to search for characteristic investment planning. For the cities of interest, the given time series of city tax revenues and investments were fitted with exponential functions of the form

$$TAX_k = a_1 \cdot b_1^k \qquad k = 0, 1, 2, \ldots n \qquad \text{(A1)}$$

$$INV_k = a_2 \cdot b_2^k$$

using a least square fit. The curve fitting also provided a convenient filter to remove the short-term disturbances. Next it was necessary to relate the investments (INV) to the tax revenues (TAX). As both quantities are described by exponential functions the relationship between the two will also be an exponential function of the form given in Eq. (A1), that is

$$F_k = INV_k / TAX_k = a_3 \cdot b_3^k \qquad k = 0, 1, 2, \ldots n \qquad \text{(A2)}$$

If we thus find an appropriate F we can reproduce the investments behavior from the taxes or

$$INV_k = TAX_k \cdot F_k \qquad \text{(A3)}$$

The addition of a disturbance to the tax revenues (in form of allotments) will be passed on to the investments, the intensity depending on the functional relationship F. We thus get

$$INV_k = (TAX_k + ALL_k) \cdot F_k \qquad \text{(A4)}$$

To obtain a measure of the sensitivity of the investments to a disturbance in the tax revenues we compare the undisturbed investments INV with the disturbed INV^+ using a mean square deviation measure computed from

$$MSD = \frac{1}{n+1} \sum_{k=0}^{n} | INV_k - INV_k^+ | \qquad \text{(A5)}$$

To compare the sensitivities of several cities it is useful to normalize the MSD by dividing it by the standard deviation of the investments computed as follows

$$\sigma = \sqrt{\frac{1}{n+1} \sum_{k=0}^{n} (INV_k - \overline{INV})^2} = \sqrt{\frac{1}{n+1} \sum_{k=0}^{n} \left(INV_k^2 - \frac{1}{n+1} \left(\sum_{k=0}^{n} INV_k\right)^2 \right)} \quad (A6)$$

The above equations were implemented in GRIPS producing the diagram shown in Fig. A1. The resulting equations as produced by GRIPS are given in Fig. A2. The correspondence between the variables used by GRIPS and the ones used in the above equations is as follows·

E1	=	TAX
E2	=	F
E3	=	ALL
E4	=	INV
F10	=	σ
F11	=	MSD/σ

Equations A1 through A6 could have been solved by hand, however, computing all terms for n = 6 and about a dozen cities turns out to be time consuming. The use of a computer is, therefore, preferred. GRIPS was chosen because of its fast and practically error-free method of constructing a simulation program. For the above application one notes that besides the need for certain standard functions (such as multiplication) there is also a requirement for accumulation. This can be done by GRIPS element S. Consider the Euler method employed by GRIPS to carry out integration:

$$S1(t) = S1\ (t - \Delta t) + \Delta t \cdot SI \quad (A7)$$

where SI is the sum of the inputs to an S-block. If we let $\Delta t = 1$ then the operation indicated by Eq. A7 is simply one of accumulation of the inputs (assuming zero initial value of S1). To compute the sensitivities of the investments with respect to disturbances in tax revenues the integration interval is chosen to be one (i.e. $\Delta t = 1.0$) and the length of computation is taken as 6 (empirical data was only available for seven years, i.e. k = 0, 1, 2, ... 6). The absolute sensitivity as expressed by the MSD of Eq. A5 and the normalized sensitivity as given by the relationship

$$NS = MSD/\sigma \quad (A8)$$

were computed by GRIPS for a number of cities. The results for one city are given in Fig. A3. The corresponding disturbance (i.e. allotments) added to the tax revenues was specified as a table function reproduced in Fig. A4. It should be noted that GRIPS will produce a time series for the sensitivities. Only the last values of these series (i.e. for t = 6) represent the sensitivity values as specified by Eqs. A5 and A8.

A high value of MSD or NS for a given city indicates a low sensitivity i. e. a relatively independent investment activity. A comparison of the histories of the investment activities for the cities studied with the computed sensitivities showed a considerable degree of agreement[14].

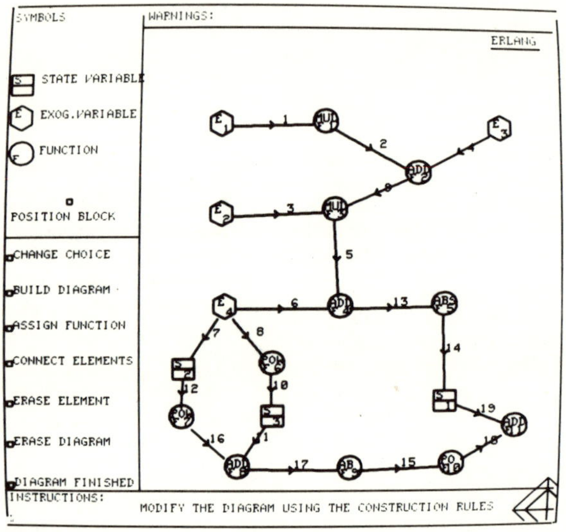

Fig. A1 - GRIPS diagram of econometric model.

SYSTEM EQUATIONS FOR THE MODEL:ERLAN1   22-NOV-76

STATE EQUATIONS

```
DS 1 =  P14*F 5

DS 2 =  P 7*E 4

DS 3 =  P10*F 6
```

AUXILIARY EQUATIONS

```
F 1 =  P 1* E 1

F 2 =  P 4* E 3  +  P 2* F 1

F 3 =  P 9* F 2

F 4 =  P 5* F 3  +  P 6* E 4

F 5 = ABS  ( P13* F 4 )

                         2.00
F 6 = ( P 8*E 4)

                         2.00
F 7 = ( P12*S 2)

F 8 =  P11* S 3  +  P16* F 7

F 9 = ABS  ( P17* F 8 )

                         0.50
F10 = ( P15*F 9)

F11 =  P18* S 1  /  P19* F10
```

PARAMETERS FOR THE MODEL:ERLAN1

P #	VALUE
1	0.1654E+02
2	0.1000E+01
3	0.7353E+00
4	0.1000E+01
5	-0.1000E+01
6	0.1000E+01
7	0.1000E+01
8	0.1000E+01
9	0.1000E+01
10	0.1000E+01
11	0.1000E+01
12	0.1000E+01
13	0.1000E+01
14	0.1667E+00
15	0.1000E+01
16	-0.1667E+00
17	0.1667E+00
18	0.1000E+01
19	0.1000E+01

INITIAL CONDITIONS

S #	VALUE
1	0.0000E+00
2	0.1000E-07
3	0.1000E-07

INPUTS (EXOGENOUS VARIABLES)

```
E 1 = (  1.121    )**T
E 2 = (  1.014    )**T

E 3 = TABLE FUNCTION WITH POINT PAIRS (T,X)
 0.000E+00  0.400E+00   0.100E+01  0.237E+00   0.200E+01  0.632E+00
 0.300E+01  0.322E+01   0.400E+01  0.481E+01   0.500E+01  0.355E+01
 0.600E+01  0.249E+01

E 4 = TABLE FUNCTION WITH POINT PAIRS (T,X)
 0.000E+00  0.203E+02   0.100E+01  0.192E+02   0.200E+01  0.182E+02
 0.300E+01  0.209E+02   0.400E+01  0.243E+02   0.500E+01  0.280E+02
 0.600E+01  0.316E+02
```

Fig. A2 - Equations and parameters of model.

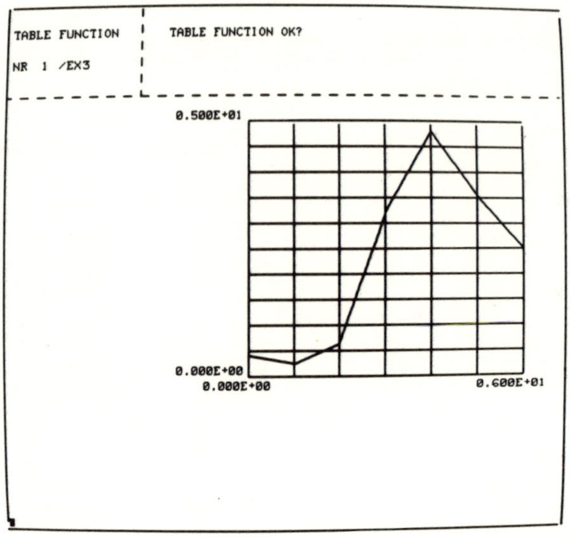

Fig. A3 - Table function of tax allotments (disturbance).

SENSITIVITY OF INVESTMENTS TO TAX ALLOTMENTS

DATE & TIME OF SIMULATION RUN : 22-NOV-76 , 8:54

TIME	S 1	F10	F11
0.0000	0.0000E+00	0.4083E-04	0.0000E+00
6.0000	0.4019E+01	0.8632E+01	0.4655E+00

Fig. A4 - Absolute sensitivity (S1) and relative sensitivity (F11) of investments to tax allotments.

APPENDIX B: GRIPS SYMBOLS, BUILT-IN FUCTIONS, AND EXOGENOUS FUNCTIONS

Symbols used by GRIPS

A complete list of symbols used by GRIPS is given below together with their name, mathematical meaning and their limitations.

Table 1 - GRIPS Symbols

SYMBOL	NAME	MATHEMATICAL EXPRESSION	Max. Number allowed	Number of Inputs
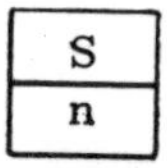	State variable	$y = \int_0^t x\,dt + y\ (o)$	50	3
	Interme-diate variable	$y = f\ (x)$	50	3
	Exogenous variable	$y = f\ (t)$	25	0
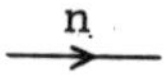	Branch	$y = cx$		1
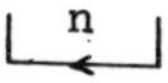	Feedback branch	$y = cx$	125	1
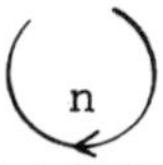	Selfloop	$y = cx$		

c = constant
x = input
y = output
n = element number
Type = function type see Table 2.

Built-in Functions available in GRIPS

The following table lists the built-in functions the user can choose from. Using these functions, almost any functional relationship required for models can be built. The table functions can be input either numerically by specifying the necessary breakpoints (up to 10 pairs allowed) or by sketching a curve using the light pen. A total of up to 50 intermediate variables representing these functions are allowed. The functions can have up to 3 input terms, except as noted below.

Table 2 - GRIPS Functions

Abbreviation	Name	Mathemat. Expression	Limitations
ADD	adder	$y = x_1 + x_2 + x_3$	
MUL	multiplier	$y = x_1 \cdot x_2 \cdot x_3$	
DIV	divider	$y = x_1/x_2$	only two inputs dividend is specified
EXP	exponential	$y = e^{(x_1+x_2+x_3)}$	
POW	exponentiation	$y = (x_1 + x_2 + x_3)^c$	
LN	nat. logarithm	$y = \ln (x_1 + x_2 + x_3)$	
LOG	logarithm base 10	$y = \log (x_1+x_2+x_3)$	
ABS	absolute value	$y = \lvert x_1 + x_2 + x_3 \rvert$	
SIN	sines	$y = \sin (x_1+x_2+x_3)$	
COS	cosines	$y = \cos (x_1+x_2+x_3)$	
HTA	hyperbolic tang.	$y = \tanh (x_1+x_2+x_3)$	
ATA	arc tangent	$y = \tan^{-1} (x_1+x_2+x_3)$	
MAX	max. value	$y = \max (x_1, x_2, x_3)$	
MIN	min. value	$y = \min (x_1, x_2, x_3)$	
DEL	delay	$y = x (t - T)$	only 10 allowed
LF1	logical function 1	$y = 0 \quad \text{if } x_1 < x_2$ $y = x_3 \quad \text{if } x_1 \geqslant x_2$	

LF2	logical function 2	$y = -1 \quad \text{if} \sum_i^3 x_i < 0$ $y = 0 \quad \text{if} \sum_i^3 x_i = 0$ $y = 1 \quad \text{if} \sum_i^3 x_i > 0$	
TF	table function		only 5 allowed with max. 10 break points

Exogenous Functions

A number of exogenous function types are available to the user. These can be combined to allow additional possibilities. For further versatility, the user may input his own function using a table function approach or by sketching the input function using the light pen. A total of 25 exogenous variables (functions) can be specified.

Table 3 - Exogenous Functions

Function	Parameters	Mathematical Representation	Graphical Representation
Delta (Impulse)	T	$e(t) = (t - T)$	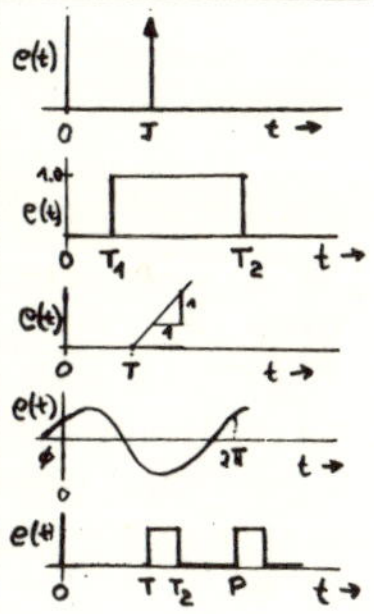
Modified Step	T_1, T_2	$e(t) = u(t - T_1) - u(t - T_2)$	
Ramp	T	$e(t) = t \cdot u(t - T)$	
Sinusoid	f, ϕ	$e(t) = \sin(2\pi ft + \phi)$	
Rectangular Wave	T_1, T_2, P		
Random Numbers evenly distributed	Rmax, Rmin, seed		
Table Function up to 3 allowed w. up to 10 Break points each			can be specified in tabular form or input graphically
Exponential function	c	$e(t) = c^t$	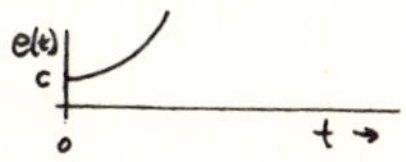

8

SENSITIVITY ANALYSIS OF SIMULATION MODELS

Walter Hudetz

1 - INTRODUCTION: THE NEED FOR SENSITIVITY ANALYSIS

Once the simulation model of a real system has been constructed, there commonly arise a number of questions concerning the quality of the model, i.e. how well does the model represent the real system? One of the problems of modelling is the collection of data and the determination of the model parameters. Invariably there will be parameters for which only approximate values can be obtained. It is therefore necessary to find some measure for the importance of model parameters with respect to the overall model behavior. One would like to determine how a small disturbance or change in a parameter will effect the model response.

There exist two basic methods to determine the sensitivity of a model towards changes in a model parameter. The first technique is rather simple and empiric. It entails the manual or possibly automatic change of the parameters of interest (one at a time) and the subsequent recording of the model response. The second method is analytic in nature and requires the derivation of the so-called sensitivity equations which when solved provide a measure of the model sensitivity to parameter variations.

Sensitivity analysis was developed as an aid in engineering and has become a rather common method in the engineering sciences. In the design of the technical systems, tolerances in system components are almost always present. It is thus mandatory to obtain information about the sensitivity of the system to perturbations in its parameters. More recently sensitivity analysis has also been applied to biological[1] and social[2] systems. There also have been some attempts to provide for automatic or programmed sensitivity analysis to be included as part of a simulation language[3].

The following paper first presents the empirical method of sensitivity analysis followed by a brief exposé of the analytic technique. Finally, using a concrete example the method of obtaining the sensitivity functions is illustrated.

2 - EMPIRICAL SENSITIVITY TESTING

In the early days of computer simulation, models of dynamic systems were developed by engineers on analog computers. The analog computer, being a parallel machine, allows for very fast computation of the modelled system's behavior. In fact, modern electronic analog computers are fast enough to display the solution on an oscilloscope in a repetitive fashion so that changes in a model parameter can be seen almost instantaneously. Thus there was a relatively efficient way to study the effect of parameter variations on the model behavior by simply changing manually the parameter of interest (on the analog computer this merely involved the change of a potentiometer setting) and observing the result on a scope. With the increased use of digital computers, this method changed somewhat. The solution time is now much longer (in the order of two or more magnitudes higher depending on model size) and it takes some time before the effect of parameter changes can be observed.

The method is straightforward and can be carried out as follows:

(1) The parameters to be varied are selected and identified in the computer program.
(2) A parameter P is altered by some small increment ΔP - usually chosen on the basis of guidelines provided by the real system - and a simulation run is performed.
(3) The resulting behavior of the model is compared with a reference run and the effect of the parameter change is determined.
(4) Steps (2) and (3) are repeated until all chosen parameters have been varied.

This technique can be programmed and performed automatically by the computer. Statistical methods can be used to evaluate the results obtained from these computations. Often it is necessary to perform several runs with changes in only one parameter to obtain critical limits in parameter values.

With large models computation time can be excessive and it is not always feasable to perform parameter studies for more than a limited sample of parameters. The model builder will select a few parameters (those he considers critical) and perform a sensitivity study on these.

3 - MATHEMATICAL SENSITIVITY ANALYSIS

This method is based on the differential calculus and involves the derivation of a set of sensitivity equations. These equations are obtained from the system or model equations and can be solved by the same methods used for solving the model equations. The solutions to these equations are the sensitivity functions. These functions exhibit the effects of a small perturbation of a parameter on the system behavior. We shall first define the sensitivity function and then show how one can obtain the sensitivity equations from the system equations. The discussion will be limited to perturbations invariant in time. For a more complete presentation on sensitivity functions and sensitivity theory see Ref. 4.

Let us take a model described by the vector differential equation

$$\dot{X} = F(X, P, t) \qquad (1)$$

$$X(t_o) = X_o$$

Where X is the state vector of dimension N, P is the parameter vector (dimension M), t is time, F is a vector function and $\dot{X}$ is the time derivative of X. The sensitivity functions of X with respect to a change in the parameters P are then defined by the matrix

$$S_i = \frac{\partial X}{\partial p_i}, \quad i = 1, 2, \ldots M \qquad (2)$$

The matrix S can be obtained by solving a matrix differential equation in S called the sensitivity equation.

The sensitivity equation is derived directly from the state equation (1) by differentiating it with respect to P to yield

$$\dot{S} = G(X, P, t) \cdot S + H(X, P, t) \qquad (3)$$

$$S(t_o) = S_o$$

where

$$G(X, P, t) = \frac{\partial f_i(X, P, t)}{\partial x_j}, \quad \begin{matrix} i = 1, 2, \ldots N \\ j = 1, 2, \ldots N \end{matrix} \qquad (4)$$

and

$$H(X, P, t) = \frac{\partial f_i(X, P, t)}{\partial p_l}, \quad \begin{matrix} i = 1, 2, \ldots N \\ l = 1, 2, \ldots M \end{matrix} \qquad (5)$$

S is an N x M matrix, G is an N x N matrix and H is an N x M matrix.

Note that Eq. (3) is a linear matrix equation with time-dependent coefficients and forcing functions (inputs). In order to solve Eq. (3) it will be necessary to obtain first the solution to the unperturbed system described by Eq. (1), as some of its state variables provide inputs to the sensitivity equation through the terms in H. This causes no special restriction when the solutions are calculated by digital computer. However, it will mean that computation time will almost double and memory requirements will also increase.

For complex systems with a large number of state variables and parameters it will not be practical to obtain sensitivity equations for each system parameter. As an example consider a system of 20 state variables (N = 20 in Eq. (1)) and 40 parameters (M = 40). To obtain all sensitivity functions this would require the solution of 40 x 20 + 20 or 820 first order differential equations, quite a job even for today's digital computers. Thus as with the empirical method the model builder will have to select a number of critical parameters for which he then obtains the sensitivity functions.

Sensitivity functions are in general time-dependent functions which provide a direct indicator for the parameter influence on system responses. Consider a simple system described by the differential equation

$$\dot{x} = f(x, p, t) \tag{6}$$

Let x (t, p) be the solution to Eq. (6). If we perturb the parameter p by a small Δp we get the solution x (p + Δp, t). Using a Taylor series expansion[5], we can express the perturbed solution as

$$x(p + \Delta p, t) = x(t, p) + \frac{x}{p} \cdot \Delta p + 0 \tag{7}$$

Where 0 represent the higher order terms in Δp of the expansion. If Δp is small we can neglect the higher order terms. We then can express the difference between perturbed and unperturbed solution (i. e. the effect of the perturbation) by product of sensitivity function ($\frac{\partial x}{\partial p}$) and the perturbation or

$$x(p + \Delta p, t) - x(t, p) = \frac{\partial x}{\partial p} \cdot \Delta p \tag{8}$$

For a constant Δp the magnitude of the sensitivity function is then a direct measure of the parameter influence on the system behavior.

Sensitivity equations can be derived for linear or nonlinear, continuous or discrete dynamic systems. Sensitivity analysis can be used to study the influence of changes in initial states of a system by simply considering the initial states to be parameters and using the same approach described above. For further applications refer to Ref. 4.

4 - AN EXAMPLE

To illustrate the use of sensitivity analysis let us consider the predator-prey model described in a previous chapter of this book. The system equations are two first order nonlinear differential equations repeated below.

$$\begin{aligned} \dot{S}_1 &= a S_1 - b S_1^2 - c S_1 S_2 \\ \dot{S}_2 &= -g S_2 + e S_1 S_2 \end{aligned} \tag{9}$$

with initial conditions $S_1/_{t=o} = C_1$ and $S_2/_{t=o} = C_2$.

To study the influence of the wolves (g) and the moose (a) growth rate on the system behavior, we first obtain the sensitivity equations for these two parameters.

Differentiating Eqs. 9 with respect to the parameter we get

$$\frac{\partial}{\partial a}\frac{dS_1}{dt} = S_1 + a\frac{\partial S_1}{\partial a} - 2b\,S_1\frac{\partial S_1}{\partial a} - (S_2\frac{\partial S_1}{\partial a} + S_1\frac{\partial S_2}{\partial a})$$

$$\frac{\partial}{\partial a}\frac{dS_2}{t} = -S_2 - g\frac{\partial S_2}{\partial a} + e\,(S_2\frac{\partial S_1}{\partial a} + S_1\frac{\partial S_2}{\partial a}) \qquad (10)$$

With the sensitivity functions defined as:

$$\frac{\partial S_1}{\partial a} = u$$

$$\frac{\partial S_2}{\partial a} = v \qquad (11)$$

and realizing that $\frac{\partial dS_1}{\partial a\, dt} = \frac{d}{dt}\frac{\partial S_1}{\partial a}$ we get from Eqs. 10:

$$\dot{u} = S_1 + au - 2bS_1u - c(S_2u + S_1v)$$

$$\dot{v} = -S_2 - gv + e(S_2u + S_1v) \qquad (12)$$

Eqs. 12 are the sensitivity equations for the parameter a. They are linear differential equations with time varying coefficients (i. e. S_1 and S_2) and inputs S_1 and $-S_2$ which represent the solutions to the system equations (9). The solution to equation 11 will be the desired sensitivity functions.

The sensitivity equations for the parameter g are derived in a similar fashion. If we define the sensitivity functions as

$$\frac{\partial S_1}{\partial g} = x$$

$$\frac{\partial S_2}{\partial g} = y \qquad (13)$$

the sensitivity equation will be

$$\dot{x} = ax - 2b\,S_1\,x - c(S_2 x + S_1 y)$$
$$\dot{y} = -S_2 - dy + e\,(S_2 x + S_1 y) \qquad (14)$$

To obtain the two sets of sensitivity functions Eqs. 12 and 14 are solved parallel to Eqs. 9. The initial conditions for the sensitivity functions are obtained by differentiating the initial conditions of the system. Since these are both constants, all initial conditions for the sensitivity equations will be zero.

The solutions to Eqs. 12 and 14 were computed using the GRIPS system. The results are shown in Figs. 1 and 2. One can see that the sensitivities vary considerably during the transient time of the system response. They settle down to some steady value somewhat after the system has settled. A comparison of the sensitivity functions is given in Fig. 3 where all four functions are plotted to the same scale. When comparing magnitudes of these functions one should always consider the corresponding parameter values and choose perturbations of equal proportion. As an example consider the effect of a 1% change in the two parameters. For parameter a with a nominal value of 2.0 this means a change $\Delta a = 0.02$. The change for parameter g with a nominal value of -20.0 amounts to $\Delta g = -0.2$. Taking the sensitivity functions at $t = 8$ years we calculate effective changes in the system response due to the above parameter changes using Eq. 7. The results are presented in table 1 below.

Table 1. Effects of parameter changes on model behavior using sensitivity functions ($t = 8.0$)

Parameter	Sensitivity Coefficients		ΔP	ΔS_1	ΔS_2
a	-0.2536	5.356	0.02	-0.005072	0.10712
g	0.5118	-0.3981	0.2	0.10236	-0.07962

Comparing the entries in above table we note that the sensitivity of the moose population (S_1) to changes in the moose growth rate (a) is considerably less than its sensitivity to the wolves growth rate (g). The opposite is true for the wolves population (S_2).

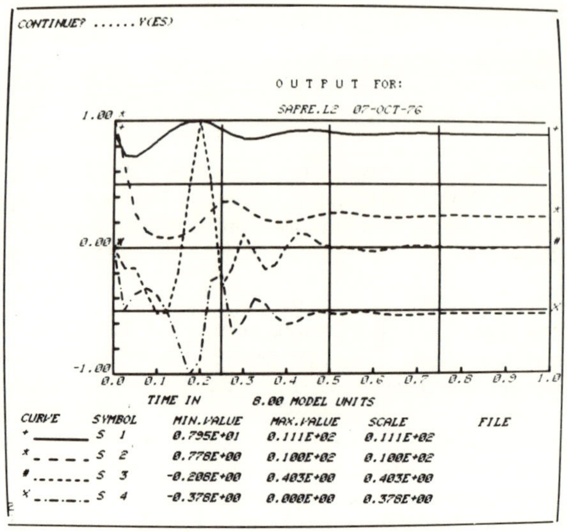

Figure 1: Model response (S1, S2) and sensitivity functions for moose growth rate (S3, S4)

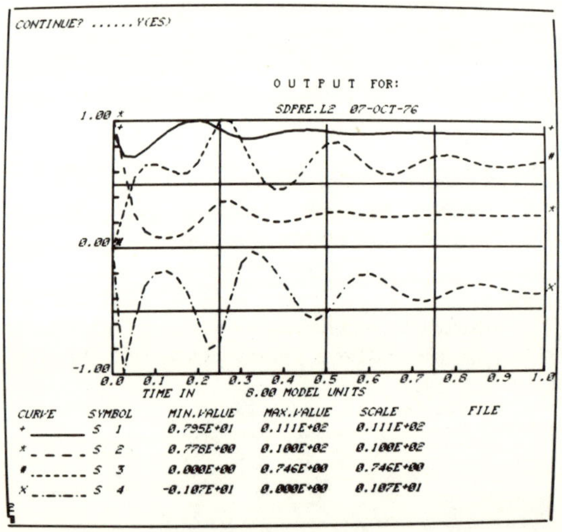

Figure 2: Model response (S1, S2) and sensitivity functions for wolves growth rate (S3, S4)

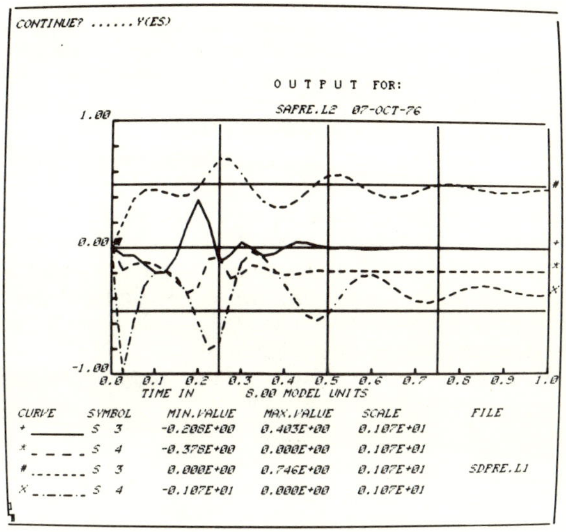

Figure 3: Sensitivity functions for moose (+, ✱) and wolves (#, X) growth rates plotted to same scale.

5 - CONCLUSION

With the more widespread use of modelling especially in the area of forecasting, it is of prime importance to use as many methods as possible, to ascertain confidence in the model. Sensitivity analysis provides a means to evaluate the importance of the model parameters. Using sensitivity analysis the model builder will be able to pinpoint those parameters which greatly influence the model response and thus have to be determined rather accurately.

Sensitivity analysis can be applied to most systems, however, for large systems, the computation effort will become a limiting factor. In any case, it is important that the model builder preselects, on the basis of his knowledge of the system which he is modelling, the more critical parameters for closer evaluation. In the future sensitivity analysis will become more automated, that is, simulation languages or programs will include, as one of their features, the possibility to perform sensitivity analysis on specified model components.

REFERENCES

1. Hudetz, W.J. , "Sensitivity analysis applied to ecosystem models". Progress in Cybernetics and System Research, Vol. 1, Hemisphere Publ. Co. 1975.

2. Willekens, F., Sensitivity Analysis, Research Memo. RM-76-49 June 1976, IIASA, Laxenburg, Austria.

3. Stübel, G., Methodologische und software-engineering-orientierte Untersuchungen für ein Unternehmensmodell verschiedener Strukturiertheitsgrade, Dissertation, Univ. of Stuttgart, Germany.

4. Tomović, R., and Vukobratović, M., General Sensitivity Theory, American Elsevier, New York 1972.

5. Sokolnikoff, I.S. and Redheffer, R.M., Mathematics of Physics and Modern Engineering, McGraw-Hill, N.Y. 1958.

9

MATCHING MAN AND MODEL: THE 'GUIDE' SYSTEM FOR INTERACTIVE MODEL HANDLING

Michael G. Strobel and Hartmut Bossel

INTRODUCTION: INTERACTIVE POLICY ANALYSIS

The catastrophic predictions for the future of the planet generated by some runs of the Forrester and Meadows models /1/, /2/ have drawn the attention of the public to the advances made in the application of computer simulation to socio-economic problems. At the same time hopes were raised that with the new technology better, i.e. more accurate, more comprehensive, and more responsible planning and policy making would ensue/3/.

A number of models of various degrees of aggregation, sophistication and complexity exist today already /4/, /5/, /6/. While much work needs to be done to build models adequate for the planning processes at various stages and for diverse planning agencies, the growing interest and competence in modelling seem to indicate that the technical demands for a comprehensive planning system can be met without great difficulties, provided the administrative and financial support is forthcoming without too much bureaucratic hindrance /7/.

However, we see a definite handicap for longterm planning efforts in the gap which now exists between the scientifically oriented development of the methodology of policy analysis, and the current implementation and execution of policy, subject to all the well-known political and economic constraints.

The considerable amount of money and man-years of work invested in the construction of dynamic models has had little impact on the actual planning process as practiced at various levels of policy making. Whatever the reason for this state of affairs the consequences for further delays tend to become intolerably costly.

In the following we will present our contribution to bridging this gap. The importance of linking the new methodology to actual decision making lies in the mutual dependency of the two factors: Neither can the development of longterm planning have any chance of success under the imposed urgency and lack of time for real life experiment without the simulation model which provides the best possible assessment of likely consequences of policy intervention; nor can model building be improved to the degree of validity necessary for responsible policy making without the benefit of direct inputs from the planners and their evaluation of the models.

The principal reason for the limited use being made by policy makers of simulation models lies in the incompatibility of the required skills and knowledge involved. The construction and running of a simulation model consists of a complicated sequence of technical manipulations and abstract transformations which have nothing in common with the managerial skills and competence acquired by those whose job it is to develop policies for real life situations. Given the attitudes and preferences of busy managers it is unreasonable to expect them to learn the many details involved in actually experimenting with present day computer models in order to arrive at an understanding of the system they wish to govern. On the other hand the costs of constructing a complete and in all detail user-oriented input and output facility for each model is prohibitive.

The obvious solution would be the development of a general interface fitting all models and designed to accommodate all users of various degrees of experience.

In the present contribution we shall discuss the GUIDE system (General User Interface for Development Evaluation) which was developed with this general objective in mind.

Section 1 reviews the specific demands on such an interface first from the point of view of the model user, and then from the point of view of the model builder, charged with the task of developing an interactive policy analysis instrument. From these requirements a set of guiding principles for the development of the interface is derived.

Section 2 provides a brief review of some functions and aspects of dynamic simulation models relevant to the further discussion.

Section 3 is addressed primarily to the model user. It presents a detailed description of the application of the GUIDE system in the input and output modes. The section also introduces the 'premodel' concept employed by GUIDE, which permits interactive model use on different levels of input parameter aggregation.

Section 4 deals with the programming steps required for attaching an existing simulation model to the GUIDE system in order to obtain an interactive policy analysis tool. The section focusses in particular on the creation of the necessary files for the generation and control of the interactive dialogue. It also contains a brief description of the service routine GUARD which provides a debugging facility for the GUIDE files, and some information on installation-specific data file handling.

Section 5 provides a commented example of the use of GUIDE for the energy part of a technology policy model, displaying all important features of the system.

Finally, in Section 6 possible extensions of the GUIDE system are discussed briefly.

1. PROBLEM DESCRIPTION

The Model User's Point of View

The transition from systems technology to planning technology will not be accomplished as long as the new tools remain experimental prototypes confined to the laboratory. Evaluation of existing models remains an academic exercise as long as practicing planners and policy makers do not use them.

The models to date are exclusively controlled by the model builder and programmer. Inevitably the models reflect his bias and perception of reality. Usually only he is cognizant of the critical model parameters and knows whether delicate balancing is necessary to keep results reasonable. Questionable model structures often remain obscure. The "conscious or unconscious technocratic manipulation" is not entirely a malevolent diffamation levelled at the model builder by his critics.

Model transparency is a definite problem by itself which should command the privileged attention of the model builder. For the time being a measure of comprehension of model structure could be gained from simply observing the model behavior under experimental input variation. From the understanding of model structure and function derives an understanding of the dynamics of the real system.

If the user is to gain experience and insight by actually running the model under his own control, the setup of experimental runs must be as effortless and as rapid as possible. The first approach should be immediate, without lengthy training periods, without weighty manuals to study.

The model should respond quickly to the most rudimentary manipulations, then relinquish control more and more as the user becomes familiar with procedures and gets a feeling for the model potential. The tempo of advance should however be entirely paced by the user.

Information requirements should be met when they arise in the course of operations or when they are demanded by the user. Technical instructions concerning the handling and content information about the significance and meaning of model-related inputs should be held available at all times. Forced information should diminish as the user concentrates more and more on the model outputs which he anticipates. Redundancy, important in the beginning when the rate of information throughput is greatest, should be phased out to make speed and efficiency the overriding concern.

Of prime importance is error tolerance. Format restrictions and sequential constraints should be kept at a minimum to avoid the most frequent sources of errors. Error recovery should be automatic or at least very quick in interaction with the user.

Location and identity of the input parameters which allow the composition of scenarios, and output parameters which contain the results, should be made accessible even to the completely inexperienced.

The loading of scenarios which may involve a great number of parameters as well as precise knowledge of their numerical values should become a manageable task even with limited competence and at an early stage of model experience. Thus fuzzy ideas expressed in rough qualitative statements which define the rate of change of a parameter as "small", "medium", or "high" should be made meaningful to the model just as they are meaningful to the user.

The possibility of working with models at various levels of abstraction would remove a major obstacle to their acceptance as planning tools.

Disaggregation of aggregated parameters should be automatic to free the model user from the burden of defining a potentially great number of parameters with limited specialized knowledge. At the same time measures should be taken to protect the user from avoidable errors such as improper summing of disaggregated parameters or proportional errors with small quantities.

In order to insure maximum transfer of learning, procedures of model handling should be standardized. The user should not have to go through the confusion of the novice every time he wants to examine and work with a different model.

The Model Builder's Point of View

The coupling of the general interface to the specific model remains the task of the model builder. He alone knows the model intimately, has all the technical information and thus can judge the form and content of communication best suited to present his model to the user. The interface must therefore also meet the demands of the model builder if it is to be adopted as a standard procedure.

Convenience of use is likely to be the most important requirement. The amount of work necessary to attach a model to the interface should be kept at a minimum. Thus the formal rules to be observed should be few and easy to learn.

There should be no need to change anything in the model core proper of an existing model.

The number of parameters and their designation as input or output should be unconstrained. The model builder should however retain a large measure of control over the preliminary operations to be performed if the model cannot deal with raw input and places restrictions on the parameter content. These operations should then be indicated by the model builder and performed by the interface.

If for instance the parameters are organized in groups and cannot be treated singly, such as the different percentages of a given parameter summing to unity, the interface must assure that all parameters belonging to the group are treated, and the proper summation obtained independent of the user's attention. If hierarchical dependencies exist among parameters, the consequences of changes at higher levels should be recognized and implemented for the lower levels.

The model builder should be able to restrict parameter manipulation at some point in anticipation of consequences. Thus it may be intolerable for a model to change two particular parameters at the same time. The interface should acknowledge the model limitations and communicate them to the user authoritatively.

Furthermore the provision of model builder control should be open-ended. Since the interface cannot know all of the possible model builder requests, any specific additions should be easily implemented without major programming effort, and above all without changing the interface structure.

Communication with the user should be in natural language. Translation of messages and information text should be possible without any major programming effort on the main body of the interface.

The model builder should also be provided with computer assistance to make his model attachment error-free and conforming to his intentions as speedily and effortless as possible.

Guiding Principles

From the analysis of both the model user's and the model builder's expectations of the interface we deduce the following overall required system characteristics:

1. Generality: The system should be independent of model attributes, programming language and computer installation.
2. Adaptability: The various user and model builder demands should be accommodated equally well. The system should be flexible enough to permit partial use for some problems such as data base inspection, scenario generation, or model validation. It should also accept additions easily.
3. Intelligence: User behavior, his information needs at various points in time, different stages of competence, and diverse topics of interest should be anticipated and accommodated accordingly. Information throughput should be regulated as a function of the learning process of the user.
4. Error tolerance: Insensitivity to user mistakes, and robustness against logical faults should be guaranteed in order to prevent frequent and needless program exits with inexperienced or inattentive users. Errors of

the model builder when connecting his model to the interface should be eliminated with program assistance.

5. Simplicity of interface: The model builder should be freed of all restrictions concerning the treatment of parameters and should not be burdened with the acquisition of much technical knowledge.
6. Simplicity of use: The system should be largely self-explanatory. It should be accessible to all interested users without prior theoretical instruction (manuals) or specialist assistance (training).
7. Completeness: The same system should be able to handle input and output requirements with maximum use of common modules.

There are a few additional desirables worth mentioning:

The system should be compact, economical in core memory space, efficient in computer-time usage, portable to different hardware, and well-documented (so copying would be easy and purchase unnecessary) and finally, perhaps, it should also work.

2. DYNAMIC MODELS AS PLANNING TOOLS

In the following section we describe briefly dynamic computer models in order to introduce some of the technical terms which will be used in the program description. The initiated reader should skip to the next section.

Dynamic models are computer programs which represent, in the form of mathematical equations, functional relationships between components as they are observed or perceived in the real world.

For example a population can be adequately represented by an integer, i. e. the number of people in that population. Birth and immigration will add to this number, while death and emigration will subtract from it. The functional relationship between the component factors of population, birth, death, immigration and emigration can be written as $P_t = P_{t-1} + B + I - D - E$, where P_t is the number of people at time t and P_{t-1} the number of people at the time of the last observation. The introduction of time as a variable makes the value observed dependent on the number of observation intervals which have elapsed since the beginning of the calculations. The state of the system can be observed at any given moment and the change over time renders the model dynamic.

Systems in the real world tend to be complex and the model builder can reflect this complexity in his model by stating all the relationships he can think of or which he considers relevant to his model of reality. He could for instance make the number of deaths dependent on the food situation as reflected in agricultural production and imports, which in turn are dependent on the available capital produced by the industrial output, and so forth.

In order to keep his model realistic the model builder must rely on historical data up to the present. He can then check the structure of his model by comparing model output with history. For the run of the model these historical data over time ("time series") are essential. The prolongation of these time series into the future constitutes of course mere guesswork. However, since all the variables in the model influence each other directly or indirectly over the various functional dependencies and feedback loops, this guesswork amounts to predicting alternative futures given certain values for certain "parameters". Thus if birth rate were made to drop, the population at some future date would diminish with consequences in all other parts of the model: Less food would be necessary, less housing, less energy, consumption would diminish, - perhaps. The complexity of reality makes it rather difficult to predict exactly what would in fact happen. Perhaps more food would be necessary and more energy because the average individual would be richer, more demanding and more wasteful.

It is the possibility of letting a great many relationships influence each other under precisely stated assumptions and of determining the consequences, which gives the computer model its enormous power and advantage over conventional planning methods of intuitive comprehension, verbal consensus and common sense.

The speed with which the great number of calculations are accomplished enables one to experiment repeatedly with different assumptions for the future in different parts of the model, i. e. with different "scenarios". The time series for the assumed future values of the parameters with the most likely outcome, or the outcome with the least surprise, are then arbitrarily termed the "standard scenario".

The time series of individual scenario parameters can be altered in accordance with a chosen policy before inputting them to the model as the basis for a simulation run which then produces a representation of the consequences of the chosen policy. In this way a potential policy can be tested before actually being applied to the real system.

Computer simulations have for many years been extensively used in the technical domain in order to gain experience with the behavior of complex systems under various conditions. Process and control simulations in the chemical industry, or flight simulation are examples. The use of the flight simulator in pilot training and aircraft development allows the pilot or engineer to completely familiarize himself with the various responses of a complex system without the threat of catastrophic failure. Here the situation is analogous to the socio-economic systems we are presently interested in: The complexity of the various interactions is impossible to foresee with any accuracy by natural means, and the consequence of errors is disaster.

The construction of valid computer simulation models of socio-economic systems is a costly and time-consuming enterprise. The special knowledge required to assemble the data, determine the structure, write the computer program and validate the emerging model may demand several man-years for the simulation of a system of some complexity. Given a valid model, however, one then has a representation of reality with the advantage that it is clearly stated, reduced in complexity, and managable. With this instrument it is then possible to examine the likely behavior of the real system in response to various conditions, limitations, and interventions. In principle, the user can experiment with the model either by systematically changing controlling parameters or by intuitively formulating and applying "policies" until he has a firm grasp of the characteristics of the system and a thorough knowledge of its behavior potential.

The construction process, which involves a gradual composition of disjoint subsystems with many possible linkages and often delicate numerical balancing to achieve realistic model behavior, may lead to a profound understanding of the functional dependencies and reactions within the system on the part of the model builder. The model user can gain an understanding of the model behavior either by systematic study of responses to experimental control inputs (and often also stochastic disturbances) according to some comprehensive experimental plan. He may attempt to carry out predetermined missions i.e. reach certain goals, given the constraints of the environment and the model dynamics (the typical application mode of flight simulators), or perhaps just 'play around' with the model. All three modes of model use can be productive and should therefore be allowed for.

Presently, however, the models neither allow playful manipulation nor the easy and flexible execution of systematic and goal-oriented policy studies. In fact the technical sophistication required to run a simulation model of the complexity of the Mesarovic-Pestel world model makes it accessible to only very few people. If the information potential vested in these models is to be used in actual practice the models must be made much more responsive to the professional and psychological needs of the intended users, i.e. the planners and policy makers who do not possess the knowledge of simulation languages, programming rules and computer handling which are now required to construct and run a non-trivial computer model. The GUIDE system to be discussed in the following section is our contribution to the solution of this problem.

3. STRUCTURE AND FUNCTIONING OF 'GUIDE'

Simulation models communicate results of the model run via output parameters, i.e. values of selected variables which carry information meaningful for the evaluation of the state of the simulated system. Similarly the model receives information necessary to describe the initial state of the system and directives about trends and limiting conditions from input parameters.

These parameters constitute the surface of the model where the user makes contact with it. The handling of the parameters, their selection, loading, processing, and representation can be, and often is,a difficult task.

The simplification of this task is precisely the raison d' être for GUIDE. Fig. 1 shows the relationship between the GUIDE concept and the simulation model.

GUIDE is a comprehensive software system written in FORTRAN IV. Although FORTRAN is not the most modern language, it certainly is the most "portable" one. The majority of computers today have a FORTRAN compiler and the programming effort to implement a FORTRAN program on any given installation is acceptable. GUIDE was developed specifically for the Mesarovic-Pestel world model, but with a view to maximum generality such that it can be used for any search and keyboard-oriented data acquisition problem in the interactive mode.

The adaptation of a specific model to GUIDE is accomplished in three steps:

1. The data base with the historical data and the standard scenario is connected to GUIDE via an input tape.

2. Each of the model parameters is then made accessible through a search tree. The tree enables the user to find any parameter in the model through a systematic search from general concepts to the specific label of the parameter.

   Let for instance this specific parameter in a population model be the people of Canada. The search through the general concepts of continents (America, Asia, Europe, etc.), subcontinents (North-, South-America, etc.), and countries (USA, Canada) would lead to the intended parameter in three decisions or selections from the successive sets of alternatives. The resulting trace (112 in our example) uniquely defines the parameter. The tree is written in natural language on a text file and connected to GUIDE via a second input tape.

3. The correspondence between the trace and its parameter is established by a simple conversion table which is read by GUIDE into core memory.

The effort demanded from the programmer for the construction of these files is kept at a minimum. Formatting rules are very few. The conceptualization of the tree, accompanying informative texts, and treatment of the designated parameters are left entirely to the model builder. Files and tables for output parameters are constructed in the same manner. All technical information for the use of GUIDE in input and output mode is supplied by the system, which eliminates the necessity of user training or expert assistance.

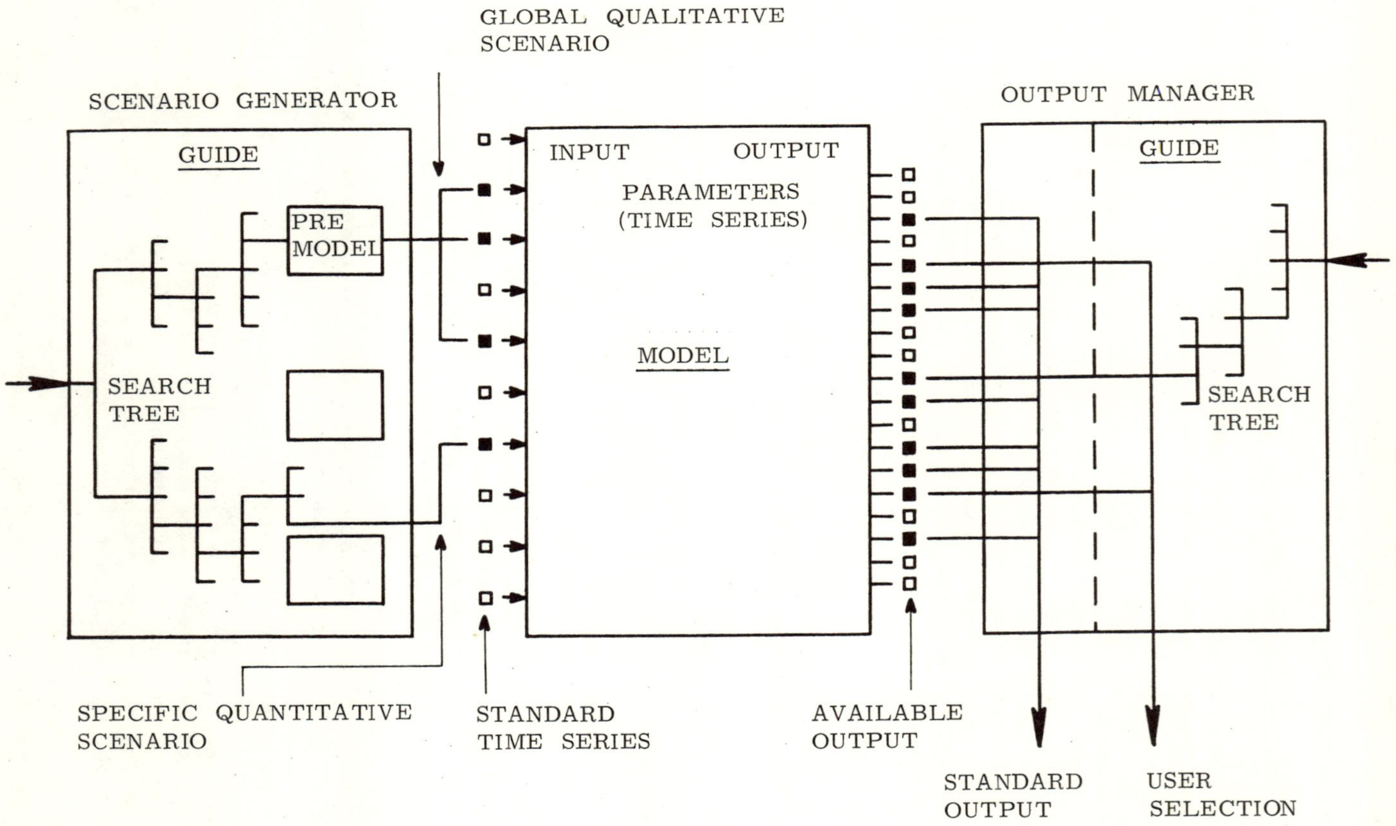

Figure 1

The GUIDE concept in relation to the computer model

GUIDE in Input Mode

The program flow is presented in Fig. 2a, 2b, 2c.

GUIDE is called from a MAIN program which associates the three input files with the logical unit numbers, connects the keyboard and the teletype or CRT screen, and defines the size of the output graphic (small for teletype, and large for line printer as output device). The format for the conversion table is left to the programmer and is transmitted to GUIDE through an array in the argument list. The program starts in input mode.

On its first entry, and only then, GUIDE presents some general information about keyboard handling and then asks the user whether he is familiar with the procedure. A new user at his first approach will receive some instructions about the system, in particular he will be presented with a list of command keys which control the system and summon technical help when he needs it.

The dialog then determines the time horizon over which the model run is envisaged. The program takes the current year as the present. From the starting year and the time span the program establishes how far back historical data should be used and how far into the future the calculations should be carried. With the time frame the user may also inspect extensive data banks for historical information only, perhaps entirely without engaging the model.

A hierarchical search procedure is now initiated. For the novice-user informative texts concerning the content, meaning, or significance of parameter descriptions provided by the model builder are printed ahead of the set of alternatives to choose from. These texts are important for the understanding of the parameter labels which are kept as short as feasible, but a stereotype repetition at every pass through the tree quickly becomes irritating and the user can drop them with the command 'O' (Omit parameter information). The program however keeps this information available at all times and presents it on command 'I' (Information request).

Each member in the set of alternatives is prefaced by a one-digit number which serves as an identifier for the user. He makes his choice by typing the identifying digit and the system calculates from these numbers the trace leading to the parameter.

If the user needs to know more about the consequences of his choice before he can decide, he may request a View of the next lower level ('V'). After providing a complete description of all the sets of alternatives which follow from the present level the program awaits the user's decision before continuing in the search tree.

When a node is found which represents an input parameter (GUIDE extracts this information from the text file), the user is offered a scenario input opportunity. If the user declines the offer the program continues to the next

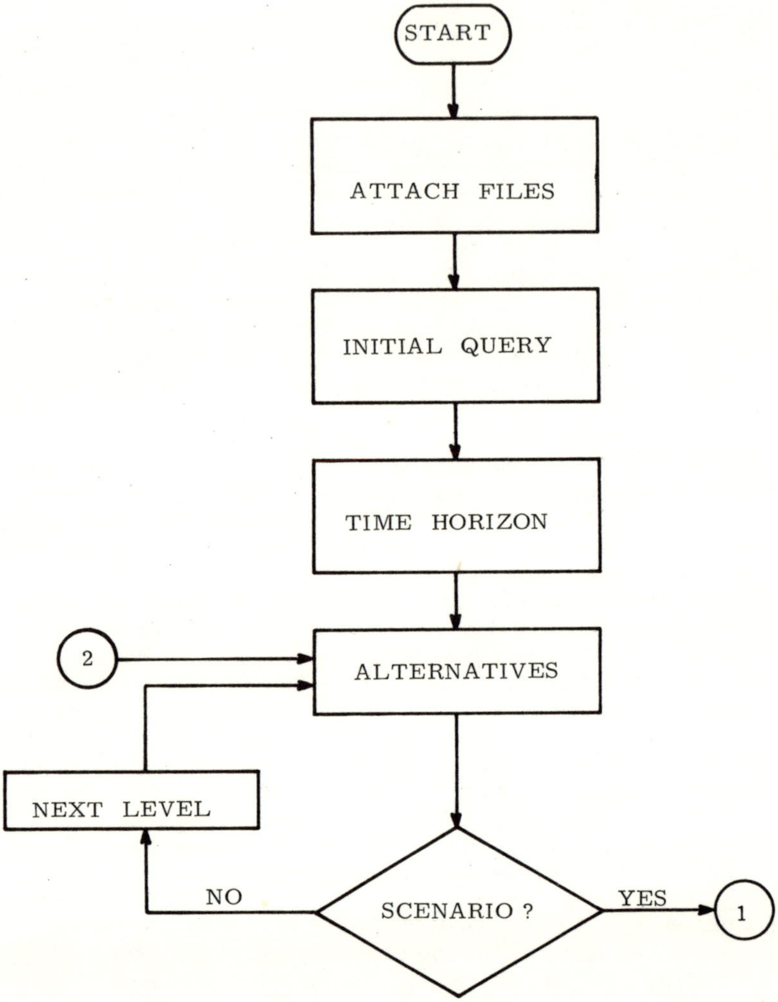

Figure 2a

GUIDE search module

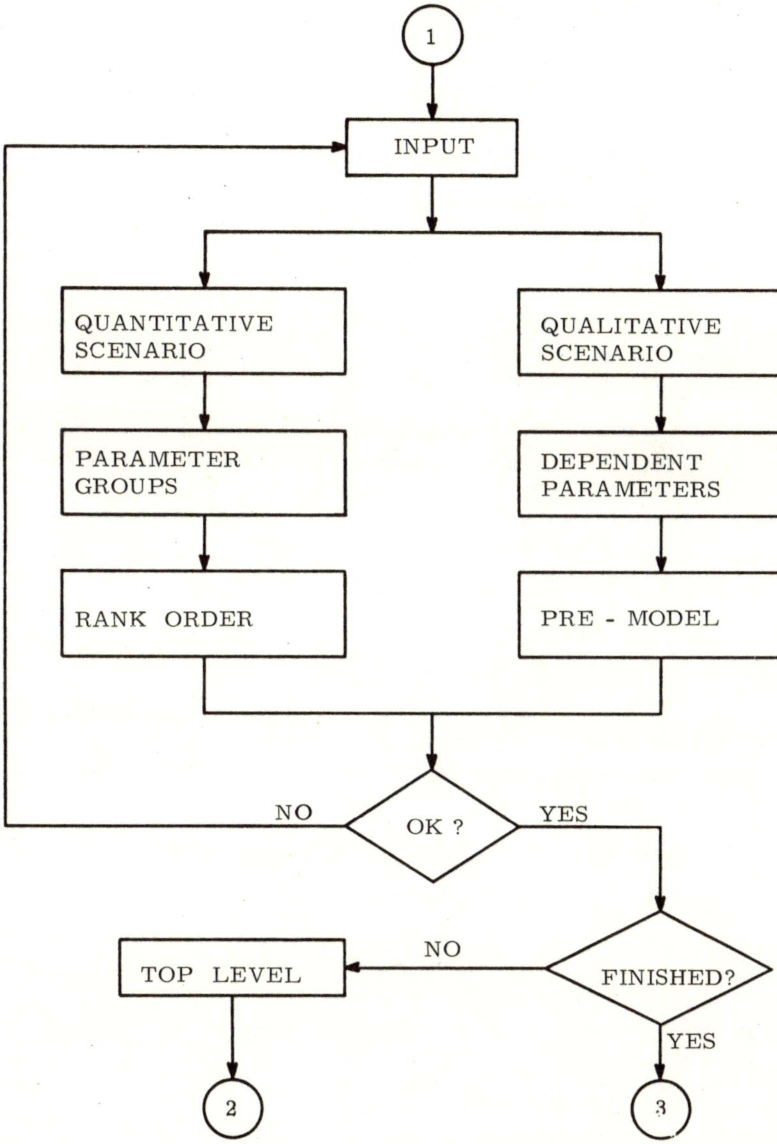

Figure 2b

GUIDE scenario input module

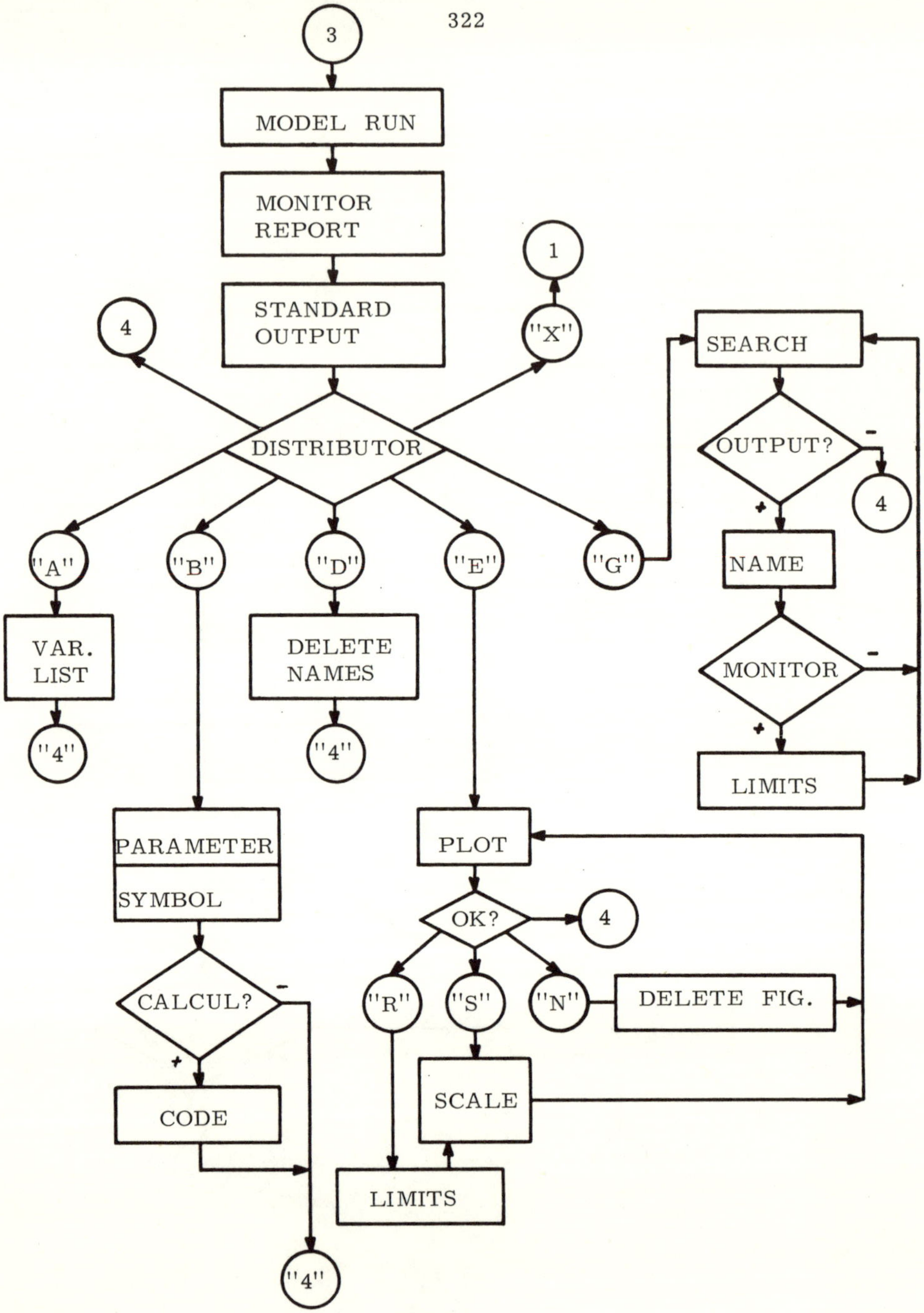

Figure 2c

GUIDE output module

lower level, or returns to the top level if the node was a terminus.

Scenarios can be of two types: G l o b a l scenarios involving inputs at an aggregated level which are distributed over the dependent disaggregated parameters automatically by the program; or s p e c i f i c scenarios addressing a single parameter. The former will always have the form of a qualitative (fuzzy) input, while the latter may be either qualitative or numerical (precise) as chosen by the user. Qualitative input consists simply of Plus- or Minus-signs indicating concepts of "more" or "less", "strong increase", "small decrease" etc. according to the parameter context. GUIDE translates these fuzzy statements into numerical values with the help of pre-models which will be discussed in more detail below. /8/

After the user has signaled that he would like to input a scenario, GUIDE writes out the time horizon and fills in historical data to the present. It then prompts the user to input his own scenario.

The program will accept numerical data as integers or decimal fractions, which again may be written in American point notation, European comma notation, or in scientific E-notation. There are no field or tabulator rules. The input is properly spaced automatically, spotty input is interpolated, missing data at the end of the time series are filled in with the last available datum. This results in a level input and avoids the dangers of extrapolation. Qualitative input is recognized as such and appropriate action taken. If necessary the user is told where a typing error occurred and the program insists on correction before accepting any more input.

The input is then presented properly aligned with the related years in the headline and the user may check it over before overwriting the standard scenario. The program then asks "OK?". If the user refuses acceptance the program prepares for a new input.

The user may also request to see the Standard scenario ('S') for his orientation whereupon the program writes out the appropriate data and repeats its prompting for the user's input. Since the data in the parameter file are not a part of the GUIDE system they may be of any form, length and composition. In order to present the data file content to the user in the limited space available on a screen with optimal information content, GUIDE constructs a floating point format for each datum such that at least 4 significant digits with the decimal point will be printed and all trailing zeros will be suppressed.

Should however the user change his mind, he may let the program know that he Waives a scenario ('W') and it continues the search process without input.

Often parameters are grouped in such a fashion that they represent proportional parts of an aggregated parameter and therefore must sum to 100 percent or unity. For example, available primary energy is a composite of several types of energy, every one of which contributes a definite proportion to the total. If the proportion of one of these parameters is changed, others have to be adapted accordingly. GUIDE selects the parameter with the smallest contribution to be adapted first, realizing that errors in small numbers weigh heaviest. It then presents all remaining parameters of the group in the order of their numerical magnitude, except for the last one which it calculates itself to ensure proper summation. It will signal a "bad scenario" if the sum exceeds 100 or unity because of inadmissible changes in the free parameters. If the model builder has indicated that no summation constraints exist, GUIDE will not insist on completing the last parameter of the group. Before overwriting the standard scenario of any of the group parameters they are submitted for the user's approval.

In the case of a global scenario, GUIDE accepts the qualitative input series and converts the indicated rates of change to numerical values individually for each parameter. The user is informed of the new scenario data for each parameter which the program determines automatically. He cannot immediately express his approval or disapproval, since global changes are made en block. However he can address any individual parameter and effect a numerical scenario input according to his own concepts. Since GUIDE presents the parameters affected by global changes by their internal number rather than by their label in the text file, the user can shortcut the search tree and request the parameter in question directly or Unguided ('U').

The professional user who is likely to be familiar with the internal numbers of the parameters will benefit from this feature which speeds up scenario composition considerably. Also the model builder in the validation phase of his model may find direct access to parameters convenient.

During the input and search phase the user is supported by a number of command keys which control either the flow of the search process or give access to sources of information.

Thus the user may want to select more than one parameter from a set of alternatives. With the command Maintain level ('M') the program will stay at the present level of the search tree and submit the same set of alternatives for another decision. If the user finds himself in a wrong branch of the tree he may return to the top level by requesting 'Z' Zero level to start a new search process. 'Y' Yes and 'N' No are natural answers to the OK? question.

The user may also for inspection purposes change the time horizon at any stage of the input phase (and change it back to the original) with 'K' (Kalendar). GUIDE prints the appropriate prompting line and accepts a new starting year and time span. In this fashion the user can move a window over the length of the data base and the scenarios for the future.

At any point in the dialog the inexperienced user may request Help ('H') if he gets confused about the proper action to take. GUIDE holds technical advice ready at all junctions anticipating user demands. Finally the List of command keys can be called up by typing 'L' anytime and thus there is no need to learn by heart the association of the mnemonic keys with their action.

When all scenario input is finished, a new parameter vector is available for a model run. GUIDE can call the model itself if the model kernel is a FORTRAN program, or it can return to the MAIN program which then initiates a model run in accordance with installation procedures. With 'X' (EXit) GUIDE automatically changes to output mode.

The Pre-model Concept

Qualitative inputs, as discussed in the previous section, consist of fuzzy statements about rate of change which are translated to numerical values with the help of pre-models. Qualitative inputs make it possible to change whole blocks of parameters on an aggregated level, provided the globally indicated change can be disaggregated and distributed, properly transformed, over individual parameters. The rules of transformation are determined by the model builder. He has the prerogative to judge the amount of change on each parameter which should correspond to the meaning of, say, "a small increase".

It should be noted at this point that the transformation process is biased by the perception of the model builder, which may not in all cases suit the user. Should the user have his doubts about the judgement of the model builder, he can access the parameter in question directly to impose his own point of view (in contrast to other simulation methods where parameter changes are made deep within the model).

The option to input aggregated and only qualitative scenarios represents a major convenience for the user of complex models. To get a feel for the reaction of the simulated system he can with very little effort probe whole areas of the model. Alternatives which look promising can then be tested and examined at a more concrete level. As long as the user has not acquired the precise knowledge necessary to make realistic numerical parameter changes he can nevertheless operate the simulation model with approximate ideas and achieve results with reasonable trends corresponding to the problem he is interested in. He can change a great number of parameters with one stroke and can thus escape the burden of inputting detailed values for each of the parameters in question.

Figure 3 illustrates the scenario generation at various levels of aggregation in the parameter access tree of an economic model. (Alternatives which are not chosen are only indicated and then abandoned.) The user is interested in the consequences of increasing the life time of capital equipment.

He can start his investigation on a highly aggregated level. He could for example indicate a small increase in the life time of capital investment from 1975 to 1985, then a large increase from 1985 to 2000 and so forth. In this case all economic sectors and branches are changed accordingly. At a somewhat less aggregated level he could indicate an increase in capital investment life time for the production sector only, which would result in appropriate changes in the five production branches. At the fully disaggregated level the user could increase the life time of capital investment specifically in the appliance

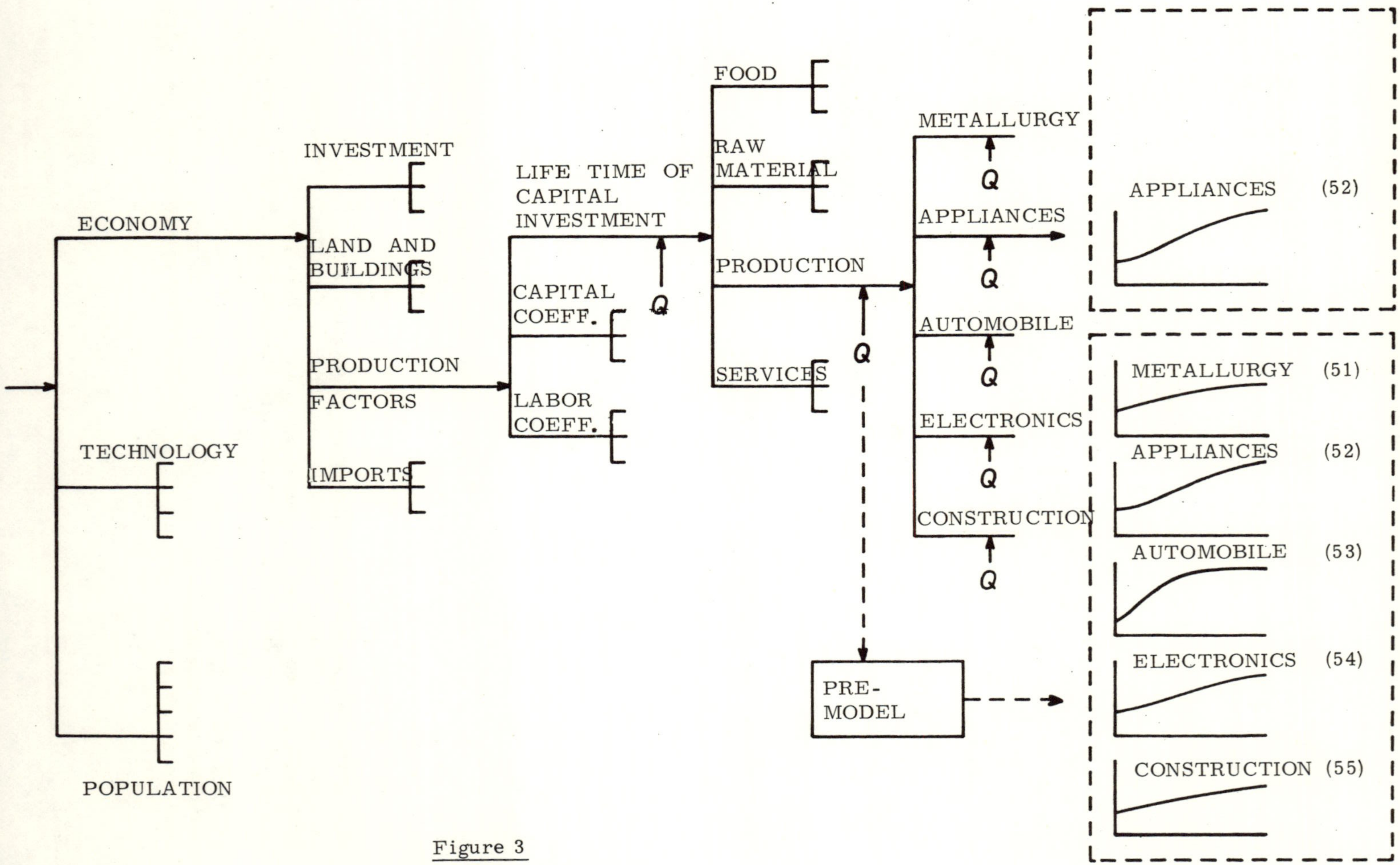

Figure 3

GUIDE tree structure
for an economic model

industry. Even here he could still use qualitative statements if he is not sufficiently knowledgable about the numerical values.

GUIDE obtains qualitative scenario inputs through the keyboard from the user according to the following scale

Rate of growth

	negative (decline)				positive (growth)		
	high	intermediate	small		small	intermediate	high
user input:	---	--	-	Ø	+	++	+++

These intervals usually correspond approximately to an exponential scale of -8, -4, -2, 0, +2, +4, +8 percent (annual) change in accordance with psychophysical and perceptual research / 9 /. In each case however the actual transformation coefficient is provided through the pre-model. Thus, "high positive" rate of growth for populations would translate to about 2% p. a.

From the time series data which contain actual values of the parameter up to the present, the rate of change from the keyboard, and the transformation coefficient from a table provided by the model builder, GUIDE calculates the required value of the parameter as a function of time. With the time period held constant the value of the function at time (t) is the product of the initial value and the growth factors of the successive periods:

$$x_n = x_1 \prod_{i=1}^{n-1} F_i$$

where

x_1 = initial value

x_n = value at time n

F_i = growth factor of period i
 = e^{rcp}

r = growth rate from keyboard

c = coefficient from table

p = period

In our population example a "strong rate of growth" would be indicated on the keyboard by the user as '+++' which corresponds to 8 intervals. GUIDE would find in the table for the population parameter the coefficient of .25, chosen by the model builder to attenuate one unit of change by a factor of 4. The rate of change would thus be 8 x .25 = 2% p. a. With this growth rate and a period of 5 years the growth factor would be $e^{(8/100)(.25)(5)} = 1.1052$. and a population of 4×10^9 would increase to 4.4×10^9 by 1980. This value would be inserted in its proper place in the time series together with the values for the remaining years to be calculated accordingly till the end of the time horizon.

Pre-models can be made as complex as the model builder cares to make them. The presently discussed approach has the advantage of great economy and efficiency. The model builder simply defines the coefficient of change for each parameter which amounts to one column in the conversion table. GUIDE assembles the available information from the data and the keyboard and proceeds to generate the required data. With this device any model can be provided with the qualitative and global scenario facility without much inconvenience. For the user the advantages are considerable: Apart from the constraint to possess expert knowledge, the amount of work demanded to change perhaps hundreds of parameters makes numerical errors difficult to avoid. The error risk is particularly small with potential professional users who have quite definite ideas about "low", respectively "high" rates of growth or decline.

In addition, the model builder retains a measure of control over model runs by foolhardy users. This control could be pushed easily one step further. GUIDE could always compare numerical inputs by the user with the amount of change defined as normal or standard by the model builder in the transformation table and send a message when reasonable limits are exceeded. One such monitor function is already implemented and will be discussed in the output section.

GUIDE in Output Mode

The user initiates a model run by exiting from the input mode ('X'). GUIDE returns after all calculations have been completed in the output mode. By that time it has connected the text file which enables a guided search to all model output parameters. This file corresponds to the text file of the input parameters and is constructed by the model builder according to the same rules. Also the output conversion table has replaced the corresponding input table and has been read into core memory. The output data file has been connected to the input tape which earlier contained the historical and scenario data. The only formal difference in these files lies in the conversion table which instead of the pre-model coefficients contains a four-character short name for those parameters which are designated by the model builder to appear in the standard output.

Standard outputs are a convenient device to give an inexperienced model user the chance to obtain essential results of a model run without any knowledge or effort on his part. The model builder decides which of the parameters convey the most important results or the results easiest to interpret and enters a short name of the parameter into the conversion table together with the number of the graph in which they are to appear. GUIDE gathers all these parameters and builds a list of names. A maximum of five parameters are then grouped to a graph and output is started automatically until the list of names is exhausted.

The output consists of a table of the numerical values over the previously determined time horizon, complemented by a graphical representation of the parameters as a function of time. The graph is headed by the short name, the symbol, the limiting values of the function, and the scale over which it is plotted.

Scaling is provided by the program respecting the principle of proportionally correct representation to the detriment of precision (for which the table could be consulted). For parameters with only positive values the null coordinate is always at the bottom of the graph. For parameters with negative values the null coordinate is placed on the most appropriate horizontal divider. Scale factors are chosen as powers of 10 to ranges of 1, 2, 4, 8 which result in scales that can easily be fitted to the coordinates. The abscissa is labelled with the appropriate time steps.

The program then requests a decision whether this graph should be accepted into the session output sequence, whose composition is retained in all the simulation runs of a session. If the answer is negative, this particular composition of parameters is dropped from the session output, although the parameters would still remain on the name list. They could be incorporated into some other graphs in different compositions.

The name list contains after the first model run only those parameters the model builder has selected for the standard output. The user can add to this list the parameters of his choice, selected by a search process identical to the input parameter selection.

The user may call for a Guided search ('G') through the output parameter access tree under the same rules as in the input mode. If GUIDE encounters a node representing an output parameter it asks the user whether it should include it in the output list. If the answer is affirmative, the user is prompted to supply a short name (1 to 4 letters) for the parameter. At this point he can also decide whether he wants this parameter monitored for critical values. In this case he enters the upper and lower limits beyond which GUIDE should report on deviations. The conditional reports keep the session output from getting cluttered, and at the same time attention is drawn to parameters which become interesting only when they reach extremes. This monitor function relieves the user from a great deal of tedious checking and frees his attention for the parameters in the focus of his interest.

During the search through the decision tree the same commands are active as in the output mode. Thus the user can bypass the search procedure if he knows the internal parameter number of his choice ('U'), and directly assemble the list of names from which he composes the graphs.

The Assembly list can be printed or displayed for reference by typing 'A'. Deletions in the list ('D') are executed by typing the identifying numbers which appear in the list before each short name. GUIDE reprints the new assembly list with updated numbering.

The command 'B' (Build a figure) causes GUIDE to prompt the composition of a new figure. GUIDE indicates the running index of the new figure and expects an identifying number for the first parameter to be entered. Together with the internal parameter index it copies the short name from the assembly list and waits for the symbol with which the parameter is to be labelled in the graph. Up to 5 parameters are acceptable for a graph, more would result in rather confused pictures on the 20 x 60 point resolution monitor screen of the usual terminal.

The user signals the End of his composition by 'E'. He may compose as many graphs in advance as he wishes. With 'F' he requests Figure output and GUIDE prints the table and the graph of the figure chosen. The OK? question permits the user to incorporate the figure into the session output or to erase it after inspection ('N').

Often the automatic scaling procedure obscures the relationship between similar functions and the user may want to see all variables plotted on a common scale. He can order Standardization of the scale by typing 'S'. GUIDE plots the new graph without repeating the table.

Again the user may prefer his own scale and signal his wishes to the program by 'R' (Rescale to reference). GUIDE will then accept the minimum and maximum values corresponding to the lower and upper range boundaries and output a new graph. With this feature it is also possible to achieve a magnifying glass effect by choosing limiting values in a relatively narrow range.

Finally, if the user has forgotten the meaning of the short name version of the parameter, he may request a list of the full names of all parameters in the figure by typing 'P'.

With 'F' the user can call any figure in the session output list and leaf through consecutive graphs, so that graphs can be more easily compared.

A further feature implemented in GUIDE is the possibility to first operate on the parameters before outputting the results. Often the relationship between two parameters is the variable of interest, or the parameter needs to be transformed to other units of measurement such as feet to meters. The user has the choice of 9 Calculations to be performed on the parameters by terminating a composition with 'C' rather than with 'E'. The program then accepts the code number of the desired calculation and executes it prior to outputting the corresponding figure. The following calculations are presently implemented:

1. Calculate the difference between parameter A and B.
   (Y = B - A)
2. Sum the series of parameters A, B, C...
   (Y = A + B + C...)
3. Plot the ratio of two parameters
   (Y = A/B)

4. Integrate a parameter with respect to time.
   $(Y = \sum A \Delta T)$
5. Plot the rate of change of a parameter.
   $(Y = \Delta A / \Delta T)$
6. Plot the log transformation of a parameter.
   $(Y = \log A)$
7. Plot the inverse function of a parameter.
   $(Y = 1/A)$
8. Multiply the parameter by a constant.
   $(Y = C \times A)$
9. Show the correlation of two parameters.
   (A : B)
   In the latter case the customary time axis on the abscissa is replaced by the second parameter as one parameter is plotted as a function of the other. The resulting scattergram shows the strength and the sign of the correlation.

Should a calculation become necessary which is not implemented in the above list it would be very simple to replace a superfluous one with the desired calculation. In the subroutine where the operations are performed (TRANS) the FORTRAN line containing the assignment statement of the superfluous calculation would have to be replaced. No great programming skills are necessary to effect this change.

As in the input mode, the user can summon Help ('H') at every step of the dialog. GUIDE provides technical information relevant to the next step to be taken. For example, if after having requested 'C' (Calculations) he does not know the code number of the calculation he wants to have performed, 'H' will produce the list he is looking for.

Again 'L' will List the command keys if the user cannot remember them. And 'X' will cause GUIDE to EXit from the output mode and return to the input for the preparation of a new model run.

In the course of a working session with a model the user accumulates rapidly a repertoire of experimental results which contains the outcomes of the various scenario games in a clear, differentiated and retrievable fashion. He has access to the figures at all times, he can freely change between the various phases of input preparation and output processing and thus should come to understand the model behavior in a relatively short time.

For the model builder the convenience in output handling does not impose undue loads. No new conventions need to be learned since input and output files are constructed by identical rules. The only difference is the replacement of the pre-model coefficients by the short names of the selected output parameters, a trivial change as far as file construction is concerned.

4. ATTACHING A MODEL TO GUIDE

The last section concentrated on the aspects of GUIDE concerning the potential model user. The accent was placed on providing an interesting variety of useful devices to aid the learning process and the policy analysis of the user, sustain his motivation, protect him from frustrations and organize his memory.

The following section describes the aspects of GUIDE concerning the model builder, who is the primary user. For, if the model builder does not attach his model to GUIDE it has only limited practical value by itself. The accent here is on simplicity and convenience. Although connecting a model to GUIDE does involve some work, there are differences in magnitudes compared to the investment of time and effort required to make a model - any model - responsive to an interactive dialog and provide it with all the conveniences discussed previously. In fact the construction of input-output handling facilities for the energy model ESPINT/10/ required some 900 man-hours of highly qualified technical personnel. By contrast, the setting up of a fully interactive input dialog for a model of similar complexity using the GUIDE system required some 20 man-hours.

The programmer has to (1) construct a text file for the search tree, (2) develop a conversion table, and (3), connect the files, including the data files, to GUIDE.

Text File Syntax

In order to illustrate the construction of a text file we use the tree structured in Fig. 3. On the lowest level there is the list of parameters which provide the model with the necessary data and scenario time series: 1, ...51 metallurgy, 52 appliances, 53 automobile, 54 electronics, 55 construction, 56 ...... 144. This group of parameters belongs to the production sector which shares the next higher level of the tree with three other sectors and so on. We want to code this tree such that GUIDE can lead the user to any given parameter on the lowest level. In addition we want to provide explanatory texts for the user to facilitate his understanding of the intermediate concepts we will use to organize the tree. In the following we present a valid code of all concepts in Fig. 3, with the abandoned branches only indicated. The rules of file construction can be easily deduced from the examples.

Text file example

```
"Which simulation model would you like to work with?"
:1"Economy" :1"Technology" :1"Population"
$
"Which model sector are you interested in?"
:1"Investments" :1"Land and buildings" :1"Production factors" :1"Imports"
:2" .....   :3" ..... .
$
```

```
"Choose from the following production factors."
:3"Life time of capital investment "30:3" Capital coefficient"
:3"Labor coefficient" :1" ..... :2" ..... :4" .....
$
"Which production sector are you interested in?"
:1"Food" :1"Raw materials" :1"Production" :1"Services" :2"..." :3"...
$
"Select the production branch"
:3"Metallurgy"12 :3"Appliances"12 :3"Automobiles"12 :3"Electronics"12
:3"Construction"12 :1" ..... :2" ..... :4" ..... :5" ..... :6" .....
$
```

Explanation of the rules

The search tree is organized in l e v e l s. Each level is terminated by a '$' in column 1 of an otherwise empty record.

All T e x t is enclosed in quotes (").

N o d e s consist of 3 components: the Link, the Name and the Qualifier, which are written as a unit. Nodes are separated by space(s).

The L i n k is preceded by a colon (:) and points towards the origin of the node on the previous level. On the first (top) level all Links are :1. On the second level the Link :1, points towards "Economy" which is the first node on its level. On the third level the Link :3 points toward "Production factors" which is the third node on its level. On the next level :1 points towards "life time of capital investment which is the first node on its level, and on the last level :3 points toward "Production" which is the third entry on its level.

The sequence of entries is immaterial; more than one Link can precede a node if there is convergence in a tree or if concepts are the same.

The N a m e is enclosed in quotation marks ("). It is a short description of a concept or a parameter.

The Q u a l i f i e r is a 2-digit number which contains the instructions to GUIDE for the treatment of this node according to the following scheme:

	Digit 1	Digit 2	
Not a parameter	Ø	Ø	Not member of a group
Parameter (continue)	1	1	Group sums to 100 or unity
Parameter (stop)	2	2	Group, no constraints
Global scenario	3		

If the qualifier is omitted it is interpreted as ØØ. All digit combinations are valid and meaningful (digit 1 ≠ Ø).

In the example there are only dummy nodes on the first two levels. The first qualifier appears on level 3, node 1 (3∅). "life time of capital investment" is a node permitting a global scenario. No groups are involved. A similar qualifier appears on the next level for "Production". The qualifiers for the first five entries on the last level (12) indicate specific parameters which belong to a group, but which do not add to a totality, i. e. they do not express percentages of production but rather output in dollar values.

Extension of existing codes

These rules suffice to quickly convert a decision tree to a GUIDE text file. A few details omitted in this description of the rules can be found in the GUIDE handbook /11/.

The bulk of the work lies in the conceptualization of the hierarchical access. The simplicity of the rules is no hindrance to construct rather complex trees, yet the amount of work is kept to a minimum.

Should the need arise to perform other operations on the input parameters than the ones already provided, the 2-digit scheme permits 100 codes for the qualifiers to instruct GUIDE of the model builder's prescriptions. Within GUIDE a subroutine called from the decoding point could then assume the job without further modifications to the existing system.

The Conversion Table

The function of the conversion table is to convert the trace through the decision tree to a parameter index. We use the already built (partial) tree to demonstrate its construction.

Suppose the target is the automobile industry parameter which was arbitrarily labelled No. 53. That is in the running numbers of parameters the 53rd contains the data for the automobile industry. (The READ statement of GUIDE addressing this time series would have to read record No. 53.) The user would have chosen among the presented alternatives from level to level as follows:

On level 1 No. 1 (Economy)
On level 2 No. 3 (Production factors)
On level 3 No. 1 (Life time of capital investment)
On level 4 No. 3 (Production)
On level 5 No. 3 (Automobile industry)

Arranged from left to right the path through the decision tree would read as 13133. In the conversion table the parameter 53 would be associated with 13133, (written in the next column of the same line). For each trace one and only one parameter index is possible and necessary. A parameter index may however be associated with more than one trace if it can be accessed over different routes. Therefore the number of lines in the conversion table may exceed the number of parameters.

There is no prescribed order for the arrangement of the table other than that the first column must contain the parameter index, the second must contain the trace. The third should contain the pre-model transformation coefficient in the input table (for the output cf. below).

The format is left to the programmer and is transmitted in the IFT array as variable format in the argument list of the CALL GUIDE statement (cf. below). It should be noted that the trace and the coefficient are to be declared real numbers to avoid integer overflow on small machines for a long trace.

The function of the pre-model coefficient is to attenuate or magnify the effect of whole number input from the keyboard for qualitative scenarios. In most cases the coefficient will probably be unity (i. e. a qualitative input of "+" would correspond to a 2% annual growth rate). In our example in a previous section, a population increase of.5% corresponding to a "+" input was achieved by a transformation coefficient of .25 in the input table. Precise calibration of rates of change is possible (cf. the growth function in the section on the pre-model concept).

For the output table the third column contains the short name (maximum of 4 letters) of the parameter. If the name is missing, the parameter is not included in the standard output list. This simple device allows the model builder to demonstrate the model in his absence. If the model builder is interested in the organization of the graphs, he can arrange the sequence of parameters such that the graphs contain (in groups of 5) the parameters of his choice.

In the Format statement the names are to be declared Hollerith type and are to be read with A4 specification.

If the input conversion table has the following form:

bb53bbb13133bbbbb1.5 (where b = blank)

the Format transmitted would read:

(I4, 2F8.1)

If the output conversion table has the following form:

bb21bbbbb121bbbbPOPL

the Format transmitted would read:

(I4, F8.0, 4X, A4)

The GUIDE Auxiliary Routines Deck (GUARD)

GUIDE assumes the text file and conversion table to be error free. It has no means of detecting programmer errors. In order to assist the programmer in debugging the text file and conversion table, GUARD has been developed with four checking functions which will be discussed separately.

The programmer runs GUARD as an independent MAIN program and submits the text file and the conversion table. GUARD responds with four alternative output modes which can be chosen according to the stage of the debugging process.

The first pass checks for syntax errors in the text file. GUARD prints an image of each line of the text file and indicates the column on which it has detected an error together with the error diagnostic.

The programmer then corrects the errors and resubmits the file to GUARD until it passes check mode 1 without errors.

Check mode 2 concerns the linkage structure of the text file. Since the nodes are written successively on a line, the counting process involved to determine the proper link on the next lower level of the decision tree can become confused in large trees. GUARD dissassembles the levels each entry to a line with the running index of the node and the link(s). Visual tracking of the structure is now quite easy.

In check mode 3 the conversion table is examined for logical errors. GUARD generates from the links in the text file all traces and compares them with those in the table. If a trace is found it determines whether the corresponding node is a parameter in the text file, whether it is unique, whether some parameters are left dangling and whether the table contains traces which cannot be generated. It also checks the validity of the qualifier.

Finally in check mode 4, GUARD generates the decision tree for visual inspection.

The debugging of large trees thus becomes an easy task and the probability of falsifying model runs due to programmer errors while coupling the model to GUIDE is very low.

GUARD is written in FORTRAN IV, like GUIDE. It is an independent package which is only interesting to programmers. The use of GUARD is extremely simple and no special knowledge is required for working with it. Technical details can be found in the GUIDE and GUARD handbook /11/.

Installation-specific Data File Handling

In most instances the data file, which contains historical statistics about the input parameters, and the standard scenario for the future, will exist on a mass storage device (tape or disk). The data files for both the input and output parameters are preferably put onto random access devices. Otherwise (for small data bases) data could be read into core memory. For sequential access a GUIDE subroutine could be used but READ statements in the program accessing data would have to be accommodated. The text file and the conversion table are likely to be prepared off-line on cards or dayfiles and the model results are written onto peripheral storage devices available to the installation.

In order to accommodate the diverse methods of file handling by the many operating systems, GUIDE is written as a subroutine to be called from a MAIN program. This MAIN program has the following basic structure:

```
1  Associate the input text file with input unit IU1
             the conversion table with IU2
             the data file with IU3
   CALL  GUIDE  (MOD, II, IO, IU1, IU2, IU3, LP, IFT)
   CALL  MODEL
   Associate the output text file with IU1
             the conversion table with IU2
             the output parameter file with IU3
   CALL  GUIDE  (MOD, II, IO, IU1, IU2, IU3, LP, IFT)
   GO  TO  1
```

The argument list of the CALL statement contains

- MOD = Input or output mode of GUIDE
  MOD should be = 0 on first entry, from then on GUIDE sets the operating mode automatically.
- II = Input unit, i.e. the logical unit number of the keyboard from which GUIDE is to be controlled.
- IO = Output unit, i.e. the logical unit number of the output device of the user dialog, (teletype or CRT monitor).
- IU1 - IU3 = logical unit numbers of the input tapes.
- LP = controls the size of the graphs in the output mode. For teletype and CRT size use LP = 1, for line printer (132 char./line) use LP = 2.
- IFT = Input format for the conversion table (see previous section on conversion table).

At installations where peripheral devices cannot be assigned within a FORTRAN program, it may become necessary to change the logical unit numbers IU1 through IU3 for the output mode to IU4 through IU6 and preassign the three files accordingly. Details about GUIDE installation-specific problems are discussed in the handbook /11/.

5. COMMENTED EXAMPLE OF A GUIDE APPLICATION

We now give an example of the application of GUIDE to develop a model scenario and manipulate the model output by a user with little experience. We will use a fully implemented energy model with 144 input parameters. Since we are only interested in the demonstration of GUIDE we will use the same text file, conversion table and data for input and output. Ordinarily these would of course be different (Fig. 4 and 5).

```
 IN WHICH PART OF THE MESAROVIC-PESTEL WORLD MODEL
WOULD YOU LIKE TO WORK ?"
:1"POPULATION"  :1"EDUCATION"  :1"TECHNOLOGY"  :1"ECONOMY"
$
"IN WHICH SECTOR WOULD YOU LIKE TO WORK ?"
:3"RESOURCES"  :3"LABOR"  :3"ENERGY"
$
" WHICH ASPECT OF THE ENERGY SECTOR ARE YOU INTERESTED IN?"
:3"ENERGY INPUT"  :3"END ENERGY CONTRIBUTIONS"
:3"PRIMARY ENERGY INPUTS"  :3"CONVERSION EFFICIENCIES"
$
"ENERGY USAGE IN THE SECTORS OF THE ECONOMY
 (METRIC TON EQUIVALENT / MIO $ GROSS VALUE ADDED)"
:1"BASIC MATERIALS"  :1"CONSUMER GOODS"  :1"INVESTMENT GOODS"30
:1"SERVICES"
"CONTRIBUTIONS OF THE DIFFERENT END ENERGIES
 TO SECTORAL END ENERGY USE (PERCENT)"
:2"BASIC MATERIALS"  :2"CONSUMER GOODS"  :2"INVESTMENT GOODS"
:2"SERVICES"
"PRIMARY ENERGY REQUIRED TO PROVIDE ONE UNIT OF END ENERGY:
 WHICH FORM OF END ENERGY?"
:3"COAL"  :3"LIQUID FUEL"  :3"GAS"  :3"ELECTRICITY"
:3"DISTRICT HEATING"
"AVERAGE CONVERSION EFFICIENCY FROM PRIMARY TO END ENERGY (PERCENT):
 WHICH FORM OF END ENERGY?"
:4"COAL"10 :4"LIQUID FUEL"10 :4"GAS"10 :4"ELECTRICITY"10
:4"DISTRICT HEATING"10
$
"WHICH SECTOR OF THE ECONOMY?"
:1"AGRICULTURE"20 :1"ENERGY"20 :1"MINING"20 :1"BUILDING MATERIALS"20
:2"FOOD INDUSTRY"20 :2"TEXTILE INDUSTRY"20 :2"GARMENT INDUSTRY"20 :2"WOO
D,PAPER, AND PRINTING INDUSTRY"20 :2"CHEMICAL INDUSTRY"20 :3"RAW METALS
INDUSTRY"20 :3"METAL WORKING INDUSTRY"20 :3"AUTOMOBILE INDUSTRY"20 :3"MA
CHINE BUILDING AND ELECTRICAL"20 :3"CONSTRUCTION"20 :4"RETAILING"20
:4"TRANSPORTATION"20 :4"HOUSING"20 :4"GOVERNMENT"20 :4"OTHER SERVICES"20
 :5"AGRICULTURE"  :5"ENERGY"  :5"MINING"  :5"BUILDING MATERIALS"  :6"FOOD I
NDUSTRY"  :6"TEXTILE INDUSTRY"  :6"GARMENT INDUSTRY"  :6"WOOD,PAPER,AND PRI
NTING INDUSTRY"  :6"CHEMICAL INDUSTRY"  :7"RAW METAL INDUSTRY"  :7"METAL W
ORKING INDUSTRY"  :7"AUTOMOBILE INDUSTRY"  :7"MACHINE BUILDING AND ELECTRI
CAL INDUSTRY"  :7"CONSTRUCTION"  :8"RETAILING"  :8"TRANSPORTATION"  :8"HOU
SING"  :8"GOVERNMENT"  :8"OTHER SERVICES"
"WHICH PRIMARY ENERGY?"
:9:10:11:12:13"COAL"12 :9:10:11:12:13"SOFT COAL"12
:9:10:11:12:13"OIL"12 :9:10:11:12:13"NATURAL GAS"12
:9:10:11:12:13"HYDRO AND NUCLEAR ENERGY"10
$
"CONTRIBUTIONS OF THE DIFFERENT END ENERGIES
 TO SECTORAL END ENERGY USER (PERCENT)"
:20:21:22:23:24:25:26:27:28:29:30:31:32:33:34:35:36:37:38"COAL"11
:20:21:22:23:24:25:26:27:28:29:30:31:32:33:34:35:36:37:38"LIQUID FUEL"11
 :20:21:22:23:24:25:26:27:28:29:30:31:32:33:34:35:36:37:38"GAS"11
:20:21:22:23:24:25:26:27:28:29:30:31:32:33:34:35:36:37:38"ELECTRICITY"11
 :20:21:22:23:24:25:26:27:28:29:30:31:32:33:34:35:36:37:38"DISTRICT HEAT
ING"11
"AVERAGE CONVERSION EFFICIENCY
 FROM PRIMARY ENERGY TO THE END ENERGY SELECTED"
:39:40:41:42:43"PERCENT EFFICIENCY"20
$
*
```

Figure 4

Text file for energy part of technology model.

Input

Param. No.	Trace	Growth factor
1	33111	.33
2	33112	.1
3	33113	.5
4	33114	1.
5	33121	.5
6	33122	.25
7	33123	.5
121	33322	.25
122	33323	1.
123	33324	.5
124	33325	1.5
125	33331	.5
126	33332	.25
127	33333	.33
141	3342	.33
142	3343	1.5
143	3344	.5
144	3345	1.
140	333111	.5
140	333121	.25
140	333131	.5

Output

Param. No.	Trace	Name
1	33111	AGRC
2	33112	ENRG
3	33113	MING
4	33114	BLDG
5	33121	FOOD
6	33122	
7	33123	
8	33124	
9	33125	
20	332111	COAL
21	332112	
22	332113	GAS
23	332114	ELEC
24	332115	
25	332121	
26	332122	
27	332123	
28	332124	
29	332125	
30	332131	
31	332132	
32	332133	

Figure 5
Conversion table for energy part of technology model. (excerpt)

The user (U) controls GUIDE (G) from a terminal keyboard and receives answers over the teletype.

(1)

```
HELLO !
THIS IS YOUR FRIENDLY GUIDE TO THE MODEL PARAMETERS.
RESPOND ON KEYBOARD AS SUGGESTED BY DISPLAY.
TERMINATE ALL RESPONSES WITH <CR>.
"RUB OUT" ERASES ERRORS.
```

1 GUIDE has been called by the MAIN program and issues preliminary instructions for an inexperienced user.

```
ARE YOU FAMILIAR WITH THE PROCEDURE ?     (2)

N                                         (3)

GUIDE AND INPUT COMMAND KEYS :            (4)
===============================
H=HELP !
I=INFORMATION REQUEST
K=KALENDAR - TIME HORIZON
L=LIST COMMAND KEYS
M=MAINTAIN LEVEL
N=NO
O=OMIT PARAMETER INFORMATION
S=STANDARD SCENARIO
T=TERMINATE SEARCH
U=UNGUIDED ACCESS TO PARAMETERS
V=VIEW LOWER LEVEL
W=WAIVE SCENARIO
X=EXIT : RUN MODEL
Y=YES
Z=ZERO LEVEL RESTART

OUTPUT COMMAND KEYS:
=====================
A=ASSEMBLY LIST
B=BUILD FIGURE
C=CALCULATE OPERATION
D=DELETE FROM LIST
E=END OF FIGURE
F=FIGURE OUTPUT
G=GUIDED SEARCH
H=HELP !
L=LIST COMMAND KEYS.
X=EXIT : TO INPUT MODE
```

2 G wants the user to indicate his competence.
3 U admits ignorance.
4 G serves the list of command keys.

```
DETERMINE TIME HORIZON                          (5)
FIRST YEAR:   TIME SPAN     INTERVAL
    1975         50            10               (6)

SCENARIO INPUT MODE.                            (7)

IN WHICH PART OF THE MESAROVIC-PESTEL WORLD MODEL
WOULD YOU LIKE TO WORK?
      1=POPULATION
      2=EDUCATION
      3=TECHNOLOGY
      4=ECONOMY
3
```

5 G starts input procedures by establishing the time horizon.
6 U responds with a 50 year future-oriented period, in 10 year steps.
7 G announces input mode, then displays alternative parts of the world model.

```
                                                (8)
TECHNOLOGY                                      (9)
====================

IN WHICH SECTOR WOULD YOU LIKE TO WORK?
      1=RESOURCES
      2=LABOR
      3=ENERGY
3                                               (10)
```

8 U selects 3 (Technology).
9 G acknowledges choice and offers model sectors.
10 U chooses 3 (Energy).

```
ENERGY                                          (11)
====================

WHICH ASPECT OF THE ENERGY SECTOR ARE YOU INTERESTED IN?
      1=ENERGY INPUT
      2=END ENERGY CONTRIBUTIONS
      3=PRIMARY ENERGY INPUTS
      4=CONVERSION EFFICIENCIES
```

11 G narrows choice to parameter groups.

```
V                                                  (12)

          ENERGY INPUT                             (13)
               BASIC MATERIALS
               CONSUMER GOODS
               INVESTMENT GOODS
               SERVICES
          END ENERGY CONTRIBUTIONS
               BASIC MATERIAL
               CONSUMER GOODS
               INVESTMENT GOODS
               SERVICES
          PRIMARY ENERGY INPUTS
               COAL
               LIQUID FUEL
               GAS
               ELECTRICITY
               DISTRICT HEATING
          CONVERSION EFFICIENCIES
               COAL
               LIQUID FUEL
               GAS
               ELECTRICITY
               DISTRICT HEATING
```

12 U needs more information and asks for a preview.

13 G prints next lower level of the decision tree.

```
1                                                  (14)

ENERGY INPUT                                       (15)
====================

ENERGY USAGE IN THE SECTORS OF THE ECONOMY
(METRIC TON OF COAL EQUIVALENT (MTCE)/ MIO $ GROSS VALUE ADDED)
     1=BASIC MATERIALS
     2=CONSUMER GOODS
     3=INVESTMENT GOODS
     4=SERVICES
```

14 U selects 1 (Energy input).

15 G prints the industry sector alternatives.

```
V                                                  (16)

          BASIC MATERIALS                          (17)
               AGRICULTURE
               ENERGY
               MINING
               BUILDING MATERIALS
          CONSUMER GOODS
               FOOD INDUSTRY
               TEXTILE INDUSTRY
               GARMENT INDUSTRY
               WOOD, PAPER, AND PRINTING INDUSTRY
               CHEMICAL INDUSTRY
          INVESTMENT GOODS
               RAW METALS INDUSTRY
               METAL WORKING INDUSTRY
               AUTOMOBILE INDUSTRY
               MACHINE BUILDING AND ELECTRICAL INDUSTRY
               CONSTRUCTION
          SERVICES
               RETAILING
               TRANSPORTATION
               HOUSING
               GOVERNMENT
               OTHER SERVICES
```

16 U wants another preview.

17 G obliges.

```
3                                                  (18)

INVESTMENT GOODS
====================

GLOBAL SCENARIO ?                                  (19)

                                                   (20)

  1985  1995  2005  2015  2025                     (21)
                       0                           (22)
```

18 U selects 3 (Investment goods).

19 G "Do you wish to input a Global Scenario here?"

20 U answers with (CR) carriage return, which G interprets as "Yes".

21 G prints the years of the time horizon and expects global, qualitative input.

22 U specifies for the decade to 1985 a slight decrease, a faster decrease till 1995, some decrease till 2005; from then on no more change.

```
PARAMETER #  10                        (23)
---------------

  1975   1985   1995   2005   2015   2025
   85.  69.59  46.65  38.19  38.19  38.19

PARAMETER #  11
---------------

  1975   1985   1995   2005   2015   2025
   92.  75.32  50.49  41.34  41.34  41.34

PARAMETER #  12
---------------

  1975   1985   1995   2005   2015   2025
   82.  67.14    45.  36.84  36.84  36.84

PARAMETER #  13
---------------

  1975   1985   1995   2005   2015   2025
   78.  63.86   42.8  35.05  35.05  35.05

PARAMETER #  14
---------------

  1975   1985   1995   2005   2015   2025
  107.   87.6  58.72  48.08  48.08  48.08

FINISHED ?                              (24)

?                                       (25)
```

23 G looks up the parameters involved (No. 10, 11, 12, 13, 14), changes them accordingly and submits them for inspection. The user knows which parameters are addressed from the preview.

24 G wants to know whether U has made all scenario changes.

25 U hasn't; he wants to go back to the top level.

26 G prints top level alternatives.

```
WHICH ASPECT OF THE ENERGY SECTOR ARE YOU INTERESTED IN?
     1=ENERGY INPUT
     2=END ENERGY CONTRIBUTIONS          (26)
     3=PRIMARY ENERGY INPUTS
     4=CONVERSION EFFICIENCIES
2
```

(Dialog continues in normal fashion until G hits on a parameter.)

```
END ENERGY CONTRIBUTIONS
====================

CONTRIBUTION OF THE DIFFERENT END ENERGIES
TO SECTORAL END ENERGY USE (PERCENT)
     1=BASIC MATERIAL
     2=CONSUMER GOODS
     3=INVESTMENT GOODS
     4=SERVICES
2

CONSUMER GOODS
====================

WHICH SECTOR OF THE ECONOMY?
     1=FOOD INDUSTRY
     2=TEXTILE INDUSTRY
     3=GARMENT INDUSTRY
     4=WOOD, PAPER, AND PRINTING INDUSTRY
     5=CHEMICAL INDUSTRY
5

CHEMICAL INDUSTRY
====================

CONTRIBUTION OF THE DIFFERENT END ENERGIES
TO SECTORAL END ENERGY USE (PERCENT)
     1=COAL
     2=LIQUID FUEL
     3=GAS
     4=ELECTRICITY
     5=DISTRICT HEATING
2
```

```
LIQUID FUEL
====================
                                                  (27)
PARAMETER SCENARIO ?
                                                  (28)


  1975   1985   1995   2005   2015   2025
   34. S                                          (29)   (30)

   34.     25.  21. 25   17. 5  13. 75    10.     (31)
   34.  27   20    14   10   8                    (32)

   34.     27.     20.     14.     10.     8.     (33)
OK?

Y                                                 (34)

DISTRICT HEATING
====================                              (35)

   1975   1985   1995   2005   2015   2025
     3. S

     3.      5.      7.      9.     11.     12.
     3. W
                                                  (36)
COAL
====================

   1975   1985   1995   2005   2015   2025
     7. S

     7.      7.      7.      6.      5.      5.
     7. W

GAS
====================

   1975   1985   1995   2005   2015   2025
    25. S

    25.     29.     33.     37.     39.     40.
    25. W

ELECTRICITY
====================

   1975   1985   1995   2005   2015   2025
     34.     32.     33.     34.     35.     35.   (37)
OK?
                                                   (38)
FINISHED ?

Z                                                  (39)
```

27 G "Here is a parameter scenario possible".
28 U "Fine" (CR)
29 G prints time horizon. The first datum is filled in for 1975, then G waits for input.
30 U would like to see the standard scenario first ('S')
31 G G prints out the data and returns to prompting for input.
32 U wants the scenario changed such that the proportion of liquid fuel in the chemical industry drops to 21 % by 1985 and to 8 % by 2025.
33 G interpolates, aligns data and prints them out for approval.
34 U approves.
35 G submits all parameters in the group for appropriate changes.
36 U declines ('W')

37 G has summed the parameters to 100% and prints out the change in the last one to compensate for the input.
38 U accepts. (But he should have looked at the standard first.)
39 U is still not finished.

```
WHICH ASPECT OF THE ENERGY SECTOR ARE YOU INTERESTED IN?
       1=ENERGY INPUT
       2=END ENERGY CONTRIBUTIONS
       3=PRIMARY ENERGY INPUTS
       4=CONVERSION EFFICIENCIES
3

PRIMARY ENERGY INPUTS
====================

PRIMARY ENERGY REQUIRED TO PROVIDE ONE UNIT OF END ENERGY:
WHICH FORM OF END ENERGY?
       1=COAL
       2=LIQUID FUEL
       3=GAS
       4=ELECTRICITY
       5=DISTRICT HEATING
2
```

```
LIQUID FUEL
===================

WHICH PRIMARY ENERGY?
      1=COAL
      2=SOFT COAL
      3=OIL
      4=NATURAL GAS
      5=HYDRO AND NUCLEAR ENERGY
3

OIL
===================

PARAMETER SCENARIO ?                                    (40)

                                                        (41)


  1975  1985  1995  2005  2015  2025
   97.S                                                 (42)(43)

   97.   96.   96.   95.   94.   93.
   97.               0                                  (44)

   97.  79.42 65.02 65.02 65.02 65.02                   (45)
OK?

Y



FINISH

X
                                                        (46)
```

40 G finds another parameter and offers the opportunity for a scenario.
41 U accepts.
42 G prompts input.
43 U requests standard.
44 U inputs qualitative scenario. Continuing decline of oil as primary energy source until 2005, then no more change.
45 G translates to numerical values by using pre-model coefficients. Submits for ok.
46 U has finished. G changes to output mode after having called the model.

```
RESULT OUTPUT MODE.

WHICH ASPECT OF THE ENERGY SECTOR ARE YOU INTERESTED IN?
      1=ENERGY INPUT
      2=END ENERGY CONTRIBUTIONS
      3=PRIMARY ENERGY INPUTS
      4=CONVERSION EFFICIENCIES
L
                                                        (47)
GUIDE AND INPUT COMMAND KEYS :
============================                            (48)
H=HELP !
I=INFORMATION REQUEST
K=KALENDAR - TIME HORIZON
L=LIST COMMAND KEYS
M=MAINTAIN LEVEL
N=NO
O=OMIT PARAMETER INFORMATION
S=STANDARD SCENARIO
T=TERMINATE SEARCH
U=UNGUIDED ACCESS TO PARAMETERS
V=VIEW LOWER LEVEL
W=WAIVE SCENARIO
X=EXIT : RUN MODEL
Y=YES
Z=ZERO LEVEL RESTART

H
                                                        (49)
PICK YOUR CHOICE BY TYPING A NUMBER; THEN <CR>

1

ENERGY INPUT
===================

ENERGY USAGE IN THE SECTORS OF THE ECONOMY
(METRIC TON OF COAL EQUIVALENT (MTCE)/ MIO $ GROSS VALUE ADDED)
     1=BASIC MATERIALS
     2=CONSUMER GOODS
     3=INVESTMENT GOODS
     4=SERVICES
0
                                                    (50)
```

47 U requests the list of commands.
48 G prints output command keys.
49 U asks for technical help.
50 U inputs an illegal character (0) which G ignores.

```
1

BASIC MATERIALS
===================

      1=AGRICULTURE
      2=ENERGY
      3=MINING
      4=BUILDING MATERIALS
1

AGRICULTURE                                   (51)
===================

 OUTPUT ?                                     (52)
Y

 NAME : AGRC                                  (53) (54)

MIN. AND MAX  VALUES FOR MONITOR             (55)

N                                             (56)

 MORE VARIABLES ?                             (57)
M
                                              (58)
      1=AGRICULTURE
      2=ENERGY                                (59)
      3=MINING
      4=BUILDING MATERIALS
2                                             (60)

      1=ENERGY INPUT                          (61)
      2=END ENERGY CONTRIBUTIONS
      3=PRIMARY ENERGY INPUTS
      4=CONVERSION EFFICIENCIES
1

ENERGY INPUT
===================

      1=BASIC MATERIALS
      2=CONSUMER GOODS
      3=INVESTMENT GOODS
      4=SERVICES
3

INVESTMENT GOODS
===================

      1=RAW METALS INDUSTRY
      2=METAL WORKING INDUSTRY
      3=AUTOMOBILE INDUSTRY
      4=MACHINE BUILDING AND ELECTRICAL INDUSTRY
      5=CONSTRUCTION
4

MACHINE BUILDING AND ELECTRICAL INDUSTRY
===================

 OUTPUT ?
Y

 NAME : MAEL

MIN. AND MAX. VALUES FOR MONITOR



 MORE VARIABLES ?
M

      1=RAW METALS INDUSTRY
      2=METAL WORKING INDUSTRY
      3=AUTOMOBILE INDUSTRY
      4=MACHINE BUILDING AND ELECTRICAL INDUSTRY
      5=CONSTRUCTION
1
```

- **51 G** Agriculture is an output parameter.
- **52 U** "Yes I want it".
- **53 G** "Under which Name?"
- **54 U** "AGRC".
- **55 G** "Do you want this parameter monitored? If so, enter limiting values".
- **56 U** No monitoring (CR).
- **57 G** "Do you want more variables?"
- **58 U** "Yes from the same level". ('M')
- **59 G** prints the same set of alternatives.
- **60 U** changes his mind.
- **61 G** Doesn't mind. Returns to top level. The dialog continues. U designates 4 more variables: MAEL, METL, ELEC, GAS.

```
RAW METALS INDUSTRY
===================

 OUTPUT ?


 NAME : METL

MIN. AND MAX. VALUES FOR MONITOR



 MORE VARIABLES ?
Z

      1=ENERGY INPUT
      2=END ENERGY CONTRIBUTIONS
      3=PRIMARY ENERGY INPUTS
      4=CONVERSION EFFICIENCIES
4

CONVERSION EFFICIENCIES
=======================

      1=COAL
      2=LIQUID FUEL
      3=GAS
      4=ELECTRICITY
      5=DISTRICT HEATING
4

ELECTRICITY
===================

 OUTPUT ?
Y

 NAME : ELEC

MIN. AND MAX. VALUES FOR MONITOR



 MORE VARIABLES ?
M

      1=COAL
      2=LIQUID FUEL
      3=GAS
      4=ELECTRICITY
      5=DISTRICT HEATING
3

GAS
===================

 OUTPUT ?
Y

 NAME : GAS

MIN. AND MAX. VALUES FOR MONITOR



 MORE VARIABLES ?
N

:A
ASSEMBLY LIST
-------------
NO. NAME     MIN.       MAX.

 1 AGRC
 2 MAEL
 3 METL
 4 ELEC
 5 GAS
```

62 U wants no more variables.

63 G prompts a command (':').

(62) 64 U wants to see the assembly list ('A').

(63) (64)

(65) 65 G presents the list.

```
FIG:  1                      (66)
-------                      (67)
NO.  VAR.  NAME SYMBOL
1                            (68) (69)
      1   AGRC L
2
     13   MAEL E
3
     10   METL M             (70)
E

FIG:  2                      (71)
-------
NO.  VAR.  NAME SYMBOL
4
    143   ELEC X
5
    142   GAS  G
F                            (72)

FIGURE NO: 1                 (73)
```

66 G prompts composition of Fig. No. 1.
67 U picks No. 1.
68 G prints parameter index (No. 1), and the previously given four letter short name, then waits for the symbol with which AGRC should be presented in the graph.
69 U decides on 'A'.
70 U signals the end of this graph ('E') after two more parameters.
71 G prepares for graph No. 2.

72 U would like to see the figures now ('F').
73 G prints Fig. No. 1 (Table and graph).

```
          FIGURE  1
          =========

          YEAR        AGRC        METL        MAEL

          1975        90.00       78.00       85.00
          1985        74.00       72.60       69.59
          1995        58.00       67.20       46.65
          2005        42.00       61.80       38.19
          2015        26.00       56.40       38.19
          2025        10.00       51.00       38.19

                VAR.  SYM.    MIN.        MAX.        SCALE

                AGRC  A    0.10E+02    0.90E+02    0.10E+03
                METL  M    0.51E+02    0.78E+02    0.80E+02
                MAEL  E    0.38E+02    0.85E+02    0.10E+03

   !-----------------------------------------------------------!
   !MMMMMMMM               .           .           .           !
   !A       MMMMMMMMM      .           .           .           !
   !EAAAA      .     MMMMMMMMM         .           .           !
   ! EEEEAAAA              .  MMMMMMMMM.           .           !
   !.....EEEEAAAA......................MMMMMMMMM...............!
   !         EEEEAAA       .           .        MMMMMMMMM      !
   !           . EE AAAA   .           .           .     MMMMMM!
   !           .   EEE  AAAA           .           .           !
   !           .      EE   .AAAA       .           .           !
   !....................EEE....AAA.............................!
   !           .           EEEEEE  AAAA.           .           !
   !           .           .     EEEEEEEEEEEEEEEEEEEEEEEEEEEEEE!
   !           .           .           .   AAAA    .           !
   !           .           .           .       AAA .           !
   !..............................................AAAA.........!
   !           .           .           .           .  AAAA     !
   !           .           .           .           .      AAAA !
   !           .           .           .           .          A!
   !           .           .           .           .           !
   !-----------------------------------------------------------!
 1975        1985        1995        2005        2015        2025
OK?                                   (74)
S                                     (75)
```

74 G wants to know whether to preserve Figure 1 in the output list.

75 U wishes the graph to be drawn to standard scale ('S').

(76) 76 G plots all functions to the largest scale (100).

```
        VAR.  SYM.    MIN.        MAX.        SCALE

        AGRC  A    0.10E+02   0.90E+02   0.10E+03
        METL  M    0.51E+02   0.78E+02   0.10E+03
        MAEL  E    0.38E+02   0.85E+02   0.10E+03

  !------------------------------------------------------------!
  !           .           .           .           .            !
  !A          .           .           .           .            !
  !EAAAA      .           .           .           .            !
  !MEEEEAAAA  .           .           .           .            !
  !.MMMMEEEEMMMA...............................................!
  !         EEEEMMMMMMMMMMM.          .           .            !
  !           . EE AAAA   MMMMMMMMMMM .           .            !
  !             EEE  AAAA           MMMMMMMMMMM   .            !
  !           .    EE  .AAAA        .           MMMMMMMMMMM    !
  !....................EEE....AAA..........................MMM!
  !           .          EEEEEE  AAAA.            .            !
  !           .           .    EEEEEEEEEEEEEEEEEEEEEEEEEEEEEEEE!
  !           .           .           AAAA        .            !
  !           .           .           .   AAA .               !
  !.........................................AAAA...............!
  !           .           .           .           . AAAA       !
  !           .           .           .           .     AAAA   !
  !           .           .           .           .           A!
  !           .           .           .           .            !
 0!------------------------------------------------------------!
1975        1985        1995        2005        2015        2025
OK?
Y
```

(77) 77 U accepts.

(78) 78 G continues with Fig. No. 2.

```
      FIGURE  2
      =========

      YEAR         ELEC        GAS

      1975         31.00       86.00
      1985         31.00       87.00
      1995         32.00       89.00
      2005         33.00       90.00
      2015         33.00       91.00
      2025         33.00       92.00

        VAR.  SYM.    MIN.        MAX.        SCALE

        ELEC  X    0.31E+02   0.33E+02   0.40E+02
        GAS   G    0.86E+02   0.92E+02   0.10E+03

  !------------------------------------------------------------!
  !           .           .           .           .            !
  !           .  GGGGGGGGGGGGGGGGGGGGGGGGGGGGGGGGGGGGGGGGGGGGGGGG!
  !GGGGGGGGGGGGGG         .           .           .            !
  !           .XXXXXXXXXXXXXXXXXXXXXXXXXXXXXXXXXXXXXXXXXXXXXXXXX!
  !XXXXXXXXXXXX................................................!
  !           .           .           .           .            !
  !           .           .           .           .            !
  !           .           .           .           .            !
  !           .           .           .           .            !
  !............................................................!
  !           .           .           .           .            !
  !           .           .           .           .            !
  !           .           .           .           .            !
  !............................................................!
  !           .           .           .           .            !
  !           .           .           .           .            !
  !           .           .           .           .            !
  !------------------------------------------------------------!
1975        1985        1995        2005        2015        2025
OK?
```

```
R
DEFINE SCALE: MIN= MAX=
80 100
```

(79)

79 U wants to inspect the output for GAS more closely and wishes to impose his own scale ('R')

```
VAR.  SYM.   MIN.         MAX.        SCALE

ELEC   X    0.31E+02    0.33E+02    0.20E+02
GAS    G    0.86E+02    0.92E+02    0.20E+02
```

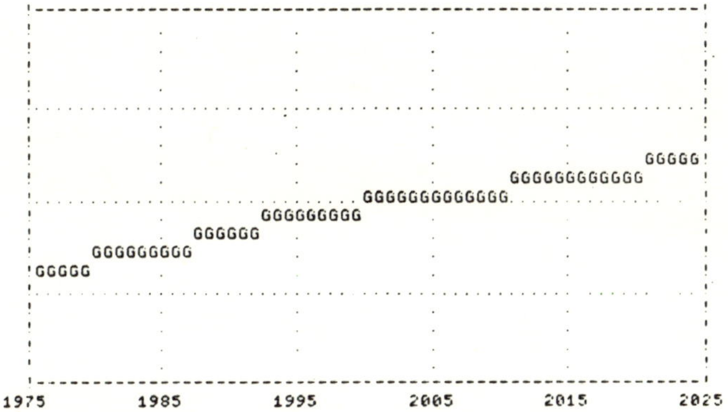


```
OK?

B

FIG:  3
-------
NO.  VAR.  NAME SYMBOL
1
      1    AGRC *
2
     13    MAEL
C
```

(80)

(81)

```
CALCULATION NO: H
```

(82)

(83)

```
CALCULATION CODE:
1=B-A;  2=A+B+..;  3=A/B;  4=SUM A,DT;  5=RATE %;
6=LOG;  7=1/A   ;  8=C*A;  9=A:B (CORRELATION)

3
```

(84)

80 U would like to compare 2 parameters.

81 U requests calculations on the two parameters. ('C')

82 U does not know the code number and asks for help. ('H')

83 G prints out the requested list.

84 U finds the ratio A/B under No. 3.

85 U wants to see the correlation between the two parameters.

```
FIG:  4
-------
NO.  VAR.  NAME SYMBOL
1
      1    AGRC +
2    13    MAEL
C

CALCULATION NO: 9
```

(85)

```
FIG:  5
-------
NO.  VAR.  NAME SYMBOL
F
```

(86)

86 U has no more input ('F').

87 G starts with Fig. No. 3, which the user has not yet seen.

FIGURE 3 (87)

```
FIGURE  3
=========

OPERATION:  A/B, ON : AGRC MAEL

        YEAR          A/B

        1975          1.15
        1985          1.11
        1995          1.11
        2005          1.09
        2015          0.94
        2025          0.90

          VAR  SYM.   MIN.        MAX.        SCALE

          A/B   *    0.90E+00    0.12E+01    0.20E+01
```

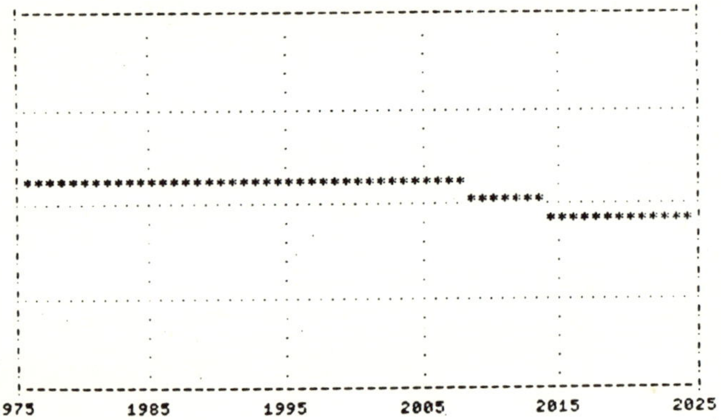


```
OK?
R

DEFINE SCALE: MIN= MAX=

.9  1.15

          VAR.  SYM.   MIN.        MAX.        SCALE

          A/B   *    0.90E+00    0.12E+01    0.25E+00
```

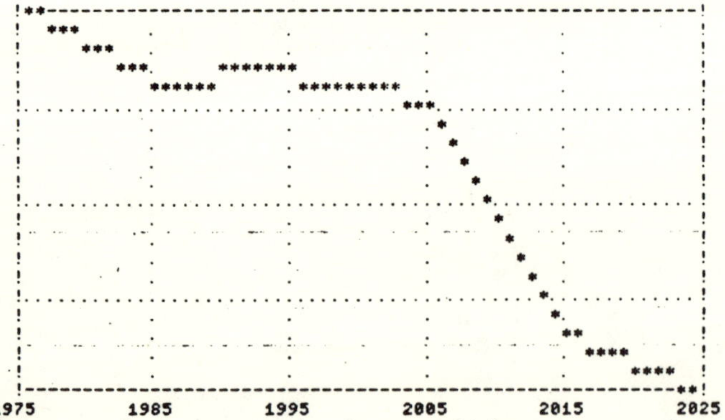

OK?

```
            FIGURE  4
            =========

OPERATION:  CORR, ON : AGRC MAEL

            YEAR           AGRC        MAEL

            1975           90.00       78.00
            1985           78.00       70.58
            1995           64.00       57.78
            2005           57.00       52.28
            2015           49.00       52.28
            2025           47.00       52.28

                   VAR.  SYM.    MIN.         MAX.          SCALE

                   AGRC   +    0.47E+02    0.90E+02    0.10E+03
                   MAEL        0.52E+02    0.78E+02    0.80E+02
```

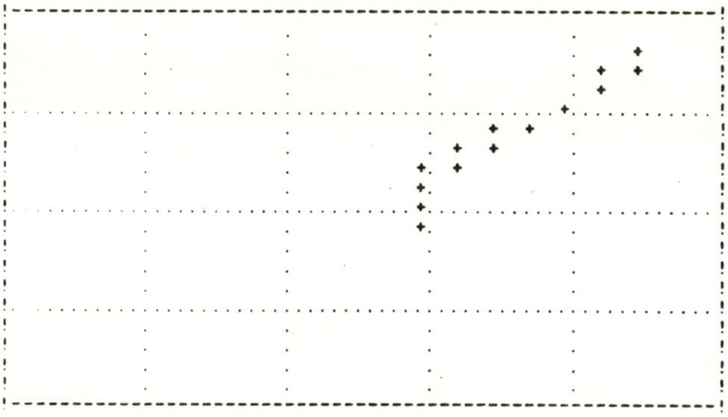

```
OK ?
A

:A

ASSEMBLY LIST
-------------
NO   NAME     MIN.        MAX.

 1 AGRC
 2 MAEL
 3 METL
 4 ELEC
 5 GAS
```

(88)

88 U wants to clean up the assembly list. He first recalls it. ('A')

```
FIG:  5
-------
NO.  VAR   NAME SYMBOL
D


DELETE FROM LIST NO.

2 4

ASSEMBLY LIST
-------------
NO.  NAME     MIN.        MAX.

 1 AGRC
 2 METL
 3 GAS
```

(89)

(90)

(91)

(92)

(93)

89 G thinks he wants more figures. G is wrong.

90 U issues the delete command ('D').

91 G asks which of the names should be dropped.

92 U deletes 2 and 4.

93 G updates the assembly list.

```
FIG:  5
-------
NO. VAR. NAME SYMBOL
G

      1=ENERGY INPUT
      2=END ENERGY CONTRIBUTIONS
      3=PRIMARY ENERGY INPUTS
      4=CONVERSION EFFICIENCIES
U

PARAMETER #: 3

 NAME : MINE

MIN. AND MAX. VALUES FOR MONITOR

120  140

 MORE VARIABLES ?
N

:X
```

(94) 94 U calls for another guided tour ('G').

(95) 95 G starts on the top level.

(96) 96 U remembers the parameter number and wants it directly ('U').

(97) 97 G asks for the number of the parameter.

(98) 98 U furnishes the number and the name.

(99) 99 U enters limiting values for monitoring.

```
SCENARIO INPUT MODE.

      1=ENERGY INPUT
      2=END ENERGY CONTRIBUTIONS
      3=PRIMARY ENERGY INPUTS
      4=CONVERSION EFFICIENCIES
X
```

(100) 100 G reappears in input mode.

```
RESULT OUTPUT MODE.

REPORT ON MONITORED PARAMETERS:
-------------------------------
PARAM.          LIMITS          YEAR.    DEVIATION

 MINE     120.00      140.00
                                1975       10.00
                                2005        0.00
                                2015       -6.00
                                2025      -10.00
```

(101) 101 G is immediately forced back into the output mode.

The model run has taken place. The monitor reports that the variable MINE has exceeded the limits 3 times and has reached a limit once.

6. EXTENSIONS FOR FUTURE VERSIONS OF GUIDE

We expect that as model builders and users work with GUIDE on various problems, and with a variety of models, there will be criticism and suggestions which we welcome in order to make GUIDE in fact the general tool it is intended to be. One addition easily implemented and probably quite useful is a statistical package which would allow the experimental results to be analysed by rigorous quantitative methods.

Users who have gained a certain degree of familiarity are likely to ask more detailed questions about internal model structure. GUIDE could be furnished with auxiliary routines to make the model structure transparent and explicit to the user.

Communication between model and user could eventually be upgraded to some form of natural language dialog with a text decoder and scenario generation on the basis of verbal description of the problem, or of the desired simulation aspects.

The proposed coupling of the GUIDE system and of the GRIPS model construction program (GRIPS is discussed elsewhere in this volume) would further contribute to reducing the dependency on programming and computer expertise in the phases of construction, operation, and modification of an interactive dynamic model. The modelling effort could then concentrate on the r e a l problems: the valid modelling of processes and systems, and the creation of practical instruments which prove their worth in daily application to actual policy analysis tasks.

7. REFERENCES

1. Forrester, J.W.: World Dynamics. Wright-Allen Press, Cambridge, Mass.: 1971.

2. Meadows, D.H.; Meadows, D.L.; Randers, T. & Behrens Ill, W.W.: The Limits to Growth. Potomac Associate/Universe Books, New York: 1972.

3. Mesarovic, M. & Pestel, E.: Mankind at the Turning Point. Dutton, New York: 1974.

4. Meadows, D.L., Behrens Ill, W.W., Meadows, D.H., Naill, R.F., Randers, J., Zahn, E.K.O.: Dynamics of Growth in a Finite World. Wright-Allen Press, Cambridge, Mass.: 1974.

5. Meadows, D.L. & Meadows, D.H.: Towards Global Equilibrium. Collected Papers. Wright-Allen Press, Cambridge, Mass.: 1973.

6. Mesarovic, M. & Pestel, E.: Multilevel Computer Model of World Development System. IIASA: Laxenburg-Vienna, 1974.

7. Mesarovic, M., Pestel, E. & Hübl, L.: Disaggregierung des Mesarovic-Pestel Weltmodells für die Bundesrepublik Deutschland. Institut für Systemanalyse und Prognose, Hannover 1975/76.

8. Zadeh, L.A.: A Fuzzy-Algorithmic Approach to the Definition of Complex or Imprecise Concepts. In: H. Bossel, S. Klaczko, N. Müller (eds.): Systems Theory in the Social Sciences. Birkhäuser, Basel; 1976, p. 202 - 282.

9. Stevens, S.S.: The Psychophysics of Sensory Function. In: W. Rosenblith (ed.): Sensory Communication. MIT Press, Cambridge, Mass.: 1964.

10. Bossel, H., Hijden, P.v.d., Hudetz, W., Denton, R.V.: Dialogprogramm zur Entwicklung und Überprüfung von Langfristkonzepten für das Energieversorgungssystem und Anwendung auf die Bundesrepublik Deutschland. Jülich: Kernforschungsanlage (Conf. 15), 1975.

11. Strobel, M.G.: GUIDE and GUARD Handbook. Institut für Systemtechnik und Innovationsforschung; Karlsruhe, 1976.

AN INTERACTIVE PROGRAM FOR ENERGY POLICY ASSESSMENT

Hartmut Bossel, Pieter van der Hijden, Walter Hudetz

INTRODUCTION: SIMULATION IN ENERGY POLICY PLANNING

Motivation and Introduction

The functioning of societies at all levels of industrial development is crucially dependent on parameters of their respective energy systems. These parameters will undergo major changes in the coming half century, as energy systems are converted to a more permanent energy base. To explore, plan, assess and prepare long-range or short-range energy policy requires comprehensive and accurate planning tools, i.e. computer models incorporating all relevant aspects of the societal system as it is affected by energy-related policies.

The present report on the development of the interactive program ESPINT for energy policy assessment is an updated version of a paper originally prepared for the 2nd International UNESCO Seminar on Trends in Mathematical Modelling in Jablonna, Poland (December 1974). Much has since been learned from the development and use of ESPINT. The development of the GUIDE system for converting any given model core into a fully interactive simulation model and policy analysis tool has been a direct consequence[1]. Irrespective of the fact that GUIDE now allows the development of an interactive program with a fraction of the time and effort expended on ESPINT, the following presentation illustrates important features of the development, the application, and the features required of an interactive policy analysis tool.

Off-Line Simulation

A structural model[2] of the energy supply system of a given region or country has been developed within the context of the Mesarovic-Pestel world modeling effort[3]. The model is basically an energy flow net containing only physically possible energy flow paths and energy conversion processes and no data whatsoever. After inputting historical and scenario data (on 109 cards in the original ESP model) the simulation model can be used off-line to study alternative scenarios for the energy supply system having the following aspects:

- different combinations of primary energy inputs (energy kinds and amounts);
- different kinds and amounts of energy imports and exports;
- different allocation of energy flows to conversion processes;
- different allocation of secondary energy flows to end-users;
- alternative technological developments;
- shifts in primary and secondary energy prices and in investment costs.

The program computes time series for the amounts of energy flows at (almost) all points of the energy system and also time series for the corresponding energy costs and investment costs.

Interactive Simulation

The preparation of a simulation run on the ESP-model requires the careful construction of a large number of time series, key punching, input of the corresponding card deck and the waiting for the computer printouts, which, despite the reproduction of time series for a large number of variables, may not contain the required information. Flexibility of use of the model and user convenience suffer under these restrictions. These deficiencies of off-line use may be partially eliminated by changing to an interactive mode. Among other things the interactive (dialogue) mode offers the following possibilities:

- operations on different levels of difficulty;
- feedback of the consequences of an input and therefore:
- possibility of an immediate correction of inputs and of
- learning by trial and error.

In the interactive approach the user may study the consequences of different decision alternatives relatively quickly during an extended dialogue on the computer terminal, thus approaching an acceptable solution in an iterative fashion.

In view of these advantages the ESP-model was changed in September/October 1974 to interactive operation (program ESPINT). The causal structure of the ESPINT-model was slightly expanded by introducing somewhat greater detail into investment cost categories.

In order to facilitate use of the program by unskilled users, the dialogue is exclusively in natural language (German, English or Dutch) and numbers. Interrogation blocks, which exceed the technical knowledge of the user or whose parameters are not to be changed, may be bypassed upon request. The program will then use the historical data of 1970, resp. the data last input to the model. In the simplest case the model may be run by specifying a total primary energy input or its annual rate of growth. In the most complicated case the user would have to supply 146 parameters for each time-step. The program logic assures that only relevant questions are asked at each point.

Following the parameter interrogation for a given time step the user may request summaries of the consequences resulting from his parameter choice on a screen, or may focus on anyone out of more than 700 variables separately. (Each one of these variables is quickly retrievable in 3 to 5 steps of a search hierarchy.) In addition there is the possibility of assessing the results for each time step with respect to seven decision criteria which influence decision-making with respect to energy systems. The assessment is later displayed in the form of a problem chart, which points out potential problem areas to the user. In developing an energy system scenario the user can at any point return to previous time steps in order to correct previous decisions and start afresh.

The computer program has been developed as a prototype of an interactive planning and decision-making tool for the use with mini-computers, which permit the relatively uncomplicated installation of audio-visual aids (floppy disk storage, CRT-displays, random access microfilm readers, random access projectors, and tape recorders). The ergonomic experience indicates that in complicated decision situations additional information will have to be presented to the user by audio-visual means to permit the user to grasp the decision situation fully and with a minimum of stress.

Uses of the Interactive Model

The interactive model of the energy supply system has been designed with two purposes in mind:

1 - to facilitate the conduction of a relatively complex planning process by a relatively unskilled user;

2 - to create a tool for the study of complex decision processes using a concrete and timely subject.

In order to satisfy the first objective, only the problem-specific causal structure is fixed in the program. Its complexity by far exceeds human information processing capacity. Into this causal structure the user must introduce his knowledge and his subjective mental models concerning indidual aspects. The program then computes the consequences.

The advantage of this approach lies in the fact that the model uses a common denominator which is equally valid for experts and non-experts of all persuasions: there can be no debate concerning the origin and direction of energy flows. The arguments begin with the quantification, especially when it concerns aspects of possible or desirable future development. These assessments are here exclusively introduced by the user. The simulation results are therefore results of <u>his</u> decision without which the program cannot be run. ESPINT simply shows the direct consequences of a given input; clearly it is not an instrument for prognoses.

Attainment of the second objective is simplified also by clear separation between objective data (physical causalities and historical conditions) and subjective data (scenarios and corresponding data).

In general, decisions are determined by several decision criteria (e. g. today decisions with respect to energy policy are no longer made on the basis of cost optimization alone). One sub-routine of ESPINT supplies indicators for seven different decision criteria relevant to energy policy, which may be assessed subjectively by the user. Using this assessment routine, it becomes possible to interactively and indirectly determine the preferences and priorities of the user. The resulting relative weights of the different decision criteria can be used to set up corresponding objective functions, which can be incorporated in optimization algorithms. The corresponding "optimal" solutions can be supplied to the user to reduce his search space. Incorporation of these aspects is planned for a later stage of program development.[4]

OVERVIEW OF THE INTERACTIVE SIMULATION PROGRAM ESPINT

A flow chart for the simulation program ESPINT is given in Fig. 1. The most important components of the program are:

- file
- interrogation routine
- structural model ESP of the energy supply system
- output programs (CRT-display or printer)

The user starts the program by typing DO ESPINT on the terminal key board. He then indicates in which of several natural languages he wants to work (presently German, English, or Dutch). Questions, informations, tables, and other texts are then displayed in this language. Following the display of the program title-page the user decides for which country or region he wants to develop or study an energy scenario (possibilities October 1974: USA, Western Europe, Netherlands, Federal Republic of Germany). Financial computations can be done in the corresponding national currencies (U.S. dollar, Dutch guilders, German marks); presently the U.S. dollar is used as the common monetary unit. The displays use the metric ton of coal equivalent (TCE) as energy unit; other energy units can be used, but the "TCE" continues to appear on the displays.

The user may now decide whether he wants to develop a new energy scenario (starting with historical data for 1970 contained in the program file), or whether he wishes to study or assess one of the scenarios contained in the data file, or finally, whether he wants to read in and to study a scenario he has prepared on a set of punched cards.

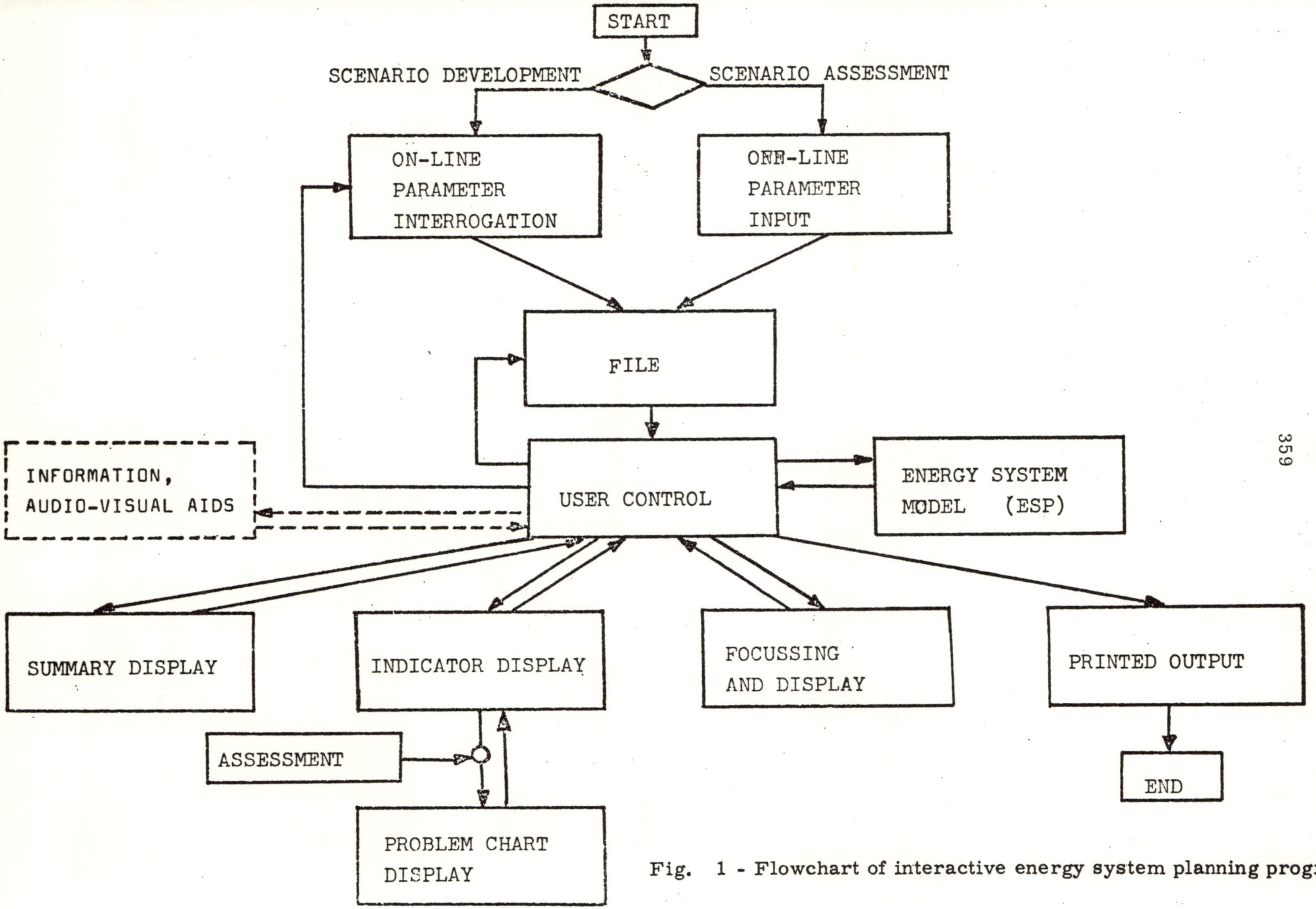

Fig. 1 - Flowchart of interactive energy system planning program

In the first case (scenario development) an interactive parameter interrogation is conducted first (described in more detail below). This procedure is repeated in time-steps of five years until the end of the simulation period (usually 2025). Depending on the objectives of the user, this interrogation may be more or less complex. The data required for the computation of the energy system follow from the interactive user's responses. If all necessary parameters are entered from the existing file or from punched cards (as in the second and third case) the interactive interrogation procedure is not used. Following the parameter interrogation or the reading in of scenario date, respectively, the user may at each time-step initiate computation of the scenario developed so far by the structural model ESP of the energy supply system and display the results on the terminal screen in three different ways:

- Summary results corresponding to the different sectors of the energy model (primary energy inputs, primary energy allocation to conversion processes, energy import and export, conversion plants, energy cost and investments, energy distribution to end-user).
- Summary of decision-relevant indicators corresponding to the decision criteria (here: adequacy of energy supply, cost, availability, rate of change, efficiency, safety, and pollution).
- Focusing on anyone out of more than 700 variables which may be computed within the program.

If he so desires the user may of course bypass any of these steps. At the end of each time-step he may continue or discontinue the process. If his decision is to continue, the program will begin again after a time-step of five years with the parameter interrogation, resp. the computation and display of results for the next time-step. If the user does not wish to continue, he may either return to a previous point in time (i.e. in order to correct an undesirable development), or he may discontinue the simulation altogether. The printout program will print the most important scenario results if desired.

DESCRIPTION OF MAJOR SUBROUTINES

Model of the Energy Supply System

The model of the energy supply system consists of a complex structure tracing flows of energy from primary energy inputs to conversion processes (with their inherent losses of useful energy) to distribution and allocation to the ultimate user. The elementary steps in this energy flows are:

(1) distribution of energy flows from a particular energy source to different energy receivers ("allocation");

(2) summation of energy flows from different sources ("collection");
(3) conversion of energy from one form to several others (useful energy plus rejected heat; some heat may be recovered).

The model breaks down into several submodels which are traversed in sequence in the course of the calculations for a given simulated year (Fig. 2):

(1) distribution of primary energy inputs;
(2) allocation of primary energy inputs to primary conversion processes or end-use;
(3) a sequence of one or several conversion processes to convert primary energy into secondary energy forms used in the user sector;
(4) distribution and transmission;
(5) allocation of secondary or primary inputs to the different users in the user sector.

The submodels are shown in Figs. 3 - 8.

The program provides merely a framework. The energy flows in the various paths of the system are exclusively controlled by the parameters provided by the user. In particular, the user must supply (1) all allocation percentages (0 to 100) in the different branches of the program, and (2) all efficiencies of conversion processes. This allows a complete tailoring of the simulation to any specific setting, whether rural village or multinational developed region, and the introduction of specific technologies and uses. It is thus the user who sets <u>all</u> the valves of the energy supply planning model himself; nothing, except all physically possible structural connections of the flow net, has been preprogrammed.

The program operates sequentially. For a given year it computes from the primary energy inputs and the allocation fractions the inputs to the various conversion processes. Using the described efficiencies, the waste energy and the useful energy are computed for each conversion process. Identical energy forms from different conversion and transition processes are then combined and allocated to the different uses. In addition to energy flows, the annual cost and corresponding plant investment are computed. New allocation fractions and efficiencies for a next point in time follow from the parameter interrogation, or from the time series supplied externally, or from the date stored in the scenario file.

In order to insure applicability to as wide a range of conceivable energy supply systems as possible, especially those of developing countries on one hand, or those of future decades on the other, we have included a wide range of possible primary and secondary energy forms and conversion processes. The primary and secondary energy forms and conversion processes considered in the program are listed in Tab. 1. For details of the energy system planning model reference is made to the respective technical

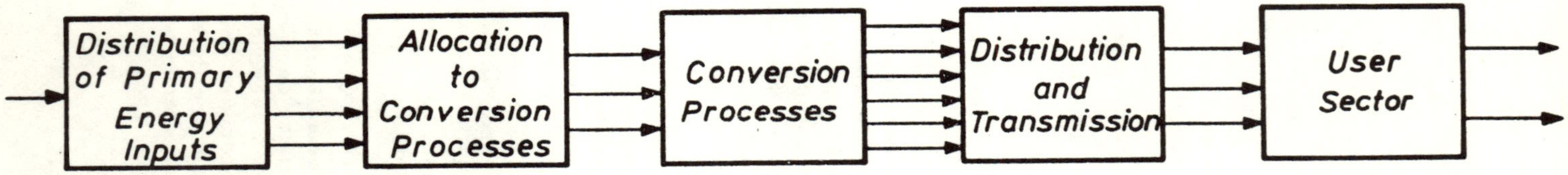

Fig. 2 - Overall Structure of Energy Supply Model

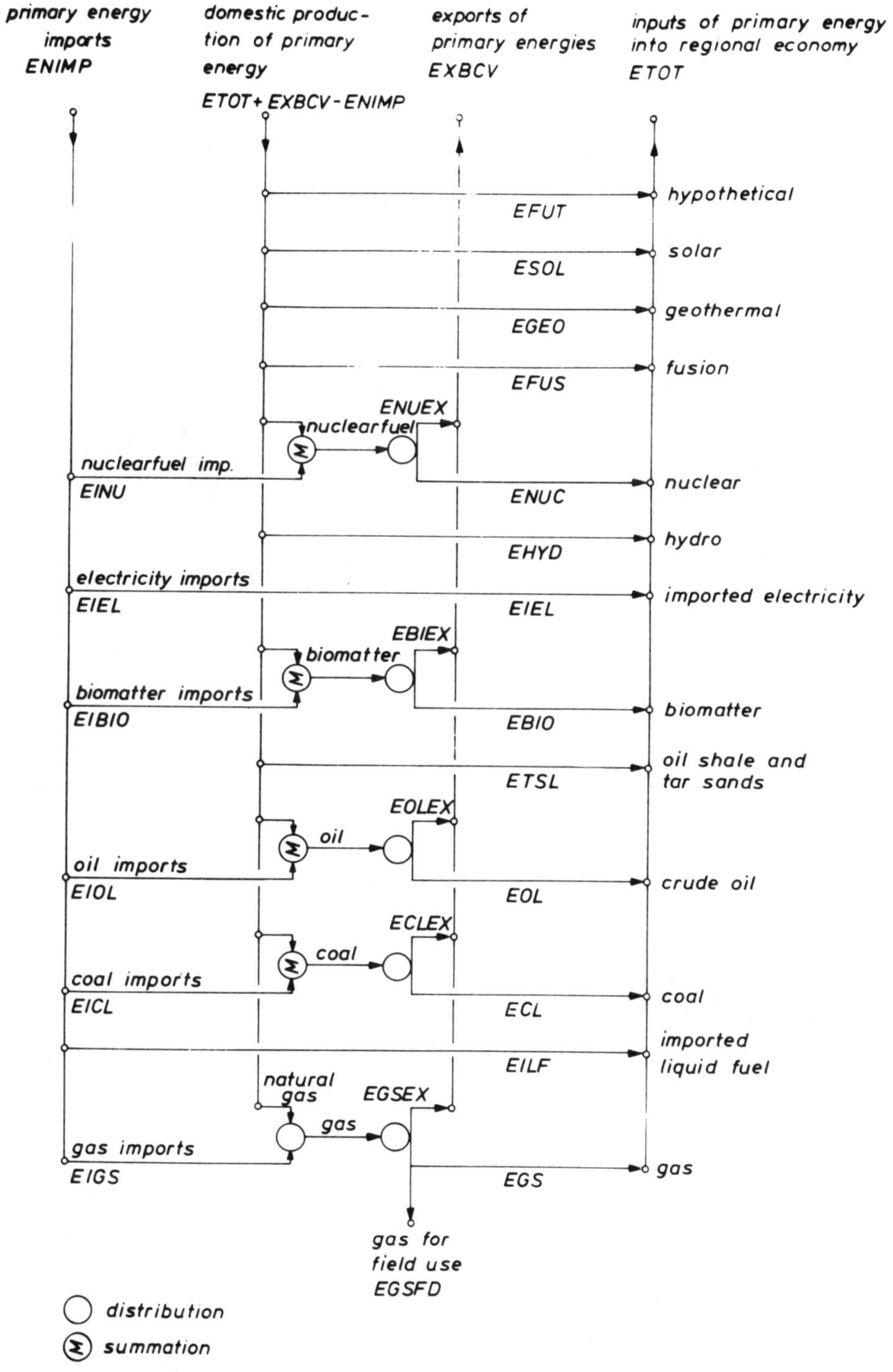

Fig. 3 Primary Energy Inputs; Imports and Exports

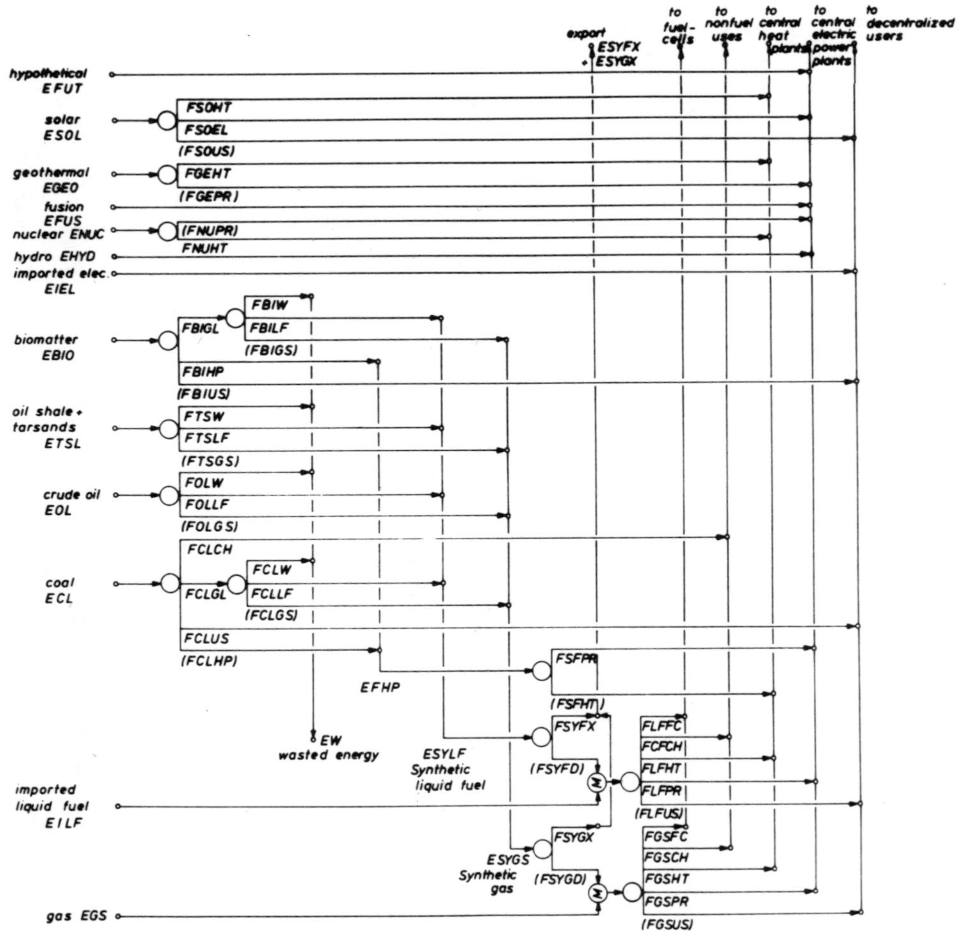

Fig. 4 Allocation of Primary Energy Inputs to Conversion Processes and Users

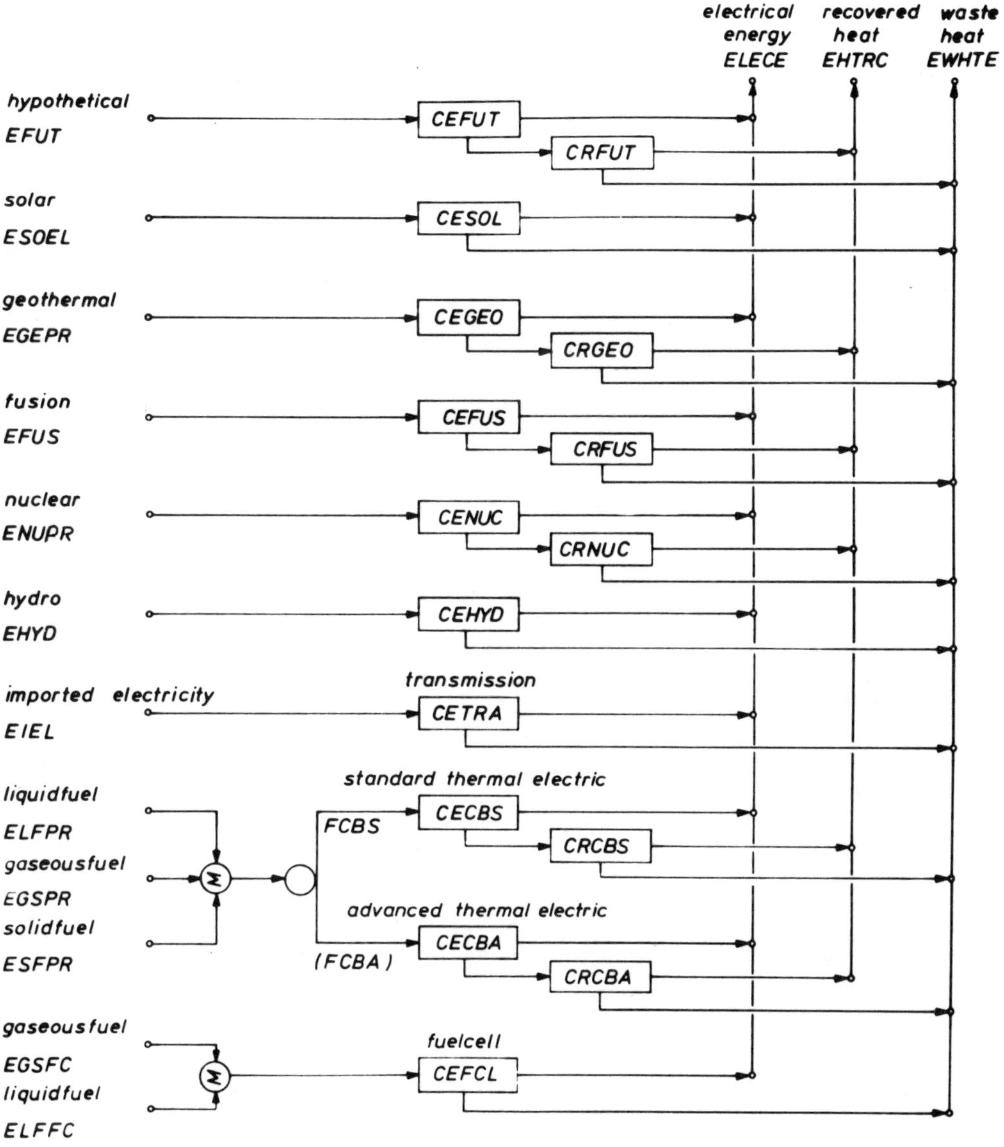

Fig. 5 Conversion to Electrical Energy

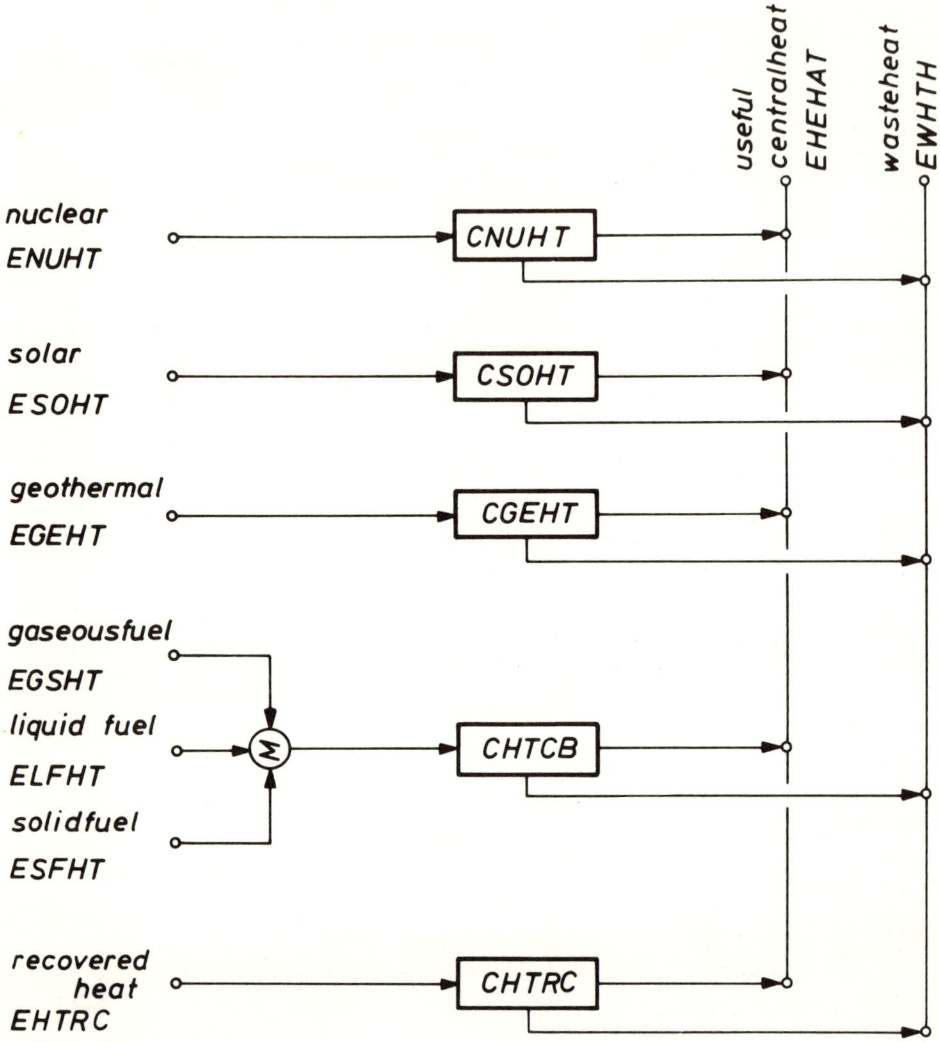

Fig. 6 Conversion to Central Heat

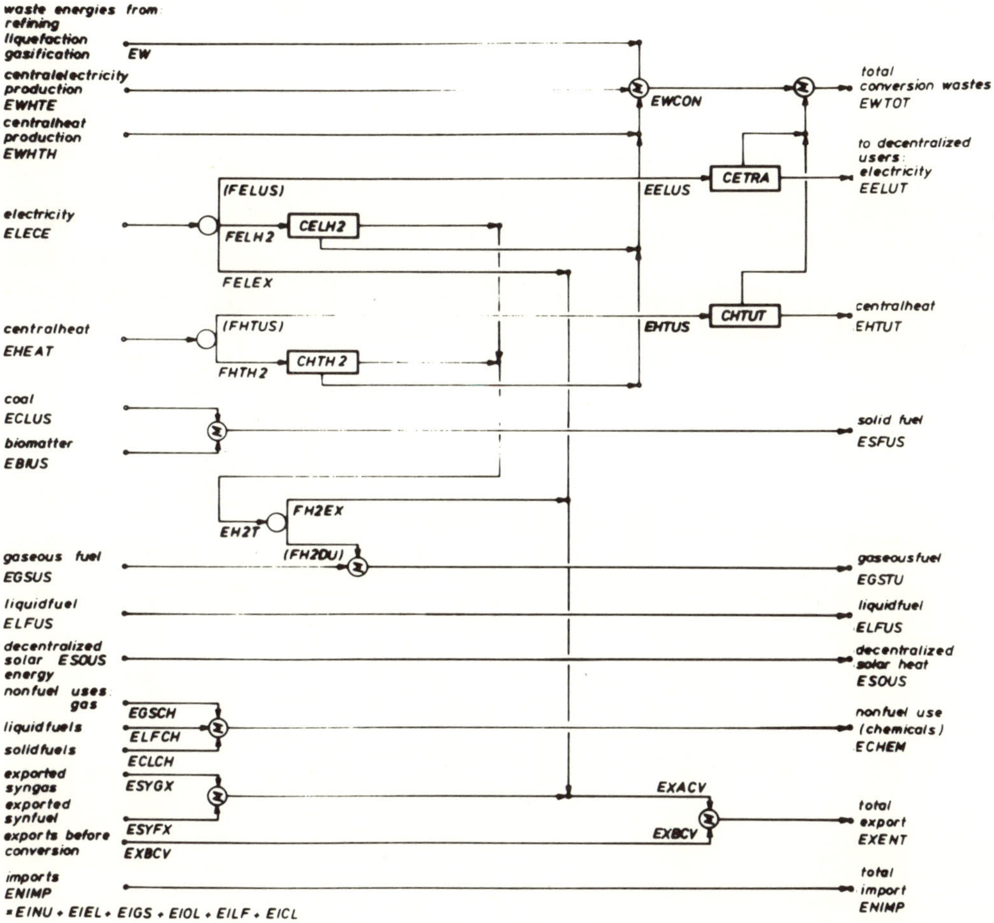

Fig. 7 Final Stages of Conversion and Inputs to Decentralized Users

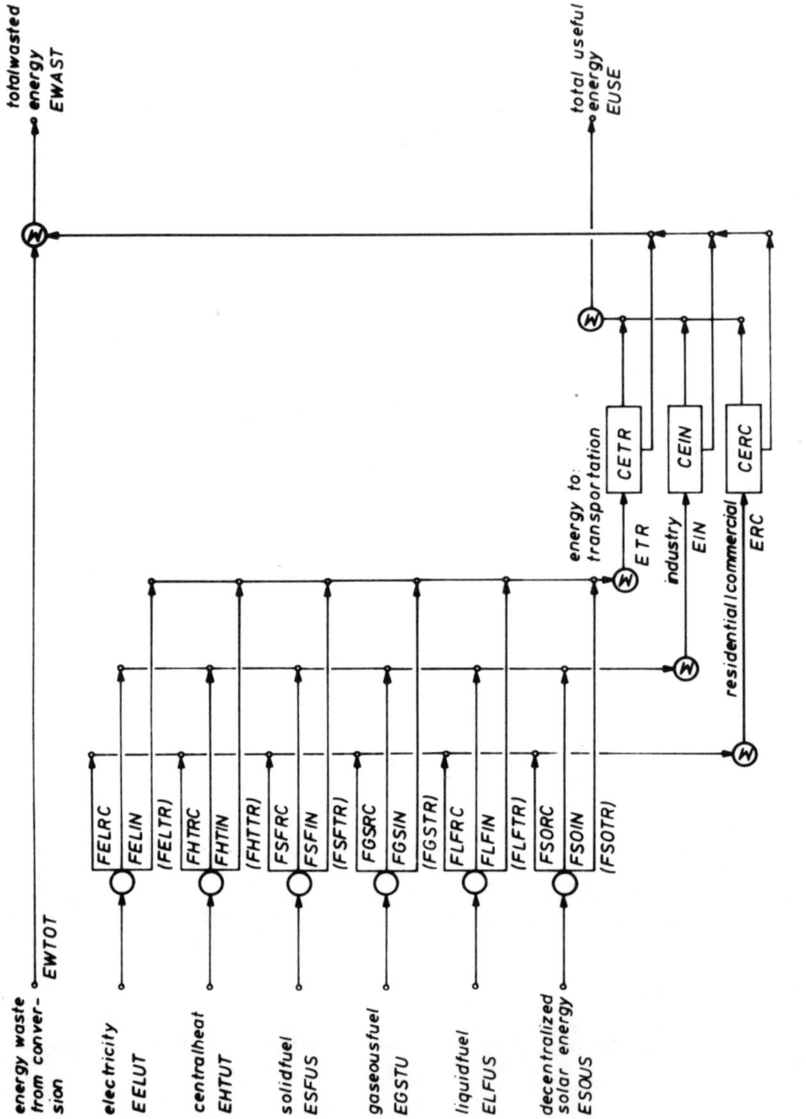

Fig. 8 Energy Allocation in User Sector

Table 1

PRIMARY AND SECONDARY ENERGY FORMS AND CONVERSION PROCESSES

Primary Energy Kinds:

- coal and lignite
- crude petroleum
- imported liquid fuels
- natural gas
- oil shale and tar sands
- wood, wastes, biomatter of different origin
- imported electricity
- hydropower
- nuclear fission energy
- nuclear fusion energy
- geothermal energy
- solar energy
- hypothetical energy

Secondary Energy Kinds:

- electricity
- central heat
- solid fuels
- liquid fuels
- gaseous fuels
- decentralized solar energy
- non-energies to chemical industry
- energy export after conversion
- rejected heat

Conversion Processes:

- gasification, liquefication, or refining of:
  - coal and lignite
  - crude petroleum
  - oil shale and tar sands
  - wood, waste, and biomatter
- generation of electricity by:
  - combustion power plants using standard technology
  - combustion power plants using advanced technology
  - hydropower
  - nuclear fission energy
  - nuclear fusion energy
  - geothermal energy
  - solar energy
  - fuel cell stations
  - hypothetical energy
- Generation of central (district or process) heat by:
  - combustion processes
  - geothermal energy
  - nuclear fission energy
  - solar energy
  - waste heat recovery from electricity generating processes
- Waste heat recovery from electricity generation by:
  - thermal power plants using standard technology
  - thermal power plants using advanced technology
  - nuclear fission energy
  - nuclear fusion energy
  - geothermal energy
  - hypothetical energy
- Generation of gaseous fuels (hydrogen etc.) by:
  - electrolysis
  - process heat

reports [5].

Print Subroutine

The output produced by the print subroutine contains on the first four pages the time series of the input parameters. On the remaining thirteen pages series and plots for approximately 35 selected result variables are displayed (see Tab. 2).

Interactive Parameter Interrogation

The parameter interrogation sequence follows the energy flows from the primary energy inputs through conversion and distribution to the end-user sectors. Logical operations within the separate interrogation blocks insure that only relevant questions are asked of the user (e.g. if the user has not indicated any input of solar energy, he will not be asked about solar energy conversion efficiencies).

The parameter interrogation is broken down into a series of steps. Steps may be bypassed if desired. In that case parameter data supplied earlier, resp. historical data of 1970 will be used by the program. During the interrogation procedure the parameter values used during the previous time-step are displayed for comparison.

In the first interrogation step the user is asked to supply the total primary energy input (in millions of metric tons of coal equivalent TCE) or its annual rate of growth (in percent per year). In addition it is determined which primary energy kinds are used and whether there is energy export or import. Next, the corresponding percentages of the different energy kinds with respect to the total energy input and the respective imports and exports are determined.

In the following step the user is asked to state the allocation percentages of the different primary energies to the different conversion processes. The efficiencies of energy conversion are determined next. Questions of the next step concern the distribution of secondary energies to the user sectors. In a final part of the interrogation program the cost per energy unit for the different primary and secondary energies, and the specific investment costs per kilowatt of effective power are determined for conversion plants and energy distribution systems.

Using the parameters obtained from the interrogation subroutine (a maximum of 146 parameters), the energy supply system model can be computed for another time-step. An example of the interrogation dialogue is given in Fig. 9.

Table 2

TABLE OF CONTENTS OF COMPUTER PRINTOUT

Page 1: Region and scenario labels; units; net primary energy input into region. Imports, exports and field use contributing to net imports

Page 2: Energy allocation fractions before conversion

Page 3: Energy distribution to users, conversion efficiencies.

Page 4: User efficiencies; primary energy prices; capital investment cost; secondary energy cost to user

Page 5: Net primary input energies (individual energies and total)

Page 6: Primary energy inputs (amounts and costs) by groups (coal and lignite; gas and liquid energies; imported electricity, biomatter, hydro power, geothermal energy, solar energy; fission and fusion; total)

Page 7: Plot of energy input amounts (same groups as page 6)

Page 8: Plot of energy input costs (same groups as page 6)

Page 9: Imports and exports of primary and secondary energies (individual energy amounts)

Page 10: Imports and exports, total amounts and total costs

Page 11: Plot of imports and exports total amounts and total costs

Page 12: Number of 1000 MWe energy conversion plants and corresponding capital investment (annual increment and cumulative)

Page 13: Plot of number of 1000 MWe energy conversion plants and corresponding cumulative capital investment

Page 14: Secondary energies to user sector: total amount and total cost, and breakdown by energy kind and user sector

Page 15: Plot of secondary energies to user sector by energy kind (electrical, heat, solar, solid fuel, gaseous fuel, liquid fuel)

Page 16: Plot of secondary energies to user sector by user sector (residential / commercial, industrial, transportation, total amount and total cost)

Page 17: Overall efficiency of energy conversion and distribution and concentrated waste heat

```
PERCENTAGES OF TOTAL GASEOUS FUEL ENERGY GOING TO:
     43 = RESIDENTIAL/COMMERCIAL SECTOR
     56 = INDUSTRIAL SECTOR
      1 = TRANSPORTATION SECTOR
            program displays previous percentages
OK?         and asks user for agreement

*N          user disagrees, wishes to change
            percentages
PERCENTAGES OF TOTAL GASEOUS FUEL ENERGY GOING TO:
    ?  = RESIDENTIAL/COMMERCIAL SECTOR
            program asks for first percentage
*
45          user inputs new value (45)
PERCENTAGES OF TOTAL GASEOUS FUEL ENERGY GOING TO:
    ?  = INDUSTRIAL SECTOR
            program asks for second percentage
*
6Ø          user inputs new value (60)

ANSWER BETWEEN    Ø AND   55 EXPECTED !!!
            program checks answer (which exceeds
*           100 percent) and prints error message
54          user corrects previous input
PERCENTAGES OF TOTAL GASEOUS FUEL ENERGY GOING TO:
     45 = RESIDENTIAL/COMMERCIAL SECTOR
     54 = INDUSTRIAL SECTOR
      1 = TRANSPORTATION SECTOR
OK?
            program computes third percentage,
*Y          displays all new values, and asks
            for agreement

            user agrees
```

Fig. 9 - Sample dialogue from the parameter interrogation

Display of Summary Results

At each time-step the user may request displays of the most important results on the console display. This summary of results is available in six frames, which roughly correspond to the different sections of the structural model of the energy system:

frame 1: total energy input and output
frame 2: energy import and export
frame 3: energy costs, number of conversion plants and active investment
frame 4: primary energy kinds
frame 5: percentages of the different secondary energies to users
frame 6: energy distribution to the user sector

As an example of the format, frame 1 is displayed in Fig. 10 In each frame several selected characteristic variables of the corresponding model section are shown, giving their values for the present time-step and for the initial year and the present annual growth rate. This display permits a rough assessment of scenario results; for a more detailed assessment the focusing subroutine or the print subroutine must be used.

Decision-relevant Indicator Display and Assessment

In arriving at energy policy decisions the decision-maker implicitly or explicitly refers to at least the following decision criteria:

(1) Adequacy of secondary energy supply (volume and mix)
(2) Capital investment cost and energy costs
(3) Long range availability of primary energy resources
(4) Speed of technological change in the energy system
(5) Efficiency of the energy system
(6) Safety of the energy system
(7) Pollution

In order to assess the simulation results with respect to these criteria, the user must have knowledge of the values of relevant state variables (indicators). From the printouts or the summaries on the terminal screen the user may obtain an impression of the situation. However, the task of assessment is made easier by presenting corresponding summaries of relevant indicators. The ESPINT simulation program presents a selection of indicators for each of the decision criteria above if desired. An example is shown in Fig. 11.(see the section "Sample Results" for other indicators). In the different frames the values of the indicator variables are displayed for the present time-step and for the initial year (1970). With this information the user may compare the situation of "today" with that of "yesterday" and can form an opinion about the development.

OVERALL ENERGY INPUT AND OUTPUT

	1970	2025	GROWTH RATE
TOT.PRIM.EN.INPUT	360.0*	1300.0*	4.7
TOT.SEC.EN.OUTPUT	260.5*	609.2*	2.4
TOTAL ENERGY WASTED BEFORE REACHING USER	72.1*	626.5*	14.0
OVERALL EFFICIENCY OF ENERGY SYSTEM	78.3	49.3	-0.7

UNITS ARE:* 10**6(MILLION)METRIC TONS OF COAL EQUIV.

Fig. 10 - Sample frame from result summary

INDICATORS OF ENERGY SUPPLY ADEQUACY

	1970	2025
POWER REACHING USER (W/CAP)	4033	9429
CORR.SERVICE IN TERMS OF 1970 TECHNOLOGY (W/CAP)	4033	9429
ENERGY MIX GO USER SECTOR (PCT)		
ELECTRICITY	14	50
GAS	5	14
LIQUID FUEL	50	6
COAL AND OTHER SOLID FUEL	28	5
CENTRAL HEAT	0	22

YOUR OVERALL ASSESSMENT OF THIS INDICATOR SET?
(0=SATISFACTORY, 1=WORRISOME, 2=UNSATISFACTORY,
3=SERIOUS, 4=UNACCEPTABLE)
?
*

Fig. 11 - Sample frame from indicator display and assessment routine

An assessment question is tied to each of the frames in the series (cf. Fig. 11; the user may choose to skip the assessment by typing in a"0" (zero)). The user can express his dissatisfaction with the situation as described by the indicators for a given decision criterion by typing in the corresponding number on a 5-point integer scale (values from 0 to 4). The assessments are stored during the interactive process and may be reproduced, if desired, in the form of a "problem chart" (s. below). In this manner the user may gain a coherent picture of his assessments, indicating to him problem categories on which he has to concentrate during the interactive scenario development phase. This assessment option may also be used for the assessment of one and the same energy scenario by different persons or interest groups. In this case different priorities and preferences are quite vividly displayed in the different resulting problem charts.

Focusing Routine

More than 700 main variables or derived quantities may be computed by the ESP model of the energy supply system. Obviously printing all these variables and time series, resp. presenting them on the screen makes little sense. A selection has therefore been made for the print routine giving the time series of the 146 input parameters and in addition time series for approximately 35 computed variables. In many cases, especially for a more detailed study of an energy scenario, the information contained in these variables will not suffice for a complete assessment. In these cases, the program should have the capacity to focus on a certain desired variable without overloading the user with information not relevant to him at this point.

The focusing subroutine in ESPINT allows the selective retrieval of time series for each of the over 700 variables of the program in the form of tables and as graphical display. The results are shown on the terminal screen or may be printed on the terminal printer. A selection is made in three to five steps of an interactive hierarchical search program. At each step the user inputs a one digit integer. The integers obtained in the search steps are combined to a five digit retrieval code number which identifies the wanted variable and permits its calculation in another subroutine.

The search process is shown in Fig. 12. In this example the user was interested in the time series (from 1970 to 2020) for the annual growth rate of the annual primary energy input. One may focus on this variable in four steps:

- frame 1:
  selection of:
  1-primary energy input; energy imports and exports
- frame 2:
  further restrictions to:
  3-total primary energy

```
DO YOU WISH TO FOCUS ON ANY PARTICULAR VARIABLE?
(Ø (ZERO) = NO; 1 = YES)
?
* 1

1-PRIMARY ENERGY INPUTS; IMPORTS AND EXPORTS
2-ALLOCATION TO CONVERSION OR END USERS
3-INTERMEDIATE ALLOCATION OF ENERGIES
4-ENERGY CONVERSION PROCESSES
5-ENERGY DISTRIBUTION SYSTEM
6-ENERGY ALLOCATION TO END USER SECTORS
?
* 1

1-PRIMARY ENERGY INPUTS; IMPORTS AND EXPORTS

TYPE IN NUMBER OF ITEM YOU ARE INTERESTED IN:

 1-FOSSILE AND BIOMATTER ENERGIES
 2-NONFOSSILE, NON-BIOMATTER ENERGIES
 3-PRIMARY ENERGY TOTALS
?
* 3

1-PRIMARY ENERGY INPUTS; IMPORTS AND EXPORTS
 3-PRIMARY ENERGY TOTALS


TYPE IN NUMBER OF ITEM YOU ARE INTERESTED IN:

   1-INPUT TO ECONOMY
   2-IMPORT
   3-EXPORT
   4-PRICE PER METRIC TON OF COAL EQUIV. ($/MTCE)
?
* 1

1-PRIMARY ENERGY INPUTS; IMPORTS AND EXPORTS
 3-PRIMARY ENERGY TOTALS

   1-INPUT TO ECONOMY

TYPE IN NUMBER OF ITEM YOU ARE INTERESTED IN:

    1-ENERGY FLOW PER YEAR (MEGATCE/YEAR)
    2-MONETARY VALUE OF ENERGY FLOW (GIGA$/YEAR)
    3-ANNUAL GROWTH RATE OF ENERGY FLOW (PCT/YEAR)
    4-ANNUAL GROWTH RATE OF MONETARY VALUE (PCT/YR)
?
*3
```

Fig. 12 - **Sample focusing dialogue**

- frame 3:
  further restrictions to:
  1-input to regional economy
- frame 4:
  the last step determines the variable:
  3-annual growth rate of energy flow (pct./year)

Following this the time series for the desired variable is displayed in the last frame (Fig.13). The variable is identified in the upper part of the frame by the hierarchically ordered identifications used during the search in the focusing procedure:

1 - primary energy inputs; imports and exports
  3 - primary energy totals
    1 - input to economy
      3 - annual growth rate of energy flow (pct/year)

Briefer: annual growth rate of total primary energy input, or the desired variable. The numerical values of the variable are displayed on the left hand side. On the right hand side the time series is displayed graphically, where results are always normalized to the maximum absolute value within the time period. Positive values are indicated by a plus (+), negative values by a minus (-) sign.

DETAILS OF IMPLEMENTATION

Some Program Statistics

The original ESP off-line simulation model of the energy system consisted of approximately 8 subroutines containing approximately 1000 statements. Making this program interactive required the expansion of the program to approximately 80 subroutines containing some 6000 statements.

Approximately 900 man-hours went into this effort. The application of the GUIDE system for the construction of interactive programs[6] would now reduce the effort to some 40 man-hours. While time expenditures of the order of 900 man-hours can only be justified in exceptional cases, a 40 man-hour effort for the conversion to interactive use of a policy analysis model is relatively insignificant in view of the considerable benefits of interactive simulation compared to off-line model use.

With minor exceptions, all ESPINT dialogues have been programmed using random access files. For each subroutine a separate file exists for each of the languages used. The files for the language used are identified at the beginning of each run and the program logic can then proceed identically independent of the language used.

```
1-PRIMARY ENERGY INPUTS; IMPORTS AND EXPORTS
 3-PRIMARY ENERGY TOTALS

   1-INPUT TO ECONOMY
    3-ANNUAL GROWTH RATE OF ENERGY FLOW (PCT/YEAR)
1970      1                    Ø++++++++++++++
1975      2                    Ø++++++++++++++++++++++
1980      Ø                    Ø++++++++
1985      Ø                    Ø+++
1990      Ø                ----Ø
1995      Ø             -------Ø
2000      Ø            --------Ø
2005      Ø                    Ø
2010      Ø                    Ø
2015      Ø                    Ø
2020      Ø                ----Ø
TYPE A "Ø" WHEN READY TO CONTINUE
*
```

Fig. 13 - Result frame following focusing dialogue

The program has been implemented both on the Siemens 4004/151 computer system and on the PDP 11/40 minicomputer with 28 K word usable memory. In the latter case the whole program has to be split into several chunks which are stored on disk file and are only transferred to the core storage when they are actively being used. The program is designed for type-writer key boards and CRT-screens as normal input-output devices, but it has also been used with a standard line printer or a standard teletype.

As the energy supply system model itself is very uncomplicated, computing times are minimum. In fact, in using the focusing routine, which requires extensive computations, computing delays cannot be noticed on the screen. While computing time is negligible, the time required for completing an interactive assessment or scenario development session in the original ESPINT version is not. Assessment of stored energy scenarios takes approximately five minutes per time-step or roughly an hour for the twelve time-steps involved from 1970 to 2025. The scenario development mode is even more time-consuming. One complete pass through the parameter interrogation subroutine takes approximately 20 minutes. This translates to a time requirement of approximately 4 hours if extensive changes are made at each time-step. Normally this will not be the case and the procedure can be completed in shorter time.

The inclusion of interactive scenario sketching techniques as they are employed in GUIDE (keyboard input), GRIPS[7] and INSAP[8] (light pen interactive graphics) reduces the scenario input time by an order of magnitude, since now an entire parameter time series is entered in one operation (the original ESPINT requires an input at each time-step).

Further Development

Experience with ESPINT has suggested desirable improvements which would probably contribute to eventual widespread acceptance of interactive policy analysis tools.

In fairly complicated decision situations such as the present one, it becomes very difficult to keep the user oriented at all times by use of a single information channel (a terminal screen or the line printer) alone. Instead, in order to stay oriented, the user should be given information about the decision situation using different communication media.

- A working screen or printer is required to display the dialogue.
- Information pertaining to the present dialogue should be displayed on one or several screens. Random access microfilm, microfiche, or slide projection could be used for this purpose at reasonable cost.
- The user must be given an information environment corresponding to the simulated point in time at which he is asked to make a decision. This necessitates display of projections into the near future as well as display of some historical results.
- In addition to information about his imbedding in the time situation, the user must be supplied with information concerning imbedding in

the overall decision process. This requires the display of flow charts and perhaps of the system relationships relating to the current dialogue.

The eventual use of random access microfilm or microfiche readers, floppy disk storage of color images, random access projection, and audio and video recordings with interactive policy analysis programs should not distract from the fact that the modeler's first responsibility is the creation of a reliable and valid model, and not of a futuristic assemblage of electronic gadgetry. As a particularly valuable and desirable improvement over keyboard dialogue we regard the use of interactive graphics (light pen), both in particular for speeding up complex dialogues by "checking-off" answers on the screen, and for sketching information (function, relations, scenarios) directly on the screen. We feel that interactive programs should make the widest possible use of this feature. The replacement of the somewhat tedious dialogue in the present scenario development by interactive processing of scenario sketches (e.g. sketched time graph of coal input into a given economy) results in an interactive planning and scenario development process which is much quicker and much more acceptable to the average decision-maker than the original approach.

SAMPLE RESULTS

In order to demonstrate the use of ESPINT in policy analysis, we now present results of a study of energy policy alternatives[9].

"Standard" Scenario for the Federal Republic of Germany

The scenario results given in Figs.14 -17 represent present government policy (the amended fourth Atomic Program[10]) extended to the year 2025. In particular, this program envisions a strong increase in the amount of primary energy supplied by nuclear sources. The distribution of primary energy inputs is shown in Fig.14. Nuclear power is phased in rapidly starting about 1980 to 1990, producing a large growth in electricity supply. Also, about 1995 it is assumed that the high temperature gas reactor goes commercial, producing process heat for various purposes. Due to diminishing oil supply, liquid fuels decrease about 1985 to 1990 despite a moderate amount of coal liquefaction and gasification starting about 1995 to 2000. The diminishing natural gas supply is augmented by coal gas after 1995, leading to somewhat increasing supplies of gas to end-users. In the conversion sector moderate increases in conversion efficiencies are assumed and some use is made of rejected heat. Fig. 15 presents the 32 indicators related to the seven decision criteria for the year 1970, 2000, and 2025. Fig. 16 shows examples of the consequences of this scenario as computed using the focusing subroutine. We wish to draw attention only to variable no. 41531, the number of nuclear electric power plants in operation (in units of 1000 megawatts electric). This number climbs from 3 in 1975 to 32 in 1985 to 163 in the year 2000 and finally to 363 in the year 2025.

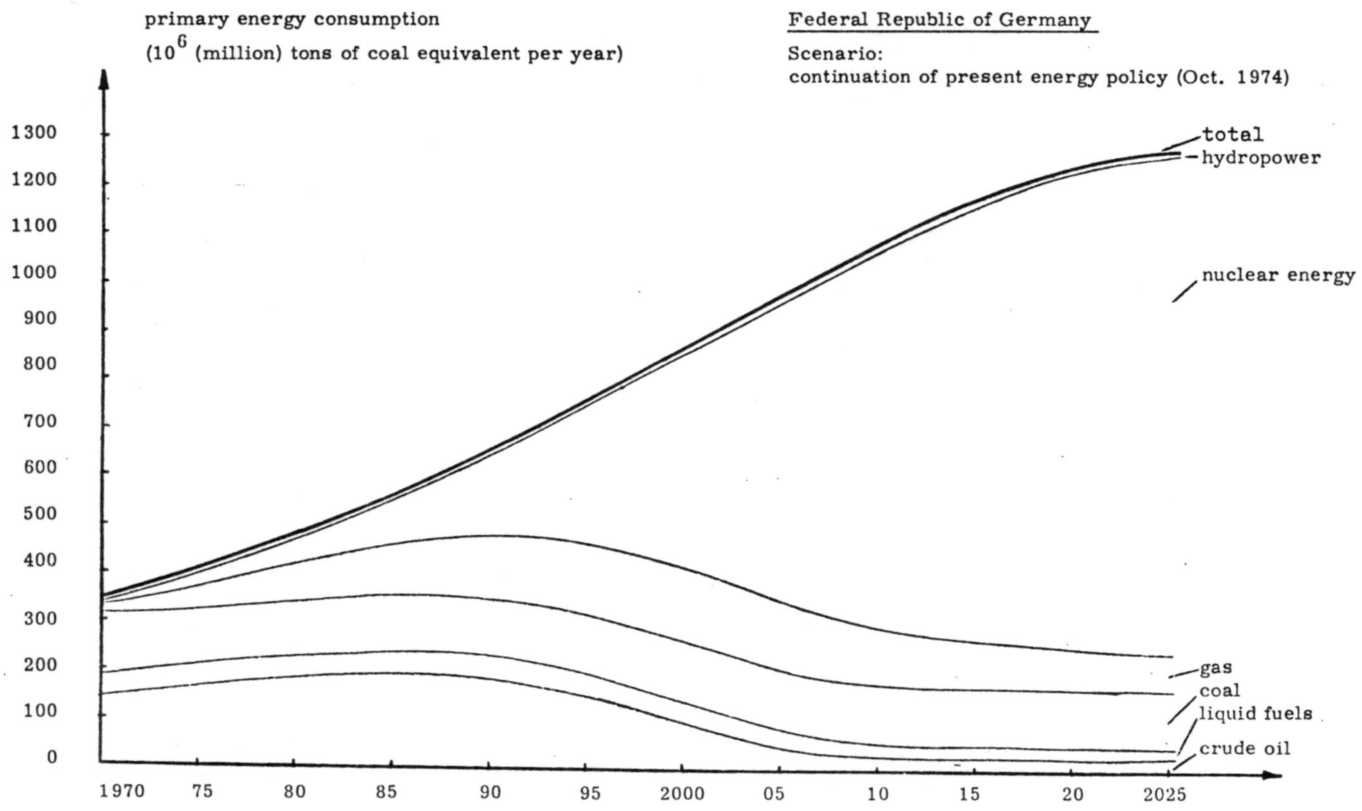

Fig. 14 - Primary energy inputs
Scenario: Federal Republic of Germany,
continuation of present energy policy WGER 1)

INDICATORS OF ENERGY SUPPLY ADEQUACY	1970	2000	2025
POWER REACHING USER (W/CAP)	4033	6994	9429
CORR.SERVICE IN TERMS OF 1970 TECHNOLOGY (W/CAP)	4033	6994	9429
ENERGY MIX GO USER SECTOR (PCT)			
ELECTRICITY	14	37	50
GAS	5	21	14
LIQUID FUEL	50	21	6
COAL AND OTHER SOLID FUEL	28	13	5
CENTRAL HEAT	0	5	22

COST INDICATORS	1970	2000	2025
AVG.COST TO USER PER ENERGY UNIT ($/TCE)	99	139	170
AVG.SPEC.CONVERSION PLANT INVESTMENT ($/KWE)	193	366	355
ANN.INVESTMENT IN CONVERSION PLANTS (MEGA$/YEAR)	0	2995	4026
ANN.IMPORT COST OF PRIMARY ENERGY (GIGA$/YEAR)	10	19	16

EFFICIENCY INDICATORS	1970	2000	2025
OVERALL ENERGY CONVERSION AND DISTRIBUTION EFFICIENCY (ENERGY TO USER/ PRIMARY ENERGY INPUT)(PCT)	72	51	46
OVERALL ENERGY SERVICE FACTOR (1970 ENERGY SERVICE/ENERGY INPUT TO USER) (1970=100)	100	100	100

INDEPENDENCE INDICATORS	1970	2000	2025
DEPENDENCE ON FOREIGN ENERGY SOURCES (PCT)	55	82	89
DEPEND.ON NONRENEWABLE ENERGY SOURCES (PCT)	94	47	18

CHANGE INDICATORS	1970	2000	2025
ANNUAL RATE OF CHANGE IN PRIMARY ENERGY INPUTS (PCT/YEAR)			
COAL	0	0	0
OIL	0	-1	-1
GAS	0	23	4
NUCLEAR	0	0	0
ANNUAL RATE OF CHANGE IN SECONDARY ENERGY OUTPUTS (PCT/YEAR)			
ELECTRICITY	0	11	12
GAS	0	18	8
LIQUID FUEL	0	0	-1
SOLID FUEL	0	0	0
CENTRAL HEAT	0	37	123

SAFETY INDICATORS	1970	2000	2025
NUMBER OF NUCLEAR POWER PLANTS (1000MWE UNITS)	0	184	576
NUMBER OF HYDROGEN PLANTS (1000MWE UNITS)	0	0	49
COAL PRODUCTION FOR DOMESTIC CONSUMPTION (MEGATCE/YEAR)	130	120	120

POLLUTION INDICATORS	1970	2000	2025
NUMBER OF COAL-FIRED POWERPLANTS (1000MWE UNITS)	21	18	18
NUMBER OF OIL-FIRED POWERPLANTS (1000MWE UNITS)	7	4	0
NUMBER OF NUCLEAR POWERPLANTS (1000MWE UNITS)	0	184	576
HEATING OIL TO RESIDENTIAL/COMMERC. USERS (MEGATCE/YEAR)	58	29	8
CONCENTRATED WASTE HEAT FROM CONVERSION PLANTS (MEGATCE/YEAR)	72	353	626

Fig. 15 - Decision criteria and corresponding indicators
Scenario: Federal Republic of Germany,
continuation of present energy policy (WGER 1)

```
1-PRIMARY ENERGY INPUTS: IMPORTS AND EXPORTS
 3-PRIMARY ENERGY TOTALS

   1-INPUT TO ECONOMY
    1-ENERGY FLOW PER YEAR (MEGATCE/YEAR)
1970     360                  0+++++
1975     390                  0++++++
1980     480                  0+++++++
1985     570                  0++++++++
1990     670                  0++++++++++
1995     760                  0+++++++++++
2000     880                  0+++++++++++++
2005     990                  0+++++++++++++++
2010    1100                  0++++++++++++++++
2015    1190                  0++++++++++++++++++
2020    1270                  0+++++++++++++++++++
2025    1300                  0++++++++++++++++++++
```

```
2-ALLOCATION TO CONVERSION OR END USERS
 1-FOSSILS AND BIOMATTER ENERGIES
  4-COAL AND LIGNITE
   2-TO GASIFIC. & LIQUEF., RESP. REFINING
    1-ENERGY FLOW PER YEAR (MEGATCE/YEAR)
1970       0                  0
1975       0                  0
1980       1                  0
1985       3                  0+
1990       6                  0++
1995       8                  0++++
2000      13                  0++++++
2005      17                  0++++++++
2010      22                  0+++++++++++
2015      28                  0++++++++++++++
2020      34                  0+++++++++++++++++
2025      40                  0++++++++++++++++++++
```

```
6-ENERGY ALLOCATION TO END USER SECTORS
 2-TOTALS WITH RESPECT TO USER SECTORS
  1-TOTAL ENERGY INPUT TO USER SECTOR

   1-ENERGY FLOW PER YEAR (MEGATCE/YEAR)
1970     263                  0++++++++
1975     279                  0+++++++++
1980     332                  0++++++++++
1985     377                  0++++++++++++
1990     416                  0+++++++++++++
1995     428                  0++++++++++++++
2000     451                  0++++++++++++++
2005     468                  0+++++++++++++++
2010     506                  0++++++++++++++++
2015     549                  0++++++++++++++++++
2020     592                  0+++++++++++++++++++
2025     609                  0++++++++++++++++++++
```

```
6-ENERGY ALLOCATION TO END USER SECTORS
 1-BREAKDOWN W.R.TO ENERGY KIND AND USER
  5-FUEL GAS
   1-INPUT TO RESIDENTIAL/COMMERCIAL SECTOR
    1-ENERGY FLOW PER YEAR (MEGATCE/YEAR)
1970       6                  0++
1975      12                  0+++++
1980      26                  0++++++++++
1985      34                  0+++++++++++++
1990      43                  0+++++++++++++++++
1995      46                  0++++++++++++++++++
2000      50                  0+++++++++++++++++++
2005      48                  0+++++++++++++++++++
2010      38                  0+++++++++++++++
2015      40                  0+++++++++++++++
2020      42                  0++++++++++++++++
2025      47                  0++++++++++++++++++
```

```
4-ENERGY CONVERSION PROCESSES
 1-CONVERSION TO ELECTRICITY
  5-NUCLEAR ENERGY TO ELECTRICITY
   3-CONVERSION PLANT NUMBER & CAP. INVESTMENT
    1-OPERATING CONVERSION PLANTS IN 1000MWE UNITS
1970       0                  0
1975       3                  0
1980      14                  0
1985      32                  0+
1990      59                  0+++
1995     105                  0+++++
2000     163                  0++++++++
2005     233                  0++++++++++++
2010     297                  0++++++++++++++++
2015     337                  0++++++++++++++++++
2020     362                  0+++++++++++++++++++
2025     363                  0++++++++++++++++++++
```

```
6-ENERGY ALLOCATION TO END USER SECTORS
 1-BREAKDOWN W.R.TO ENERGY KIND AND USER
  4-LIQUID FUEL
   3-INPUT TO TRANSPORTATION SECTOR
    1-ENERGY FLOW PER YEAR (MEGATCE/YEAR)
1970      37                  0+++++++++++
1975      44                  0+++++++++++++
1980      54                  0+++++++++++++++
1985      66                  0+++++++++++++++++++
1990      68                  0++++++++++++++++++++
1995      60                  0+++++++++++++++++
2000      48                  0++++++++++++++
2005      31                  0+++++++++
2010      26                  0+++++++
2015      23                  0++++++
2020      25                  0+++++++
2025      27                  0+++++++
```

```
6-ENERGY ALLOCATION TO END USER SECTORS
 2-TOTALS WITH RESPECT TO USER SECTORS
  6-CONCENTRATED WASTE HEAT FROM CONV. PROCESSES

   1-ENERGY FLOW PER YEAR (MEGATCE/YEAR)
1970      72                  0++
1975      79                  0++
1980     112                  0+++
1985     155                  0++++
1990     204                  0++++++
1995     273                  0++++++++
2000     353                  0+++++++++++
2005     443                  0++++++++++++++
2010     525                  0++++++++++++++++
2015     569                  0++++++++++++++++++
2020     611                  0+++++++++++++++++++
2025     626                  0++++++++++++++++++++
```

```
6-ENERGY ALLOCATION TO END USER SECTORS
 1-BREAKDOWN W.R.TO ENERGY KIND AND USER
  1-ELECTRICITY
   1-INPUT TO RESIDENTIAL/COMMERCIAL SECTOR
    1-ENERGY FLOW PER YEAR (MEGATCE/YEAR)
1970      16                  0+
1975      17                  0++
1980      24                  0++
1985      32                  0+++
1990      47                  0+++++
1995      63                  0+++++++
2000      84                  0++++++++++
2005     109                  0+++++++++++++
2010     136                  0++++++++++++++++
2015     153                  0++++++++++++++++++
2020     166                  0+++++++++++++++++++
2025     166                  0++++++++++++++++++++
```

Fig. 16 - Selected time series obtained by focusing Scenario: Federal Republic of Germany, continuation of present energy policy (WGER 1)

PROBLEM CHART

SUMMARY OF INDICATOR ASSESSMENTS

YEAR	ADEQU	COST	INDEP	CHANG	EFFIC	SAFET	POLLU
1970		X	XXX				X
1975		X	XXX	X			X
1980		XX	XXX	XX		X	X
1985		XX	XXX	XX		XX	XX
1990		XXX	XXX	X	X	XXX	XXX
1995		XXX	XXX	XX	XX	XXXX	XXXX
2000		XXX	XXX		XX	XXXX	XXXX
2005		XXX	XXX		XXX	XXXX	XXXX
2010		XXX	XXX		XXX	XXXX	XXXX
2015		XXX	XXX		XXX	XXXX	XXXX
2020	XX	XXX	XXX		XXX	XXXX	XXXX
2025	XX	XXX	XXX		XXX	XXXX	XXXX
	SUPPLY ADEQUACY	COST	DEPENDENCE	CHANGE	EFFICIENCY	SAFETY	POLLUTION

Fig. 17 - Problem chart
Scenario: Federal Republic of Germany, continuation of present energy policy (WGER 1)
(x = worrisome, xx = unsatisfactory, xxx = serious, xxxx = unacceptable)

(The number to the year 2000 is equivalent to a 1000 Megawatt electric unit on each area fourty by fourty kilometer square.) The indicator displays and the problem chart summarizing the indicator assessments (Fig. 17) point to significant problem fields which may make this scenario unacceptable to the majority of the population.

An "Alternative" Scenario for the Federal Republic of Germany

From designing, studying and assessing many different scenarios for the United States, Western Europe, and the Federal Republic of Germany, we have slowly come to the conclusion that a concentrated effort at energy conservation by increasing the efficiencies of energy use may be the least painful alternative energy policy available to these countries. Some results of such a conservation scenario for the Federal Republic of Germany are displayed in Figs. 18 to 21. In this scenario the demand for energy services is allowed to increase roughly at the present rate of 3% to approximately the year 2000 and to saturate thereafter with no further increase. At the same time it is assumed that very strong efforts are undertaken to increase the efficiencies of energy use in the different user sectors. Thus it is assumed that over a 25 year period the amount of secondary energy input into the industrial sector can be reduced by approximately 20% for a constant output in energy service. More significant savings can be expected in the residential / commercial sector and in the transportation sector, as efficiencies there are presently relatively low. Assuming a 40% drop in the secondary energy input for the same energy service in the residential/ commercial sector and a 30% drop in the transportation sector, the required primary energy input is now significantly lower than that for the standard scenario (Fig. 18). Detailed results are given in Figs. 19 to 20. The problem chart for this case (Fig. 21) indicates a solution which may be much more acceptable than the previous one. Note again that end-users receive an energy service approximately equivalent to that in the standard scenario.

CONCLUSIONS

Increasing system complexity coupled with accelerating dynamics has made the intuitive assessment and development of policies for societal systems more prone to error and failure than ever before. It is essential that reliable aids and tools for planning and decision-making are developed. These tools must be adapted to the skills and abilities of the average decision-maker. The ESPINT project is one approach to this task. It has yielded valuable information concerning the design of interactive policy analysis tools. We are aware that eventual acceptance of simulation-based decision aids depends greatly on providing an ergonomically acceptable working environment. It is in this area that efforts should be concentrated in the future.

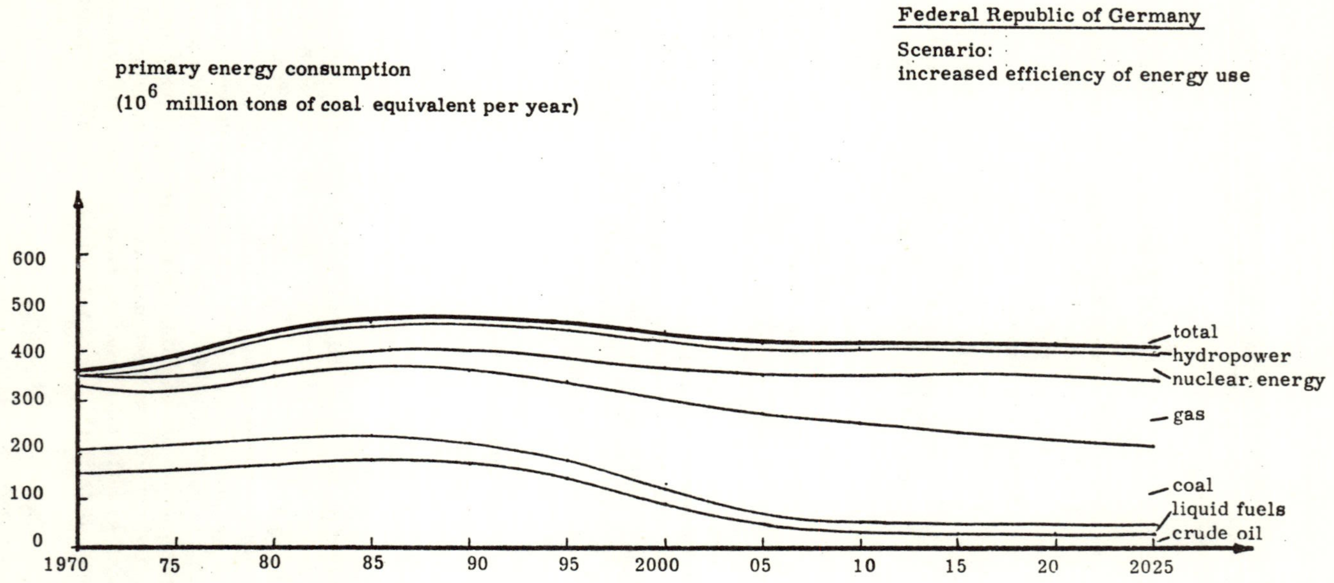

Fig. 18 - Primary energy inputs
Scenario: Federal Republic of Germany
increased efficiency of energy use (WGER 6)

INDICATORS OF ENERGY SUPPLY ADEQUACY	1970	2000	2025
POWER REACHING USER (W/CAP)	4033	4555	3626
CORR.SERVICE IN TERMS OF 1970 TECHNOLOGY (W/CAP)	4033	6700	5430
ENERGY MIX GO USER SECTOR (PCT)			
ELECTRICITY	14	21	23
GAS	5	17	34
LIQUID FUEL	50	28	18
COAL AND OTHER SOLID FUEL	28	31	20
CENTRAL HEAT	0	1	3

COST INDICATORS	1970	2000	2025
AVG.COST TO USER PER ENERGY UNIT ($/TCE)	99	104	103
AVG.SPEC.CONVERSION PLANT INVESTMENT ($/KWE)	193	252	249
ANN.INVESTMENT IN CONVERSION PLANTS (MEGA$/YEAR)	0	-840	-64
ANN.IMPORT COST OF PRIMARY ENERGY (GIGA$/YEAR)	10	13	14

EFFICIENCY INDICATORS	1970	2000	2025
OVERALL ENERGY CONVERSION AND DISTRIBUTION EFFICIENCY (ENERGY TO USER/ PRIMARY ENERGY INPUT)(PCT)	72	66	57
OVERALL ENERGY SERVICE FACTOR (1970 ENERGY SERVICE/ENERGY INPUT TO USER) (1970=100)	100	147	150

INDEPENDENCE INDICATORS	1970	2000	2025
DEPENDENCE ON FOREIGN ENERGY SOURCES (PCT)	55	61	78
DEPEND.ON NONRENEWABLE ENERGY SOURCES (PCT)	94	84	82

CHANGE INDICATORS	1970	2000	2025
ANNUAL RATE OF CHANGE IN PRIMARY ENERGY INPUTS (PCT/YEAR)			
COAL	0	2	-1
OIL	0	-7	0
GAS	0	7	0
NUCLEAR	0	0	0
ANNUAL RATE OF CHANGE IN SECONDARY ENERGY OUTPUTS (PCT/YEAR)			
ELECTRICITY	0	0	0
GAS	0	6	0
LIQUID FUEL	0	-6	0
SOLID FUEL	0	1	-3
CENTRAL HEAT	0	5	0

SAFETY INDICATORS	1970	2020	2025
NUMBER OF NUCLEAR POWER PLANTS (1000MWE UNITS)	0	17	22
NUMBER OF HYDROGEN PLANTS (1000MWE UNITS)	0	0	2
COAL PRODUCTION FOR DOMESTIC CONSUMPTION (MEGATCE/YEAR)	130	100	160

POLLUTION INDICATORS	1970	2000	2025
NUMBER OF COAL-FIRED POWERPLANTS (1000MWE UNITS)	21	27	24
NUMBER OF OIL-FIRED POWERPLANTS (1000MWE UNITS)	7	3	0
NUMBER OF NUCLEAR POWERPLANTS (1000MWE UNITS)	0	17	22
HEATING OIL TO RESIDENTIAL/COMMERC. USERS (MEGATCE/YEAR)	58	25	8
CONCENTRATED WASTE HEAT FROM CONVERSION PLANTS (MEGATCE/YEAR)	72	98	73

Fig. 19 - Decision criteria and corresponding indicators
Scenario: Federal Republic of Germany,
increased efficiency of energy use (WGER 6)

```
1-PRIMARY ENERGY INPUTS; IMPORTS AND EXPORTS
 3-PRIMARY ENERGY TOTALS
  1-INPUT TO ECONOMY
   1-ENERGY FLOW PER YEAR (MEGATCE/YEAR)
1970   360          Ø++++++++++++++++
1975   390          Ø+++++++++++++++++
1980   440          Ø+++++++++++++++++++
1985   460          Ø++++++++++++++++++++
1990   470          Ø+++++++++++++++++++++
1995   460          Ø++++++++++++++++++++
2000   440          Ø+++++++++++++++++++
2005   420          Ø++++++++++++++++++
2010   420          Ø++++++++++++++++++
2015   420          Ø++++++++++++++++++
2020   420          Ø++++++++++++++++++
2025   410          Ø++++++++++++++++++
```

```
6-ENERGY ALLOCATION TO END USER SECTORS
 2-TOTALS WITH RESPECT TO USER SECTORS
  1-TOTAL ENERGY INPUT TO USER SECTOR

   1-ENERGY FLOW PER YEAR (MEGATCE/YEAR)
1970   260          Ø+++++++++++++++++
1975   278          Ø++++++++++++++++++
1980   301          Ø+++++++++++++++++++
1985   317          Ø++++++++++++++++++++
1990   323          Ø+++++++++++++++++++++
1995   314          Ø++++++++++++++++++++
2000   294   (x)    Ø+++++++++++++++++++
2005   273          Ø+++++++++++++++++
2010   263          Ø+++++++++++++++++
2015   253          Ø++++++++++++++++
2020   246          Ø++++++++++++++++
2025   234          Ø+++++++++++++++
```

(x) corresponding energy service to user increases by 50 percent to 2000

```
4-ENERGY CONVERSION PROCESSES
 1-CONVERSION TO ELECTRICITY
  5-NUCLEAR ENERGY TO ELECTRICITY
   3-CONVERSION PLANT NUMBER & CAP. INVESTMENT
    1-OPERATING CONVERSION PLANTS IN 1000MWE UNITS
1970    0           Ø
1975    3           Ø++++
1980   14           Ø+++++++++++++++++++
1985   14           Ø+++++++++++++++++++
1990   14           Ø++++++++++++++++++++
1995   15           Ø++++++++++++++++++++
2000   15           Ø++++++++++++++++++++
2005   15           Ø+++++++++++++++++++++
2010   15           Ø++++++++++++++++++++
2015   15           Ø++++++++++++++++++++
2020   14           Ø++++++++++++++++++++
2025   14           Ø+++++++++++++++++++
```

```
6-ENERGY ALLOCATION TO END USER SECTORS
 2-TOTALS WITH RESPECT TO USER SECTORS
  6-CONCENTRATED WASTE HEAT FROM CONV. PROCESSES

   1-ENERGY FLOW PER YEAR (MEGATCE/YEAR)
1970    72          Ø++++++++++++++
1975    80          Ø+++++++++++++++
1980   106          Ø++++++++++++++++++++
1985   109          Ø++++++++++++++++++++
1990   110          Ø+++++++++++++++++++++
1995   105          Ø++++++++++++++++++++
2000    98          Ø++++++++++++++++++
2005    93          Ø+++++++++++++++++
2010    87          Ø++++++++++++++++
2015    79          Ø+++++++++++++++
2020    75          Ø++++++++++++++
2025    73          Ø++++++++++++++
```

```
4-ENERGY CONVERSION PROCESSES
 3-BIO-&FOSS. FUELS: REFINING, GASIF., LIQUEF.
  4-GASIFICATION AND LIQUEFACTION OF COAL
   3-CONVERSION PLANT NUMBER & CAP. INVESTMENT
    1-OPERATING CONVERSION PLANTS IN 1000MWE UNITS
1970    0           Ø
1975    0           Ø
1980    1           Ø
1985    4           Ø+
1990    8           Ø++
1995   12           Ø++++
2000   21           Ø+++++++
2005   33           Ø+++++++++++
2010   41           Ø++++++++++++++
2015   47           Ø++++++++++++++++
2020   54           Ø+++++++++++++++++++
2025   59           Ø+++++++++++++++++++++
```

```
6-ENERGY ALLOCATION TO END USER SECTORS
 1-BREAKDOWN W.R.TO ENERGY KIND AND USER
  5-FUEL GAS
   1-INPUT TO RESIDENTIAL/COMMERCIAL SECTOR
    1-ENERGY FLOW PER YEAR (MEGATCE/YEAR)
1970    6           Ø++
1975    9           Ø++++
1980   10           Ø++++
1985   11           Ø+++++
1990   15           Ø+++++++
1995   19           Ø++++++++
2000   25   (x)     Ø++++++++++++
2005   29           Ø++++++++++++++
2010   35           Ø+++++++++++++++++
2015   40           Ø+++++++++++++++++++
2020   43           Ø++++++++++++++++++++
2025   43           Ø+++++++++++++++++++++
```

(x) corresponding energy service to user increases by 66 percent to 2000

```
6-ENERGY ALLOCATION TO END USER SECTORS
 1-BREAKDOWN W.R.TO ENERGY KIND AND USER
  4-LIQUID FUEL
   3-INPUT TO TRANSPORTATION SECTOR
    1-ENERGY FLOW PER YEAR (MEGATCE/YEAR)
1970   37           Ø++++++++++++
1975   44           Ø+++++++++++++++
1980   54           Ø++++++++++++++++++
1985   63           Ø+++++++++++++++++++++
1990   62           Ø++++++++++++++++++++
1995   57           Ø+++++++++++++++++++
2000   41   (x)     Ø++++++++++++++
2005   27           Ø++++++++
2010   22           Ø+++++++
2015   24           Ø+++++++
2020   26           Ø++++++++
2025   28           Ø++++++++
```

(x) corresponding energy service to user increases by 43 percent to 2000

```
6-ENERGY ALLOCATION TO END USER SECTORS
 1-BREAKDOWN W.R.TO ENERGY KIND AND USER
  1-ELECTRICITY
   1-INPUT TO RESIDENTIAL/COMMERCIAL SECTOR
    1-ENERGY FLOW PER YEAR (MEGATCE/YEAR)
1970   16           Ø+++++++++++
1975   17           Ø++++++++++++
1980   23           Ø+++++++++++++++
1985   24           Ø++++++++++++++++
1990   29           Ø+++++++++++++++++++
1995   30           Ø++++++++++++++++++++
2000   31   (x)     Ø++++++++++++++++++++
2005   31           Ø++++++++++++++++++++
2010   31           Ø+++++++++++++++++++++
2015   30           Ø++++++++++++++++++++
2020   30           Ø+++++++++++++++++++
2025   29           Ø+++++++++++++++++++
```

(x) corresponding energy service to user increases by 66 percent to 2000

Fig. 20 - Selected time series obtained by focusing Scenario: Federal Republic of Germany, increased efficiency of energy use (WGER 6)

PROBLEM CHART

SUMMARY OF INDICATOR ASSESSMENTS

YEAR	ADEQU	COST	INDEP	CHANG	EFFIC	SAFET	POLLU
1970		X	XXX				X
1975			XXX				X
1980		X	XXX	XX		X	X
1985		X	XXX			X	X
1990		X	XXX			X	X
1995		X	XXX			X	X
2000		X	XXX			X	X
2005		X	XXX	X		X	X
2010		X	XXX	X		X	X
2015		X	XXX		X	X	X
2020		X	XXX		X	X	X
2025		X	XXX		X	X	X
	SUPPLY ADEQUACY	COST	DEPENDENCE	CHANGE	EFFICIENCY	SAFETY	POLLUTION

Fig. 21 - Problem chart
Scenario: Federal Republic of Germany, increased efficiency of energy use (WGER 6)
(x = worrisome, xx = unsatisfactory, xxx = serious, xxxx = unacceptable)

Footnotes

1 The GUIDE system for the generation of interactive policy analysis programs is fully discussed in the contribution by H. Bossel and M. Strobel in this volume.

2 Energy Supply Planning model ESP developed by H. Bossel at the Systems Research Center, Cleveland, Ohio, in the winter of 1973/1974. The model is described in H. Bossel, "Energy Supply Model" in: Multilevel Computer Model of World Development System, IIASA Symposium Proceedings SP-74-4, Vol. IV, International Institute of Applied Systems Analysis (IIASA) Vienna 1974. A somewhat more complete account is given in H. Bossel, "Energy Supply System: Simulation Model, Results and Evaluation", Technical Report, Institut für Systemtechnik und Innovationsforschung (ISI), Karlsruhe, March 1974.

3 Directors: M. Mesarovic, E. Pestel. See: M. Mesarovic, E. Pestel, "Mankind at the Turning Point", Dutton Press, New York 1974, or M. Mesarovic, E. Pestel, "Menschheit am Wendepunkt", DVA, Stuttgart 1974.

4 See the contribution by Chr. Deissenberg on interactive multiple criteria optimization in this volume.

5 See H. Bossel, "Energy Supply Model", op. cit.

6 See the contribution by H. Bossel and M. Strobel in this volume, op. cit.

7 For a discussion of the GRIPS system for the interactive construction of dynamic models see the contribution by W. Hudetz in this volume.

8 The INSAP system for the interactive assessment of satisfaction states and the computation of priorities is discussed in the contribution by H. Bossel and K. H. Simon in this volume.

9 Both the "standard" and the "alternative" scenario were prepared by R. V. Denton. The computations were repeated later with more recent data: see R. V. Denton "Energy Alternatives for the Federal Republic of Germany - Three Scenarios", Institut für Systemtechnik und Innovationsforschung (ISI), D 75 Karlsruhe, May 1976; also: R. V. Denton "Energie-Alternativen für die Bundesrepublik Deutschland: Drei Szenarien" in H. Bossel, D. Teufel, H. H. Wüstenhagen (eds.): "Energie - richtig genutzt", C. F. Müller, Karlsruhe 1976.

see "Viertes Atomprogramm der Bundesrepublik Deutschland für die Jahre 1973 bis 1976", Bundesministerium für Forschung und Technologie, 1973, and "Korrekturen am Energieprogramm", Handelsblatt 25. Sept. 1974. Also: "Rahmen-Programm Energieforschung 1974 - 1977", Bundesministerium für Forschung und Technologie, 1973; "Daten zur Entwicklung der Energiewirtschaft in der Bundesrepublik Deutschland", Ausgabe 1973, Bundesministerium für Wirtschaft; H. Mandel, "Primärenergieversorgung in der Bundesrepublik Deutschland" Vortrag, 11. Gespräch der List-Gesellschaft Düsseldorf, March 1974; "Rahmen-Programm Energieforschung 1974 - 1977 der Bundesrepublik", Technologie Nachrichten Nr. 096, 15. Aug. 1974

11

MAN-MACHINE INTERACTION AS AN ANSWER TO THE MULTIPLE-GOAL PROBLEM

Christophe Deissenberg

SURVEY

In many real problems the evaluation of alternative actions must take multiple heterogenous and complex indices or criteria into account. In this case, the standard mathematical optimization models cannot be applied to determine the "best" decision. What methods can then be used to help the decision-maker in his choice? What supplementary information is needed and how can it be obtained?

This article attempts to answer these questions by giving a critical overview of several man-machine interactive methods which were recently devised to solve the multiple-goal problem. Three types of methods are outlined and compared. The mathematical structure and the implementation of one of the methods, which appear to be operational for a wide range of problems, are presented in greater detail and illustrated by means of an example.

INTRODUCTION: THE MULTIPLE - GOAL PROBLEM

In this article we are considering complex decision situations characterized by a multiplicity of partially conflicting goals, all of which are desirable to some extent. For simplicity's sake these goals are assumed to be of the form [1)]

$$x_i = f^i(z_1, \ldots, z_m) \rightarrow \sup_z, \quad x_i \in R, \quad i = 1, \ldots, n.$$

We assume the functions f^i to be point-to-point mappings so that exactly one x corresponds to each z and vice-versa. The functions f^i, the set $D \subseteq R^m$ of feasible problem variables z and the corresponding set $T \subseteq R^n$ of feasible goal variables x are supposed to be clearly defined and explicitly known. The decision-maker is assumed to have an implicit overall objective function U as a function of the n single variables x_i. The function U, however, is not explicitly known. Formally, this decision-making situation can be formalized as a constrained maximization problem,

$$\begin{aligned} & U(x_1, \ldots, x_n) \rightarrow \sup, && U \text{ unknown}, \\ & \text{subject to} && \\ & x_i = f^i(z_1, \ldots, z_m), && i = 1, \ldots, n; \\ & x \in T \Leftrightarrow z \in D \Leftrightarrow && G(z_1, \ldots, z_m) = 0; \end{aligned} \qquad (1)$$

in which G describes a set of direct and functional constraints on the variables z_j.

Multiple-goal situations of the kind described above are most common in practical economic decision-making processes and have been recognized for a long time in economic theory[2]. Two examples of these kinds of problems are:

a) In macroeconomics the "stabilization policy problem": unemployment and maintenance of full-capacity output, control of inflation, reasonable rate of economic growth, maintenance of a high level of investment, and redistribution of income through taxes and transfers;

b) In microeconomics the problem of maximizing profit, cash flow, profitability, stabilizing prices and beneficiary margins, assuring future investment possibilities and growth, augmenting the market share, etc.

Note that multiple-goal problems typically appear in organizations too, in which there is not a single decision-maker but a board, each member of which is more crucially interested in certain specific goals.

However, the assumption of an explicitly known, single-valued, overall objective function is still the rule in economic theory as well as in the decision-oriented models of Operations Research. The main reason for the apparent neglect of multiple-goal situations and their specific problems is probably the difficulty in handling multiple goals in a satisfactory manner. Knowledge of n single goals is insufficient in itself in enabling the formulation of an optimization problem capable of being used for actual policy recommendations to the decision-maker. When only the n goals are known, this can lead only to the vector-maximization problem

$$\begin{aligned} &(x_1, \ldots, x_n) \rightarrow \sup, \\ &\text{subject to} \\ &x_i = f^i(z_1, \ldots, z_m), \; i = 1, \ldots, n; \\ &G(z_1, \ldots, z_m) = 0. \end{aligned} \tag{2}$$

The solution of (2), however, is not uniquely defined but consists of a whole set of points, i.e. the efficient set. Each element $\bar{x}$ of this set, i.e. each efficient point, is characterized by the fact that no feasible x exists such that $x_i \geq \bar{x}_i$, $i = 1, \ldots, n$, with the strong inequality $>$ holding for at least one i. That means there is no feasible point x which fulfills one single goal better than $\bar{x}$ without simultaneously fulfilling some other goal less well than $\bar{x}$ (Pareto optimality). Therefore, the solution of the decision problem (1) given a specific objective function U is necessarily an efficient point. Nevertheless, even when the computation of the efficient set is possible, the decision-maker is left with the problem of determining the "best" point in the efficient set. Since the efficient set is, as a rule, a complicated, n-dimensional structure, this reduced problem is not significantly simpler than the original problem of finding the best point in the feasible set.

The purpose of this paper is to present some interactive man-machine approaches which can be effectively applied in actual multiple-goal decision situations to help the decision-maker make his choice.

There is no general agreement concerning the solution of the multiple-goal problem. The solution is straight-forward in two special classes: (a) No real difficulty arises when the preference ordering of the decision-maker is lexicographic; (b) The best solution can easily be found by directly comparing alternatives when the feasible or the efficient set contains only a few points or when they can be represented in an easily understandable way, for example graphically. However, a graphical representation is, in general, only possible for $n = 2$. For $n > 2$ the feasible or the efficient set can, as a rule, only be represented analytically in the form of an equation, which in most practical situations will be too intuitively meaningless to serve as the basis for a decision.

For the general case, several interactive approaches have been studied to date. (For an excellent review, see Roy (1971).) Some of these approaches aim at the explicit specification of the overall objective function of the decision-maker or of some weaker surrogate of it, in order to permit the expression of the decision problem as a standard mathematical program. The highly interesting questions arising therefrom are central to welfare theory. However, these approaches are often too ambitious for practical application. In particular, the information which the decision-maker has to supply within the interactive process is often too complex. In any case, these approaches have mostly been studied on a theoretical level and there has been little or no attempt to apply them in actual problem solving.

We will therefore restrict our attention to the second main kind of approach, which has already reached the operational stage. The aim here is to determine a "satisfactory" solution through sequential exploration of the feasible set without having recourse to overall information about the preference ordering of the decision-maker. This exploration, however, is guided to some extent by local information furnished by the decision-maker and leads, among other things, to a progressive definition of his preferences. Procedures of this kind are typically based on an interactive procedure in which the decision-maker is faced at the first iteration with a feasible first solution. He is then asked by the algorithm to answer a few simple, intuitively clear questions, directed at revealing his evaluation of the solution (decision phase). The answers are subsequently used in a calculation phase to determine a new, "improved" solution, which forms the basis for a new iteration. The process is assumed to converge within a reasonable number of iterations to a "satisfactory" or "suboptimal" solution.

Let us already state at this point one very important characteristic of the methods we will present. The whole computation, which takes place in the problem variable space $\{z\}$, is relegated to the computer. The decision-maker can regard the entire procedure as taking place in the goal variable space $\{x\}$; he can disregard the values taken by the variables z_j, the function f^i and the constraints G. This has two advantages: a) The decision-maker can concentrate on his choice with no extraneous details to distract him; b) Practically, the only limiting factor in the use of the method is the maximal number of goal variables the decision-maker can comprehend at one time. Depending on the method, this number lies between 4 and 10 (see section III, B). The number of problem variables z_i can be much higher. The dimension of $\{z\}$ and the complexity of the functions f^i and the constraints G is limited only by the computer's capacity to solve in a reasonable amount of time the classical optimization problem corresponding to (1) when the objective function U is explicitly known.

This article is organized as follows: In part I we discuss some general characteristics of interactive methods for solving the multiple-goal problem and their consequences, and present the logic underlying the three main classes of methods. The implementation of the GEOFFRION approach, which we consider to be the most promising of the three, is discussed in part II. A numerical example is given. Part III is devoted to comparative evaluation of the different methods presented. Some conclusions are drawn relative to their practical application and to further research.

I - BASIC METHODS

Three main classes of approaches for solving the multiple-goal problem through sequential exploration of the feasible set can be distinguished:

- direct search or unstructured approaches;
- best compromise approaches (prototype: STEM method);
- interactive large-step procedures of the GEOFFRION-type.

The corresponding methods all aim at determining the best solution to a constrained optimization problem. However, the fact that they are based on a man-machine dialogue and are designed especially for assistance in managerial decision-making, implies the existence of important general properties that distinguish them in the family of optimization methods. These properties and their implications are discussed briefly in section A. The basic ideas underlying the unstructured approaches, the STEM and the GEOFFRION methods are presented in sections B - D.

A - General properties

Normally, the cost of building and optimizing a multiple-goal model do not differ significantly from the cost of building and optimizing the corresponding classical optimization model, given a known overall objective function. To be sure, the interactive procedure may occasion increased programming and computing expenditures, although this may be offset by increased willingness to tolerate an inexact solution (see below). The supplementary expenditures, however, are likely to constitute only a small fraction of the total analysis cost and will not play a decisive role in the choice of a given method.

Nevertheless, one specific cost factor places narrow constraints on the interactive methods: the high cost, for example in time elapsed, of the decision-maker's participation in the interactive process. This cost factor will be of decisive importance if the decision-maker participating in the interactive procedure is - as should ideally be the case - the "policy-maker" himself, i.e. usually a (board of) top-level manager(s) or high government official(s).

Another specific aspect of interactive procedures, which distinguishes them from regular iterative optimization problems, is the fact that "inexactitude" is introduced <u>during</u> the iterative process by the human element. Interactive procedures are based on an information exchange which takes place at each iteration between decision-maker and computer. It is likely that the decision-maker will not be able to exactly express the information he wants to communicate to the computer. Moreover, he will probably undergo a learning process during the interactive procedure, so that the information he furnishes at a later iteration may be "inconsistent" with the information he furnished at earlier iterations. On the other hand, the decision-maker will not be able to interpret exactly the information provided by the computer. In particular, he will consider small changes in the values of the variables insignificant, although even such seemingly insignificant changes may be of great importance in a standard optimization routine.

A third aspect is the fact that the decision-maker will not consider the "best solution" attained in the interactive procedure to be the decisive answer to his decision problem. Rather, he will rely on the procedure to provide him with supplementary <u>information</u> on the problem and to help him in his appreciation of relevant alternatives. In other words, <u>confidence</u> in the method is an essential factor in its practical success, and the key to the successful conduct of multiple-goal methods is the joint exercise of good judgement by executives and professional operations researchers.

From the various arguments discussed above, it is obvious that only approximate solutions can realistically be expected from interactive methods for solving the multiple criteria problem. The important issue, however, is not whether the proposed solution is optimal, but whether the method permits an <u>improvement</u> in the solution significant enough to justify its use. Therefore, a good approximation of the optimal solution is satisfactory, too. Furthermore, since the model to be optimized is itself an approximation, solutions will be acceptable which do not exactly satisfy the constraints (i.e., pseudo solutions). The consequence of this standpoint is that the formal problem of the existence of a solution becomes uninteresting except in one case. If the solution is unbounded, the problem is meaningless. In the following, we will assume that all solutions are bounded, unless stated otherwise.

Since the inexactitude of the solution and the limited number of iterations are accepted, the infinite convergence of the method is irrelevant. The initial convergence, however, is crucial. A few iterations should lead to a reasonably small neighborhood of the optimum. The convergence must be robust against possible inconsistencies in the information provided by the decision-maker. The interactive procedures altogether should be compatible with the decision-maker's eventually changing his mind; he should be helped, but not restricted, in his search.

All the methods presented in this paper satisfy the above requirements. They are not bound to a special mathematical structure of the multiple-goal problem either, but can be applied to a wide variety of models. Only the STEM method is more restrictive in its use. However, it should be clear that quick convergence to a global optimum presupposes "reasonable" formal properties of the problem. The existence of several local optima in itself is not necessarily very disturbing in an interactive setting. In most cases, experience and intuition will allow easy recognition of a given local solution as globally unsatisfactory.

The implementation of a multiple-goal procedure in a concrete case should be carefully planned, if possible in close collaboration with the executives and the staff of the firm concerned. Before it is practically used as decision aid for a given problem, the procedure should be extensively tested. The corresponding trial runs should, if possible, be conducted with middle managers. Particular regard should be given to the instructions describing the model, the method, and the way they can contribute to the solution of the concrete multiple-goal problem. It is also extremely important to organize the information exchange between decision-maker and computer so that inexactitudes and/or misunderstandings as well as time required are reduced to a minimum. In general, the information exchange should be made with the help of a time-sharing program directly on a computer console whereby the calculation results are displayed on the screen.

Before the decision-maker is allowed to use the interactive procedure for solving his concrete problem, he should be thoroughly trained in the use of the method. In his training he should receive both theoretical explanations and practice in solving typical examples. Experience has shown that this training is not only important as an instrument in increasing the decision-maker's confidence and his acceptance of the method. It is also crucial in increasing the reliability of his answers to the computer. The solution of the real problem should be repeated at least once in order to increase confidence in the results and to check for eventual learning processes and local optima. The results must be filed and analyzed ex post in collaboration with the decision-maker in order to interpret his choices and their consequences.

For the description of a practical case of implementation, see section III, A.

B - The unstructured approaches

Unstructured approaches refer to the direct application to multiple-goal problems of methods known in mathematical programming under the generic name of "Sequential Optimum Seeking by Experimentation". The designation "unstructured" is common but unfortunate, since many of these methods have a non-trivial structure. Their common characteristic is that they do not require elaborate information from the decision-maker. In general, a pairwise ranking of alternatives is all that is necessary. They neither seriously restrict the decision-maker in his search nor help him to any great extent. The rate at which they proceed toward the optimum depends on the decision-maker's luck and cannot be predicted in advance. Nevertheless, their importance should not be underestimated. These methods are generally easy to understand, easy to implement, and give very satisfactory results in situations which are not too complex.

In the simplest case the decision-maker is invited at each iteration to enter a solution x. Then the computer tells him whether x is feasible or not. (See printout and flow chart of the GEOFFRION method). Supplementary information can eventually be supplied; for example, the computer can indicate if x is efficient or not, which constraints are binding, etc. The decision-maker is completely on his own in choosing which new solution he will enter at the next iteration. Contrary to the STEM and the GEOFFRION methods, this approach can also be applied to discrete problems.

More complicated methods present the decision-maker at each iteration with a whole set of feasible solutions. He is then asked for a subjective ranking of the solutions. This ranking is used to determine the set of solutions to be presented at the next iteration, using, for example, a combined gradient and golden search method. A detailed exposition of these methods cannot be given here. The interested reader, however, may refer to the corresponding chapter in Simmons (1975) (in a classical optimization context) for an overview.

C - The STEM Method

1. General remarks. The STEM method devised by Benayoun and Tergny (1969) is applicable to linearly constrained problems in which the goal variables x_i are linear functions of the problem variables z_i. That is, it is applicable to multiple objective linear programs of the type:

$$U(x) \rightarrow \max; \quad x_i = c^i z, \quad i = 1, \ldots, n; \quad U \text{ unknown};$$

$$\text{subject to} \qquad (3)$$

$$z \in D \Longleftrightarrow (Az \leq b, \ z \geq 0).$$

with $x = (x_1, \ldots, x_n)$, $z = (z_1, \ldots, z_m)'$,

$c^i = (c^i_1, \ldots, c^i_m)$, $b = (b_1, \ldots, b_\ell)$,

A a (l x m) matrix.

The concept behind the STEM method is to sequentially explore feasible modifications (i.e., compromise solutions) of an unfeasible "ideal" solution, whereby the exploration is guided to some extent by the decision-maker's answers to simple questions posed by the algorithm. The decision-maker is not asked for information about the overall objective function U at any stage of the iterative process.

Prior to the interactive process with alternating calculation and decision phases, a preparation phase is necessary in order to calculate an "ideal" solution and the first compromise solution.

2. Preparation phase. This phase begins with the determination of the n extreme solutions which correspond to the maximization of each variable x_i considered as the unique goal. In other words, these extreme solutions are solutions to the n LPs

$$x_i = c^i_z \longrightarrow \max \qquad \text{subject to} \qquad z \in D \, , \tag{4}$$

$i = 1, \ldots, n$. Let $\tilde{x}^i = (\tilde{x}^i_1, \ldots, \tilde{x}^i_n)$ be the solution of the i-th problem (4) and $\tilde{z}^i = (\tilde{z}^i_1, \ldots, \tilde{z}^i_m)$ the corresponding value of z. The value $\tilde{x}^i_i$ represents the maximum value that the goal variable x_i can attain under the constraint $z \in D$, irregardless of the "goodness" of the values of the other goal variables.

The vectors $\tilde{x}^i$ are used to build a pay-off matrix $\{\tilde{x}^i_j\}$, the i-th row of this matrix being given by the extreme solution $\tilde{x}^i$. The main diagonal of the pay-off matrix, $\{\tilde{x}^i_i\}$, which consists of the "maxima maximorum" of the goal variables x_i, is considered to be the reference or "ideal" solution. Because of the way they were obtained as solutions to the n-problems (4), the values $\tilde{x}^i_i$, $i = 1, \ldots, n$, cannot be reached simultaneously, so that $\{\tilde{x}^i_i\}$ is unfeasible.

3. Calculation phase. The preparation phase is followed by a calculation phase in which the feasible $\bar{x}^k = (\bar{x}^k_1, \ldots, \bar{x}^k_n)$, which is "closest" in the minimax sense to the ideal solution $\{\tilde{x}^i_i\}$, is calculated as the solution of a LP (see flow chart, Fig. 1).

In this calculation, weights π_i are introduced to express the relative importance of the distance of each goal variable x_i from its ideal value $\tilde{x}^i_i$. These weights are chosen in such a way that they will be small when the value of x_i is not much improved by a change in z from its ideal value $\tilde{z}^i$ (see "Term 1" in flow chart). On the contrary, π_i will be large if x_i is very sensitive to a change in the value of z. The weights are normalized to one in order to enable easy comparison of different solutions obtained from different weighting strategies. Fig. 2 presents a printout example of the calculation phase.

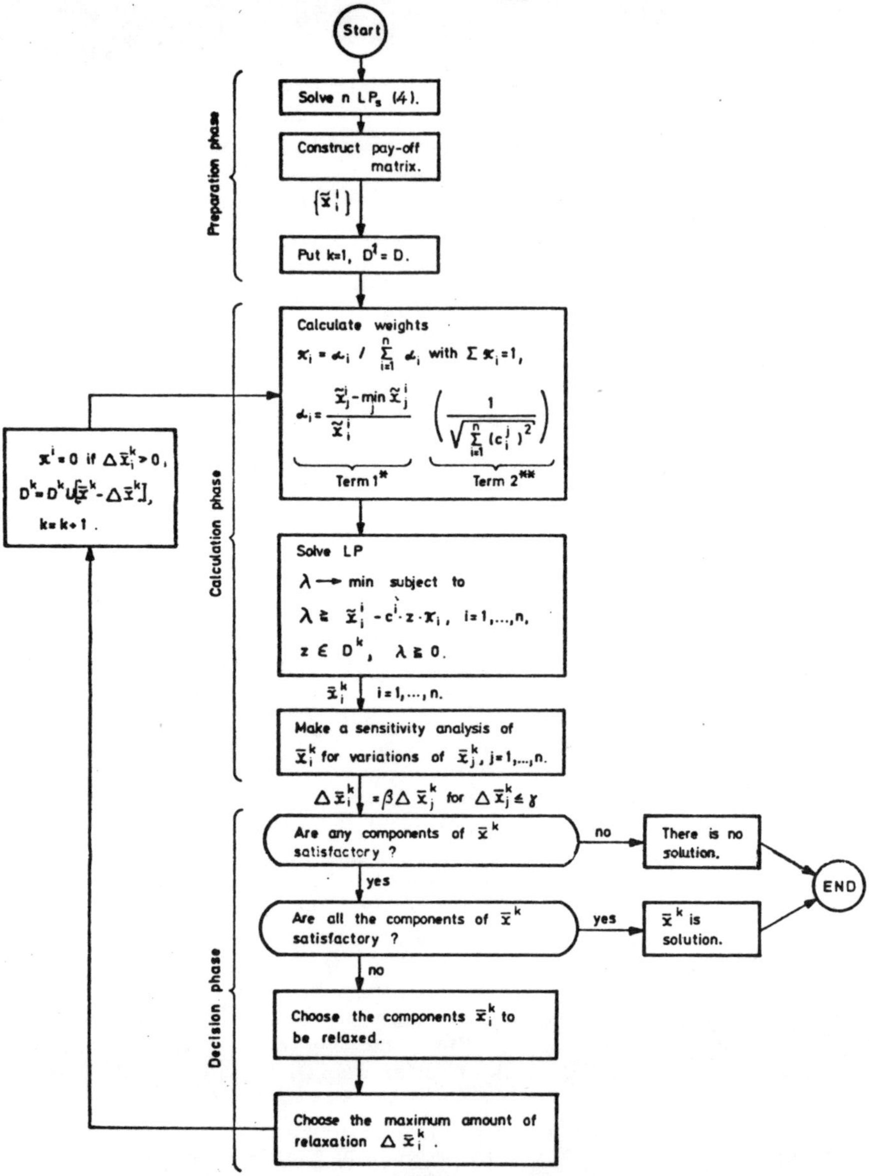

* "Minimax" term. This term becomes $(\min_j \tilde{x}_j^i - x_i^i) / \min_j \tilde{x}_j^i$ when $\tilde{x}_i^i \leq 0$.

** "Normalizing" term.

FIG.1: Flow chart of STEM

Fig. 2 - STEM method: Calculation phase printout example
(data input previously)

```
IDEAL AND COMPROMISE SOLUTIONS ARE
            COST         STOCKOUT      SALES
IDEAL       800000       6.4           1000000
COMP        1200000      9.3           700000          ] = x̄^k

ARE ALL COMPONENTS OF COMP UNSATISFACTORY? Y or N.
□:N

ARE ALL COMPONENTS OF COMP SATISFACTORY? Y or N:
□:N

IF VARIABLES ARE NOT RELAXED BY MORE THAN              ]
            200000       1.3           -3000           ]
THEN ONE UNIT RELAXATION PERMITS                       ] Sensivity
            DELTACOST    DELTASTOCK    DELTASALES      ] Analysis
COST        1            -.0000043     1.1             ]
STOCK       -60000       1             27400           ]
SALES       -2.5         -.0000018     -1              ]

ENTER ABSOLUTE AMOUNTS OF MAXIMUM RELAXATION FOR ALL VARIABLES
□:          100000.      0.            0.              ]= Δ x̄_i^k , i=1,..,3

IDEAL AND COMPROMISE SOLUTIONS ARE
            COST         STOCKOUT      SALES
IDEAL       800000       6.4           1000000
COMP        1300000      8.87          810000          ] = x̄^(k+1)
```

4. Decision phase. Following the calculation phase, the ideal solution and the compromise solution are presented to the decision-maker, who compares them and decides if the compromise solution is satisfactory or not.

Three different cases can be distinguished:

- If no component of $\bar{x}^k$ is satisfactory, the problem is declared unsolvable und computation is terminated.
- Likewise computation is terminated if all components of $\bar{x}^k$ are satisfactory. The current compromise solution $\bar{x}^k$ is then chosen as the "best compromise" or the definitive solution.
- If some of the components of $\bar{x}^k$ are satisfactory and others not, the decision-maker must accept a certain worsening or relaxation of the satisfactory components in order to permit an improvement of the unsatisfactory ones. Therefore, he is asked which satisfactory component $\bar{x}_i^k$ can be relaxed and how much relaxation $\Delta\bar{x}_i^k$ is acceptable at the most. To help him with his decision, he is presented with the results of a sensitivity analysis, which indicate the behaviour of the different goal variables in the neighbourhood of the present compromise solution $\bar{x}^k$. Then the program returns to the calculation phase.

For the next iteration, the feasible set D^k is modified according to the decision made. It is requested for the next iteration that the new value for each element of the new compromise solution, $\bar{x}_i^{k+1}$, not be less than the old value minus the accepted maximal relaxation, if any:

$$\bar{x}_i^{k+1} \geq \bar{x}_i^k - \Delta\bar{x}_i^k \; , \; \Delta\bar{x}_i^k \geq 0, \quad i = 1, \ldots, n. \tag{5}$$

That is, the new compromise solution must be in the domain defined by the decision-maker. The weight π_i is set equal to zero in the k+1 iteration whenever $\Delta\bar{x}_i^k > 0$. This expresses the fact that the decision-maker doesn't consider relaxation $\Delta\bar{x}_i^k$ to be very costly.

At the end of the procedure it may be interesting to calculate a posteriori weights such that $\pi_i/(\bar{x}_i^i - \bar{x}_i^k)$ = constant. In this way local approximations can be determined for the marginal rates of substitution between goals at the optimum.

5. Characteristics. The calculation phase of STEM can be easily programmed with the help of standard LP programs. The convergence of STEM to the best compromise solution is fast. The solution can be obtained in less than n iterations when one of the constraints of the type (5) has been relaxed at each iteration to such an extent that further relaxation is out of question. Fewer iterations are needed when during a single iteration more than one constraint is relaxed "to the limits of the acceptable". It should be emphasized here that in the case of STEM, in contrast to the unstructured of GEOFFRION approach, the stopping rule cannot be chosen according to the specific problem, but is stringently imposed by the algorithm.

In general, the compromise solutions are efficient. If not, they can always be made efficient by means of minor alterations.

STEM has one unpleasant characteristic. In later iterations it is impossible to "undo" partially or completely a relaxation $\Delta \tilde{x}_i^k$ made at an earlier stage. In this way, the decision-maker is impeded in his exploration of the feasible set. He cannot change his mind during the decision-making process or correct incorrect decisions. The only possibility of taking learning processes into consideration, which eventually may take place during the interactive procedure, is, therefore, to begin the process again from the beginning.

STEM can be considered to be the prototype of several interactive procedures, all of which:

- are designed within the framework of linear programming;
- replace the concept "best solution" with the concept " best compromise";
- use the vector $\{\tilde{x}_i^i\}$ as an "ideal solution".

These methods differ in the way in which they work toward the "best compromise". We mention here the method devised by Saska (1968) at the same time as, but independently of, STEM; the more highly developed Progressive Orientation Procedure (POP) of Benayoun and Tergny (1969); the algorithm of Belenson and Kapur (1973); the interactive procedures based on the Goal Programming Method of Charnes and Cooper (1961) (see for example Dyer (1972a). In some important aspects, however, these differ from STEM to a greater extent.) See also Aubin and Näslund (1972) and Contini and Zionts (1968).

D - The GEOFFRION Method

1. General remarks . Some of the most effective methods for the numerical solution of non-linear, constrained optimization problems are known in optimization theory under the generic name of large-step algorithms. A large-step procedure is typically defined by the following iterative steps:

Step 0. Select an (arbitrary) initial feasible point $z^o = (z_1^o, \ldots, z_m^o)$. Let $k = 0$.

Step 1. At iteration k, determine the "best"direction y_j^k, $j = 1, \ldots, m$, to improve the current point z^k. The choice of y^k is to be based on the gradient in direction of z of the objective function U at the current point z^k, $\nabla U_z(z^k)$. 3)

Step 2. Find a step-size t^k such that $U(z^k + t^k y^k)$ is maximized over all the feasible points $z^k + t^k y^k$.

Step 3. Compute the new current point $z_j^{k+1} = z_j^k + t^k y_j^k$, $j = 1, \ldots, m$. Return to step 1, where z^{k+1} replaces z^k.

The iterative process 1-3 produces a sequence z^o, z^1, ... of improving feasible points z. It ends when z^k is a local maximum or a "satisfying" point, i.e. when it is impossible to find a better point than the current one by means of local considerations.

Large-step methods have been designed for the most general types of non-linear optimization problems (see, for example, Blum and Oettli (1975)). Under appropriate regularity conditions, they converge very fast to a neighborhood of the optimum. [4)]

In his (1970) paper, Geoffrion conjectured that large-step methods could offer a very effective way of solving the multiple-goal problem (1) if the decision-maker is able to give the local information about his implicit objective function U necessary in carrying out the optimization calculation. This information is: (a)Some expression for the gradient of U at the current point and (b) the optimal step-size. In other words, the logic underlying Geoffrion's proposal is to adopt a mathematical programming technique of known efficiency, but to implement it interactively in order to do away with the need for knowledge of the overall objective function.

Since Geoffrion's original paper, this approach has been studied in detail and applied by numerous theoreticians (see, for example, Deissenberg (1976), Dyer (1973a),(1973b), (1974), Feinberg (1972), Geoffrion and Hogan (1972), Geoffrion and Dier (1972), Geoffrion et al. (1972), Wallenius (1975)). Contrary to the STEM method in which implementation is determined within narrow limits by the STEM algorithm itself, the GEOFFRION approach permits a large number of ways of obtaining the needed information from the decision-maker, and can be applied to the whole range of large-step algorithms. Since it is impossible to cover all possible versions of the method, we will present in the following the logic underlying steps 1 and 2 in an interactive large-step algorithm within the specific framework of the FRANK-WOLFE algorithm[5)], but in terms as general as possible. Except for the special form of the optimization problem serving to determine t^k, our presentation is valid for all interactive large-step algorithms if the objective function U has continuous derivations on $\{z\}$ and the feasible set D is compact and convex. Application of an interactive large-step algorithm will be discussed in more detail in part II.

2. Step 1. In a large-step procedure, the determination of the best direction y^k uses the property of the gradient $\nabla_z U(z^k)$ as the "direction of steepest ascent" of U in the vicinity of z^k. In the FRANK-WOLFE algorithm, y^k is given by $y^k = \bar{z}^k - z^k$, where $\bar{z}^k$ is the solution of a standard LP approximating the problem

$$\nabla_z U(z^k) \cdot z \longrightarrow \sup_z$$

subject to (6)

$$z \in D.$$

In other words, in this particular algorithm the direction y^k is chosen such that the product of the maximum rate of improvement multiplied by the feasible rate of improvement in this direction is maximized.

In a multiple-goal problem, U is unknown and, therefore, $\nabla_z U$ is unknown, too. Before solving the LP corresponding to (6), it is necessary to specify $\nabla_z U(z^k)$ in a decision phase on the basis of information given by the decision-maker.

In general, however, the decision-maker evaluates the current situation in terms of $x_i^k = f^i(z^k)$, $i = 1, \ldots, n$, and not in terms of z^k. Hence, he will be unable to give direct information on the partial derivatives $\partial U(z^k)/\partial z_j$. Fortunately the problem of estimating $\nabla_z U$ can easily be expressed in terms of x^k. $\nabla_z U(z^k)$ can be written

$$\nabla_z U(z^k) = \sum_{i=1}^{n} (\partial U/\partial x_i^k)\, \nabla_z f^i(z^k).$$

In this expression, $\nabla_z f^i(z^k)$ can be directly calculated from the known f^i. Note further that the solution of (6) is not affected by a positive scaling of $\nabla_z U(z^k)$. $\nabla_z U(z^k)$ can, for example, be divided by $(\partial U/\partial x_1^k)$, which, according to our assumptions, is positive. Hence (6) can be expressed equivalently as

$$\sum_{i=1}^{n} w_i^k \, \nabla_z f^i(z^k) \cdot z \longrightarrow \sup_z$$

$$\text{subject to} \qquad\qquad (6')$$

$$z \in D,$$

with $w_i^k = (\partial U/\partial x_i^k)/(\partial U/\partial x_1^k)$, $\quad i = 1, \ldots, n$.

Since the objective function has been scaled by $(\partial U/\partial x_1^k)$, we will call the goal variable x_1 the reference variable. Note that the choice of x_1 as the reference variable is arbitrary and that any other goal variable x_i could be chosen to play this distinguished role.

Thus, in order to permit the construction of $\nabla_z U(z^k)$, the decision-maker needs only to give a subjective appreciation of the current point x^k (and not z^k) in a form suitable for approximating the n-1 weights w_i^k, $i=2, \ldots, n$. (Since x_1^k was chosen as the reference variable, w_1^k is identically equal to 1). This subjective appreciation can be made from two different standpoints:

a) On the one hand $(1/w_i^k)$ is the slope of the projection of $\nabla_z U(z^k)$ on the (x_1, x_i) plane. That is, w_i^k gives the marginally "ideal proportion of change" for x_1 and x_i. Let $w_i^k = (\delta x_i/\delta x_1)$; then U increases most rapidly if x_i^k is marginally augmented by δx_i units for each δx_1 augmentation of x_1^k, all other variables being constant. Therefore, the weight w_i^k approximately corresponds to the decision-maker's answer to the question: "How much should x_i ideally increase from its current level x_i^k if x_1 is increased by δx_1 from its current level x_1^k?"

b) On the other hand, $-w_i^k$ is the slope of a tangent to the indifference curve through x^k in the (x_1, x_i) plane. In other words, w_i^k expresses the marginal rate of transformation or trade-off between x_1 and x_i at x^k. If the decision-maker is indifferent to a change in the values of x_1^k and x_i^k in the marginal amounts Δx_1 and Δx_i respectively, all other variables being constant, then $w_i^k = -(\Delta x_1/\Delta x_i)$. The weight w_i^k can therefore be approximately determined by letting the decision-maker answer the question: "What loss in x_i from its current level x_i^k would compensate exactly for a given increase Δx_1 in x_1 from its present level x_1^k?"

The relationship between the two standpoints is expressed graphically in Fig. 3. The interactive evaluation of the weights w_i^k is followed by a calculation phase. The weights are used to build the objective function of the LP corresponding to (6). The computer solves the LP determining $\bar{z}^k$ and y^k. The program then proceeds to step 2.

3. Step 2. In all likelihood the point $\bar{z}^k$ is not in the immediate neighborhood of z^k and the behavior of U can change significantly between z^k and $\bar{z}^k$. This implies that the "best" direction y^k, which was myopically determined as a function of U's behavior in the immediate neighborhood of z^k, may become a "bad" direction as one advances farther from z^k in the direction of $\bar{z}^k$. However, because of the continuity of U and its partial derivatives, there is a feasible combination $z_j^{k+1} = (1-t^k)z_j^k + t^k\bar{z}_j^k$, $j = 1, \ldots, m$, $0 \leq t^k \leq 1$, of z^k and $\bar{z}^k$ that yields $U(z^{k+1}) > U(z^k)$. The problem in step 2 is to determine the optimal step-size t^k, i.e. the value of t^k which maximizes $U(z^{k+1})$.[6]

In the interactive procedure, the optimal value of t^k is directly determined by the decision-maker. He is guided in his choice by plots of the values $x_i^{k+1} = f^i(z^k+t^ky^k)$, $i = 1, \ldots, m$, as a function of t between 0 and 1 (Fig. 4a). These plots permit a comprehensive overview of the feasible bundles x_i^{k+1}, $i = 1, \ldots, m$ as a function of the single variable t^k. Alternatively, the computer can tabulate the values of the goal variables at selected values of t. Given the important case that the goal variables are linear functions of the variables z_j, the x_i's are also linear in t (Fig. 4b).

4. Summary of the method. As a whole the application of an interactive large-step algorithm to problem (1) proceeds in the following manner:

- Step 0 (Initialization): The decision-maker chooses or is presented with an initial feasible solution $x_i^o = f^i(z_i^o)$, $i = 1, \ldots, n$.

- Step 1, a) (Decision phase): At iteration k, the decision-maker assesses his trade-off weights w_i^k by subjectively analyzing the current solution x^k. This analysis can follow either approach 2a) or 2b) above.
  b) (Calculation phase): Compute the best direction y^k from the solution of a LP formulated on the basis of both w_i^k, $i = 1, \ldots, n$, and the constraints defining the feasible set D. Plot the function $f^i(z^k+t^ky^k)$ for $0 < t \leq 1$, $i = 1, \ldots, n$.

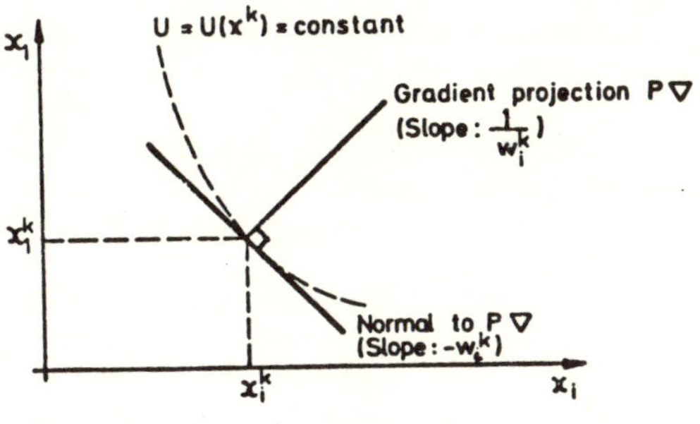
U = U(x^k) = constant
Gradient projection P∇
(Slope : 1/w_i^k)
Normal to P∇
(Slope : -w_i^k)
x_1
x_1^k
x_i^k
x_i

FIG. 3

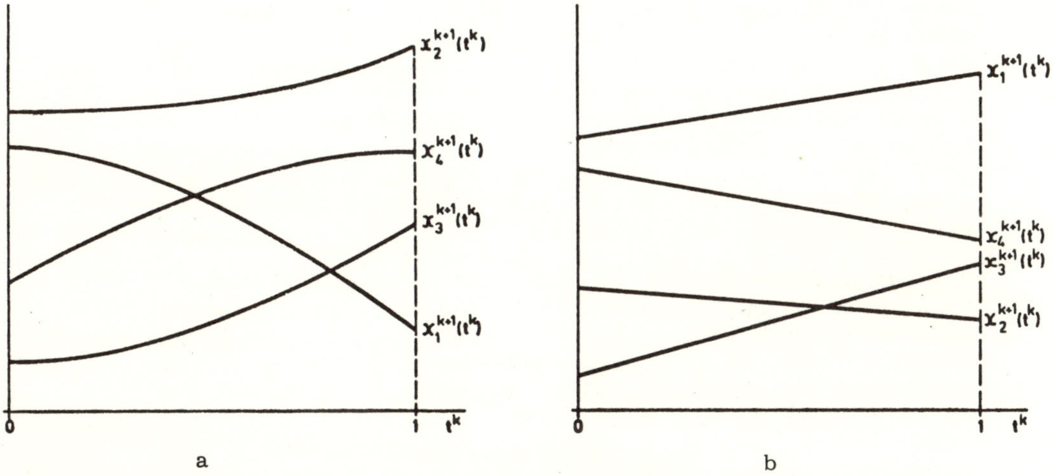
x_2^{k+1}(t^k)
x_4^{k+1}(t^k)
x_3^{k+1}(t^k)
x_1^{k+1}(t^k)
0
1
t^k
a
x_1^{k+1}(t^k)
x_4^{k+1}(t^k)
x_3^{k+1}(t^k)
x_2^{k+1}(t^k)
0
1
t^k
b

FIG. 4

- Step 2 (Decision phase): Let the decision-maker choose the "best" t^k by subjective analysis of the plots of $f^i(z^k+t^k y^k)$.

- Step 3 (Calculation phase): Use the "best" t^k from step 2 to compute the new current solution $z^{k+1} = z^k + t^k y^k$. Let $x_i^{k+1} = f^i(z^{k+1})$, $i = 1, \ldots, n$, $k = k + 1$, and return to step 1.

5. Characteristics. The calculation phase of the FRANK-WOLFE algorithm and of most other interactive large-step procedures are easy to program with the help of standard LP programs. The initial convergence of the large-step algorithms is very fast in general. In the case of the FRANK-WOLFE algorithm, Wolfe (1970) has shown that under certain regularity conditions the difference between the maximal value of the objective function, $U(x^*)$, and the current value, $U(x^k)$, is at least halved at each of the first K iterations (K unknown). That is,

$$\frac{U(x^*) - U(x^{k+1})}{U(x^*) - U(x^k)} \leq \frac{1}{2}, \quad k \leq K.$$

The improvement $U(x^{k+1}) - U(x^k)$ is in general greater, the farther x^k is from the solution x^*. Accordingly, the algorithm leads very quickly to a neighborhood of x^*.

The convergence is robust against errors in the specification of the weights w_i^k. The convergence toward x^* is assured if, generally speaking, the error on the w_i^k decreases as x^k comes closer to x^* (see Dyer (1974)). The decision-maker can modify his preference at any time. He can express his present preference through his choice of the w_i^k and t^k at the current iteration without being restricted in any way by the algorithm. The flexibility of the algorithm also gives the decision-maker the possibility to experiment at any stage of the interactive process, i.e. to use arbitrary weights w_i^k in order to see the results or to explore extreme areas of the feasible set. To determine whether or not the preferences of the decision-maker have stabilized themselves during the interactive process, it may be useful to begin the procedure again by starting from another initial point z^o and to see if both corresponding sequences $x^o, x^1, \ldots$ and $x^{o\prime}, x^{1\prime}, \ldots$ converge to the same area in x.

A significant characteristic of GEOFFRION-type methods is their high informational content. In particular it is possible to construct a family of indifference curves in the vicinity of the path $x^o, x^1, \ldots$, which is uniquely determined up to a monotonous transformation. In this way, in case of stable preferences one gets an a posteriori approximation of the behavior of the overall objective function U along with the path $x^o, x^1, \ldots$. When different paths, which all converge to the same area in x, are known, it may be possible to integrate the local information along each path to approximate the overall objective function of the decision-maker (Fig. 5).

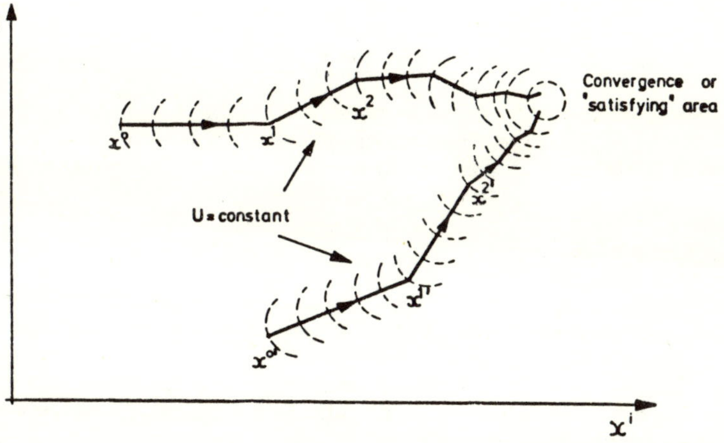

x^j
Convergence or
'satisfying' area
x^0
x^1
x^2
U=constant
$x^{2'}$
$x^{1'}$
$x^{o'}$
x^i

FIG. 5

Two paths $x^o, x^1, \ldots$ and $x^{o\prime}, x^{1\prime}, \ldots, x^o \neq x^{o\prime}$, will not converge to the same area in two cases: a) If the decision-maker has changed his mind to a significant degree between the last iteration of the first experiment and the last iteration of the second experiment; b) If there are several local optima. It may be impossible to recognize which case is true in a given situation. In any case, however, an effort should be made to analyze the reasons for the divergence. The decision-maker's opinion will, of course, play a central role in such an analysis.

II - APPLICATION OF INTERACTIVE LARGE-STEP ALGORITHMS

Having presented the logic underlying GEOFFRION's approach, we now turn to its practical application. Some aspects of implementation are discussed in Section A; Section B is devoted to an example. A flow chart is given in Fig. 6.

A - Implementation

1. Preparation. Any practical application of a large-step procedure must be carefully planned according to the "General Remarks" made in Section I, A.

2. Step 0 (Initialization): Any feasible point z^o can be chosen as the initial solution. However, the number of iterations necessary to reach a satisfying solution may be decreased to a great extent by choosing a "good" if possible efficient, starting point z^o.

A simple but effective procedure to this effect consists of letting the decision-maker choose a good x^o by himself with the help of an unstructured approach and then compute the corresponding z^o. In most practical applications another possibility is to use actual or historical values of the problem variables for z^o, possibly modified to satisfy the model constraints. Other more sophisticated methods for determining a favorable initial solution have been devised in optimization theory. Let us mention here the possibility of projecting an "ideal", feasible point given by the decision-maker on the efficient surface. (Note the analogy with the determination of the first compromise solution in STEM). For details see, for example, Dikin (1967).

The determination of a feasible z^o may not be a trivial task if the feasible set is defined by complicated functional constraints $G(z) = 0$.

3. Step 1 (Decision phase): In practical applications it may be difficult for the decision-maker to directly answer the questions corresponding to the "ideal proportional change" or the "trade-off" approaches presented in subsection I D 2. Therefore, indirect methods have been devised which permit the determination of the weights w_i^k by letting the decision-maker answer a sequence of yes-no questions generated by the computer. We present here such an indirect method devised by Dyer (1973) and extensively tested in numerous applications (see also flow chart Fig. 7 and printout example Fig. 8).

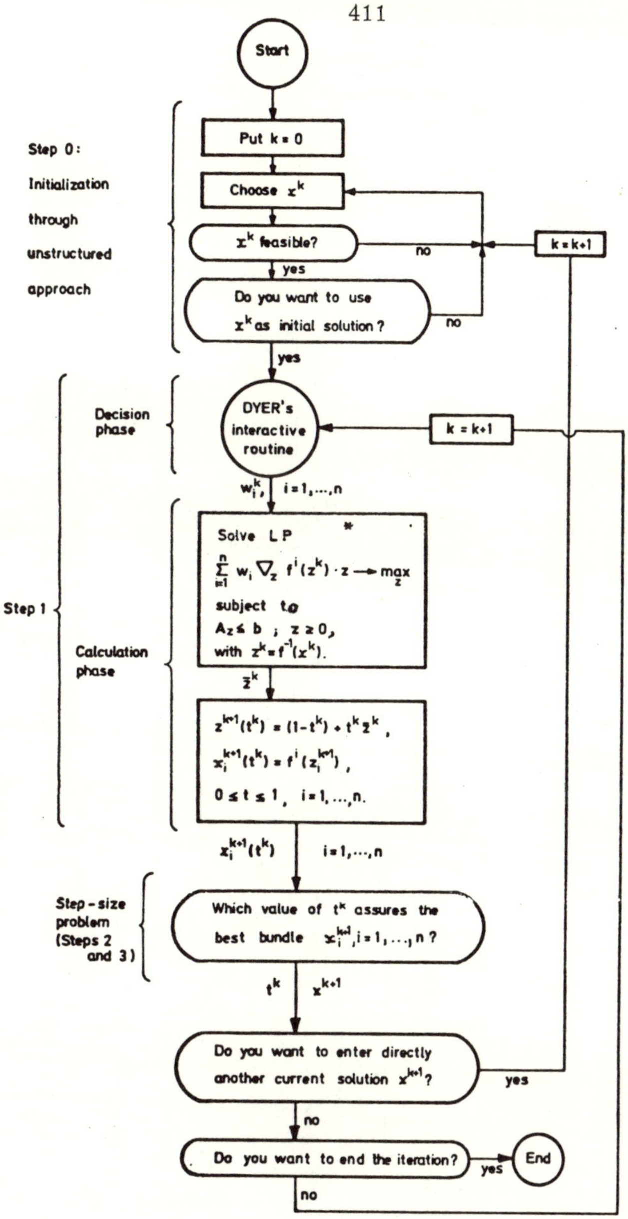

* This LP corresponds to the solution of the problem $U(x) \longrightarrow \sup$
subject to $x_i = f^i(z)$, $i = 1, \ldots, n$.
$Az \leq b$, $z \geq 0$,
with the FRANK-WOLFE algorithm.

FIG. 6 : GEOFFRION Method: Flow Chart

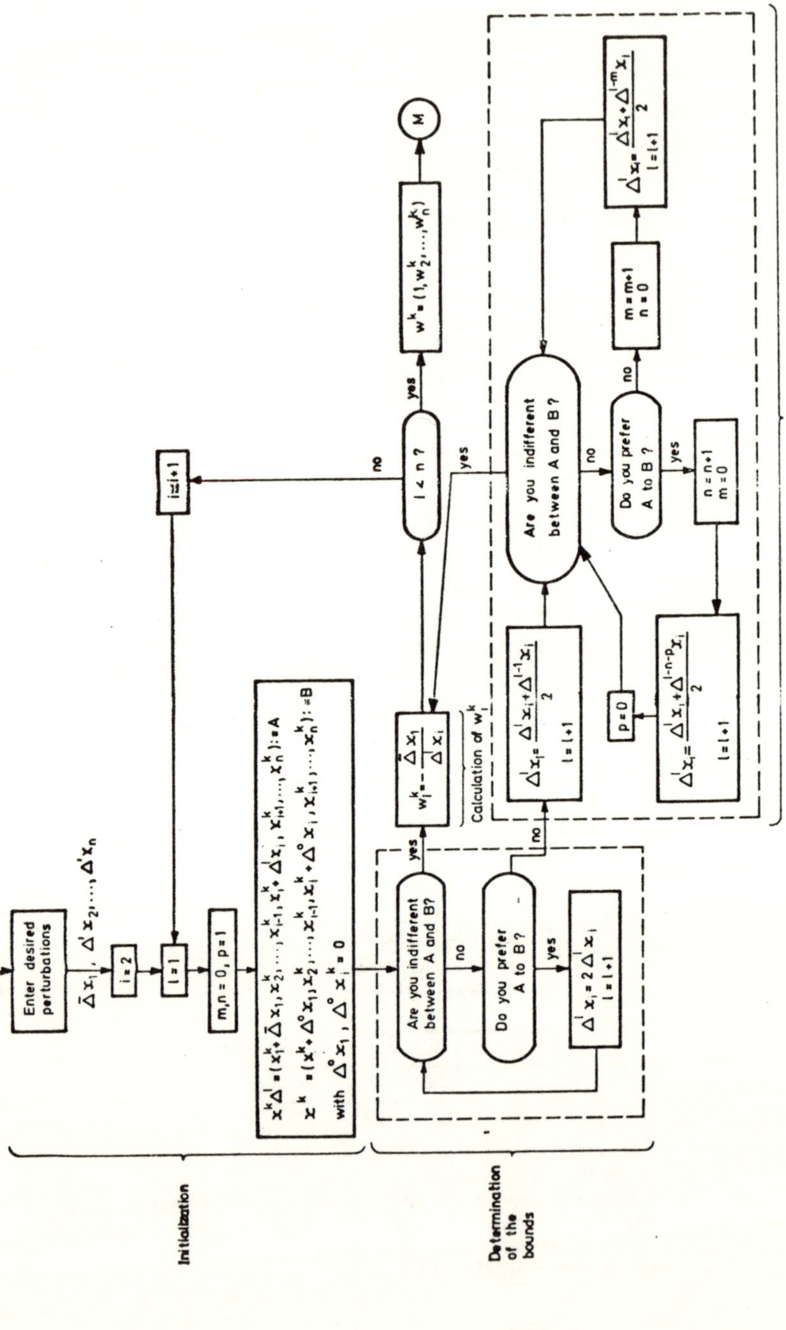

FIG. 7: DYER's interactive procedure: Flow Chart

Fig. 8 - Geoffrion's approach with Dyer's trade-off estimation routine: printout example (data input previously).

```
ENTER BEST INITIAL SOLUTION COST, STOCKOUT, SALES.              ]
□:          800000.         6.4         1000000.                ]
                                                                ]
THIS SOLUTION IS NOT FEASIBLE. CORRECT YOUR CHOICE              ]   Step 0:
□:          1300000.        9.          800000.                 ]   Initialization
                                                                ]
THIS SOLUTION IS FEASIBLE. IF YOU WANT TO USE IT AS             ]
THE INITIAL SOLUTION, TYPE "Y". IF NO, ENTER NEW                ]
SOLUTION.                                                       ]
□:Y                                                             ]

ENTER DESIRED PERTURBATIONS                                     ]
□:          -10000.         -0.5        5000.                   ]
```

$\bar{\Delta} x_1, \Delta^1 x_2, \Delta^1 x_3$

```
                A               B
COST         1300000         1290000
STOCK              9               9
SALES         800000          795000
IF YOU PREFER A (B) TYPE "A" ("B"). IF YOU ARE
INDIFFERENT, TYPE "I".
□:A

                A               B
COST         1300000         1290000
STOCK              9               9
SALES         800000          797500
IF YOU PREFER A (B) TYPE "A" ("B"). IF YOU ARE
INDIFFERENT, TYPE "I".
□:B

                A               B
COST         1300000         1290000
STOCK              9               9
SALES         800000          798750
IF YOU PREFER A (B) TYPE "A" ("B"). IF YOU ARE
INDIFFERENT, TYPE "I".
□:I
```

Determination of w_3^k.

Fig. 8 cont'd

```
THE TRADE-OFFS ARE                                        ]
COST            -1                                        ]
STOCK           -3                                        ]  The vector w^k
SALES            8                                        ]

ENTER NO. OF POINTS TO SEE IN STEP-SIZE PROBLEM           ]
□:10                                                      ]  =ℓ

COST              STOCK              SALES
1300000           9.                 800000
1310000           8.9                802000
1320000           8.8                804000
1330000           8.7                806000                  Step-size
1340000           8.6                808000                  problem
1350000           8.5                810000
1360000           8.4                812000
1370000           8.3                814000
1380000           8.2                816000
1390000           8.1                818000
1400000           8.                 820000

DO YOU WANT A DIFFERENT NUMBER OF POINTS? IF YES,
TYPE TOTAL NUMBER. IF NO, TYPE "N".
□:N

CHOOSE A PREFERRED SOLUTION FROM THE ABOVE VECTORS.
□:        137000.        8.3      81400.                  ]  =x^{k+1}; t^k=0,7.

IF YOU WISH TO END ITERATIONS, TYPE "E". OTHERWISE
TYPE "C".
□:C

CURRENT SOLUTION IS
         137000          8.3      81400
DO YOU WANT TO ENTER ANOTHER CURRENT SOLUTION DIRECTLY? Y OR N.
□:N

ENTER DESIRED PERTURBATIONS
□:
     →
```

Dyer's interactive routine is based on the "trade-off" approach. In order to determine w_i^k, it aims at finding a modified vector $x^k\bar{\Delta} := (x_1^k + \bar{\Delta}x_1, x_2^k, \ldots, x_{i-1}^k, x_i^k - \bar{\Delta}x_i, x_{i+1}^k, \ldots, x_n^k)$, $\bar{\Delta}x_1, \bar{\Delta}x_i \geq 0$, which is considered by the decision-maker to be equivalent to the current solution $x^k = (x_1^k, \ldots, x_n^k)$. The interactive procedure first determines upper and lower bounds for $x^k\bar{\Delta}$. With the help of a bisection algorithm, these bounds are gradually brought closer together until a close approximation for $x^k\bar{\Delta}$ is reached.

a) Initialization. At the beginning of the procedure the decision-maker is confronted with the current solution x^k and with the first, arbitrarily modified vector $x^k\Delta^\ell = (x_1^k + \bar{\Delta}x_1, x_2^k, \ldots, x_{i-1}^k, x_i^k - \Delta^\ell x_i, x_{i+1}^k, \ldots, x_n^k)$. Let $\ell = 1$. Since we are interested in the marginal rates of substitution w_i^k, the perturbations $\bar{\Delta}x_1$ and $\Delta^1 x_i$ must be small relative to the current values x_1^k and x_i^k, in order to keep the errors of higher order in an acceptable range. However, they must be large enough to be considered significant by the decision-maker. To ensure this last characteristic, it is convenient to let the decision-maker himself choose $\bar{\Delta}x_1$ and $\Delta^1 x_i$, $i = 2, \ldots, n$. ("ENTER DESIRED PERTURBATIONS" in example printout.)

b) Determination of the bounds. At iteration ℓ, the decision-maker is asked if he prefers x^k to $x^k\Delta^\ell$, $x^k\Delta^\ell$ to x^k, or if he is indifferent between the two. If the decision-maker prefers $x^k\Delta^\ell$ to x^k, i.e. if in his opinion the decrease $-\Delta^\ell x_i$ in the value of x_i^k is more than compensated for by the increase $\bar{\Delta}x_1$ in the value of x_1^k, then $\Delta^\ell x_i$ is doubled in the next iteration $\ell+1$ and the question is repeated until x^k is preferred to $x^k\Delta^\ell$. One iteration before, however, $x^k\Delta^{\ell-1}$ was preferred to x^k. Thus we know that the perturbation $-\bar{\Delta}x_i$, which exactly compensates for the perturbation $\bar{\Delta}x_1$, has as upper and lower bounds $-\Delta^{\ell-1}x_i$ and $-\Delta^\ell x_i$, respectively.

c) Reduction of the interval. A bisection algorithm using the general formula

$$\Delta^{\ell+1}x_i = (\text{upper bound} + \text{lower bound at iteration } \ell)/2 \tag{7}$$

is then applied to explore and narrow the interval $(\Delta^\ell x_i, \Delta^{\ell-1}x_i)$. $\Delta^{\ell+1}x_i$ is computed according to (7). It is then used as the new lower bound ($x^k\Delta^{\ell+1}$ preferred to x^k) or as the new upper bound (x^k preferred to $x^k\Delta^{\ell+1}$) in a new iteration using (7). The process is repeated until the decision-maker is indifferent between x^k and $x^k\Delta^{\ell+1}$, i.e. $\Delta^{\ell+1}x_i = \bar{\Delta}x_i$. The calculation of w_i^k follows immediately from $w_i^k \simeq -(\bar{\Delta}x_1/\bar{\Delta}x_i)$. To assure the working of the algorithm in case x^k is preferred to $x^k\Delta^1$ at the first iteration, it is practical to use the convention $x^k = (x_1^k + \Delta^o x_1, x_2^k, \ldots, x_{i-1}^k, x_i^k - \Delta^o x_i, x_{i+1}^k, \ldots, x_n^k)$ with $\Delta^o x_1 = \Delta^o x_i = 0$.

The above procedure is repeated until all n-1 weights w_i^k, $i = 2, \ldots, n$, have been calculated. w_1^k is identically equal to 1. Remark that $\bar{\Delta}x_1$ remains constant during the whole procedure. In general, w_i^k is obtained within a few iterations because of the limited ability of the decision-maker to discriminate between two similar vectors.

In the above presentation of DYER's method, changes Δx_i in the values of x_i^k, = i = 2, ..., n, were systematically modified until they exactly compensated for a given change $\bar{\Delta} x_1$ in the value of x_1^k. In other words, x_1 was used as the reference variable. As stated before, any other goal variable x_i can assume the role of reference variable. As a matter of fact, it may be interesting to let the decision-maker calculate a second set of weights, $w_i^{k\prime}$, using another goal variable x_j as the reference variable. If the decision-maker is consistent in his appreciation, we should have

$$w_j^k \; w_1^{k\prime} = (\bar{\Delta} x_1^k / \bar{\Delta} x_j^k)/(\bar{\Delta} x_j^k / \bar{\Delta} x_1^k) \simeq 1 \tag{8}$$

$$w_i^k / w_i^{k\prime} = (\bar{\Delta} x_1^k / \bar{\Delta} x_i^k)/(\bar{\Delta} x_i^k / \bar{\Delta} x_j^k) \simeq w_j^k, \; i, \; j = 1, \ldots, n, \text{ etc.} \tag{9}$$

Thus, the calculation of a second set of weights $w_i^{k\prime}$ offers a possibility of computing a measure for the "inconsistency" or "inexactitude" of the information provided by the decision-maker. If the inconsistency of the information exceeds a given tolerance limit, one may ask the decision-maker to think over his statements. A corresponding routine can easily be built into the computer program so as to include such an automatic consistence check at every iteration.

3. Step 1 (Calculation phase): As mentioned previously, the calculation phase in step 1 consists of little more than the solution of a standard LP. The LP corresponding to the FRANK-WOLFE algorithm in the case of linear restrictions is given in the flow chart. For additional cases see Simmons (1975).

Two particular outcomes of the step 1 calculation phase are of interest: a) If the solution of the LP is unbounded, the solution of (1) is unbounded and the interactive problem has no meaningful solution; b) If the solution $\bar{z}^k$ of the LP is the current point z^k itself, there is no "improving" feasible direction in the neighborhood of z^k. In other words, z^k is a (local) optimum and, from a purely mathematical point of view, the problem is solved. However, the decision-maker may consider z^k an implausible solution or may want to resume the search for supplementary information about the feasible set. It is therefore useful to give him the possibility at this point of entering directly a modified feasible point z^{k+1}. From a formal point of view, this is, of course, equivalent to starting a new search from the beginning. From a psychological point of view, however, this can make a great deal of difference.

4. Step 2: The fundamental aspects of the implementation of the step-size problem have already been discussed in part I. If the computer tabulates the values of $(1-t^k)z^k + t^k\bar{z}^k$ for ℓ equidistant values of t^k, i.e. for $t^k = 1/\ell$, $2/\ell$, ..., ℓ/ℓ, the decision-maker should be allowed to choose the number ℓ according to his subjective information needs, and/or given the possibility of modifying a previously chosen number.

If $\bar{z}^k$ is in the neighborhood of z^k, the solution of the step-size problem can produce only a small modification of the current solution. Thus, many iterations may be needed to leave the neighborhood of z^k, a feature which can be time-consuming as well as nerve-racking for the decision-maker. In this case, too, it may be advantageous to present the option: "Enter directly a modified current solution z^{k+1}". For simplicity's sake and in order to give the decision-maker the most complete freedom in his search, we propose to systematically offer such an option in step 2, regardless of the characteristics of $\bar{z}^k$.

5. Step 3: This step is trivial.

6. Stopping rule: As stated already, the calculation ends when the solution of the LP in step 1 is unbounded (meaningless problem) or when $z^k = \bar{z}^k$. However, $z^k = \bar{z}^k$ is an exact mathematical requirement which may be fulfilled only after a very high or even infinite number of iterations. Hence, it is necessary to define some other, more practical rule for terminating the iterative process.

Of course, it is possible to weaken the requirement $z^k = \bar{z}^k$ to $z^k \simeq \bar{z}^k$, i.e. to let the computation end whenever $\bar{z}^k$ is in a neighborhood of z^k. One can also impose a ceiling on the number of iterations. However, any formal stopping rule impairs the freedom of the decision-maker in his search. Therefore it seems preferable to simply let the decision-maker decide by himself when he wants to end the computation. Experience has shown that, as a rule, the path x^k, x^{k+1}, ... tends to exhibit at the end of the search some kind of cyclical behavior within the "satisfactory" area (Fig. 9).

7. Additional remarks. Let us state again that repetition of the iterative procedure, starting from different initial points, may provide useful information. The data and, in particular, the decision and the paths for x^k, should be filed and analyzed ex post with the help of the decision-maker.

8. Printout. The following printout corresponds largely to Dyer's original printout. However, Dyer's program contains an option "ENTER TRADE-OFFS DIRECTLY". Step 0 uses an unstructured interactive approach for choosing z^o. Note that the perturbations Δx_1 and Δx_2, corresponding to "costs" and "stockout" respectively, are negative. This is due to the fact that these variables are to be minimized, i.e. the program maximizes the variables "-costs" and "-stockout".

B - Example

The following numerical example was chosen solely on the basis of its simplicity, which makes it possible to easily understand the structure of the problem. Although the problem is presented somewhat like a case study, it does not at all pretend to be realistic. For case studies and more realistic examples, see the literature listed in part III. See also the example described in section III, A.

Consider a firm that produces three products 1, 2 and 3 in the respective quantities z_1, z_2, z_3. The production capacity is limited by the constraint $z_1 + 2z_2$

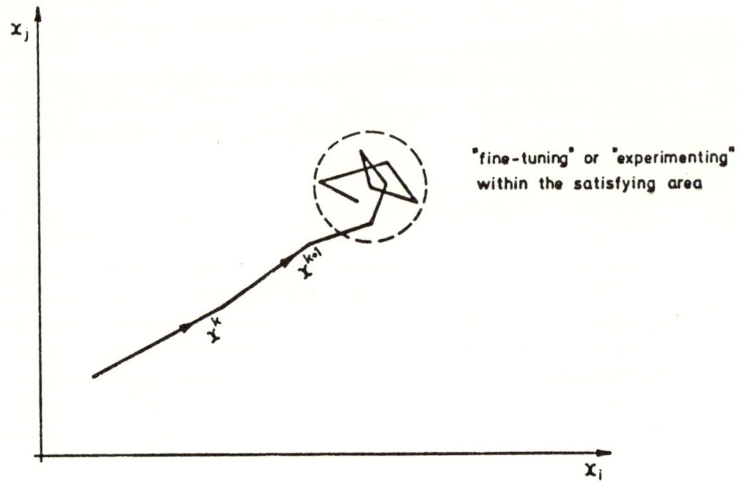
x_j
"fine-tuning" or "experimenting"
within the satisfying area
x^k
x^{k+1}
x_i

FIG. 9

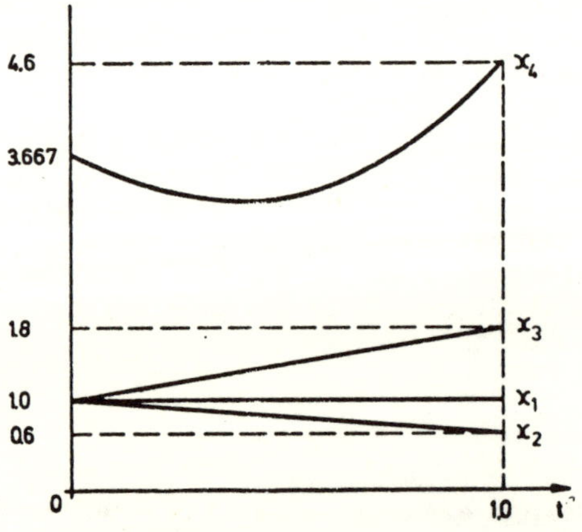
4.6
3.667
1.8
1.0
0.6
0
1.0
t
x_4
x_3
x_1
x_2

FIG. 10

$+ z_3 \leq 4$. The OR department of the firm has determined that the cost of the production of 1, 2 and 3 is $3z_1^2$, $2z_2^2$ and $3z_3^2$, respectively. The market price for 1, 2 and 3 is 4, 3 and 2, respectively. Thus the profit function of the firm is

$$\pi(z) = (4z_1 - 3z_1^2) + (3z_2 - 2z_2^2) + (2z_3 - (1/3)\, z_3^2).$$

However, profit maximization is not the only goal pursued by the management of the firm. In order to be well-represented on all markets 1, 2 and 3 and to thereby reduce the firm's sensitivity to business cycles, the management is also interested in high production levels for each product. For this reason, the firm is currently producing the same quantity of each product: $z_1 = z_2 = z_3 = 1$. Nevertheless, the management is unsatisfied with this solution. Being unable to find a satisfying solution immediately or to define an overall objective function over the four simultaneous, conflicting goals

$$z_1 \rightarrow \max, \quad z_2 \rightarrow \max, \quad z_3 \rightarrow \max, \quad \pi \rightarrow \max,$$

the management turns to its OR staff for help.

The OR men realize they are faced with the following multiple-goal problem:[7]

$$\begin{aligned} &\max U(x),\ U \text{ unknown} \\ &\text{subject to} \\ &x_1 = z_1,\ x_2 = z_2,\ x_3 = z_3, \\ &x_4 = \pi = (4z_1 - 3z_1^2) + (3z_2 - 2z_2^2) + (2z_3 - (1/3)\, z_3^2), \\ &z_1 + z_2 + z_3 \leq 4, \\ &z_1,\ z_2,\ z_3 \geq 0. \end{aligned} \qquad (10)$$

OR staff and management decide to solve this problem with the help of an interactive large-step algorithm (modified interactive FRANK-WOLFE algorithm).

After an introduction to the method, to the problem and to the use of the computer, an experiment is performed using the current operating point $z = (1, 1, 1)$, i.e. $x = (1, 1, 1, 3.667)$, as the initial solution.

Presented with x^o, the managerial board is asked to determine a trade-off weight w_2^o for x_2, the production level of product 2, versus the reference variable x_1. The weight w_2^o is estimated by using the "ideal proportional change" approach. The ratio of x_2 to x_1 in the current solution is one to one. The management, however, feels that more emphasis should be put on the production of product 1. It therefore comes to the conclusion that an ideal proportional change from the current values of these two goal variables would be 0.02 units of product 1 for every 0.01 unit[8] of product 2, or

$$w_2^o = \delta x_2 / \delta x_1 = 0.01/0.02 = 0.5.$$

Similar reasoning relating x_3 to x_1, leads to $w_3^o = 0$. That is, the management is not interested in changing the production of product 3 following a change in the production of product 1 from its present value.

The weight w_4^o is estimated by using the "trade-off" approach. The management considers the loss of 0.01 profit units exactly compensated for, in terms of its preferences, by an increase of 0.005 units in the production of product 1, so that

$$w_4 = (\Delta x_1/\Delta x_4) = -(0.005/ -0.01) = 0.5.$$

The trade-off weights w_i^o are used to compute the best direction y^o and the management is confronted with the plots of $x^o + t^o y^o$ presented in Fig. 10. Since x_1, x_2 and x_3 are linear functions of z, the corresponding plots are line segments.

The management decides that the best combination of values for x_1 - x_4 corresponds to $t^o = 1$. This value is used by the computer to calculate the new solution, $x^1 = (1, 0.6, 1.8, 4.6)$. x^1 is used as the initial solution for a new iteration. After 6 iterations, which are summarized in Table 1, the management considers the current solution x_6 satisfactory and decides to terminate the procedure.

Iteration k	x_1^k	x_2^k	x_3^k	x_4^k	Optimal step-size t^k	$U(x^k)$*	s^k
1	1	1	1	3.667	1.0	6.667	0
2	1	.6	1.8	4.6	.4	7.2	0
3	.88	.6	1.92	4.888	.12	7.248	0
4	.88	.624	1.872	4.866	.025	7.2499	0
5	.8752	.624	1.8768	4.875	.005	7.2499	0
6	.8752	.6250	1.8745	4.875	.0010	7.2499	0.0003
Optimal values *	.875	.625	1.875	4.875		7.25	0

* for $U = 2x_1 + x_2 + x_4$

Table 1

In fact, Table 1 reproduces the search process of a decision-maker a) whose preferences are represented by the overall objective function $U(x) = 2x_1 + x_2 + x_4 \rightarrow \max$, and b) who gives the exact value of x^k and t^k corresponding to his preference. In addition, Table 1 contains the values of x_i, $i = 1, \ldots, 4$, corresponding to the optimal solution of problem (10) given the above objective function U, and the values assumed by U at the different points x^k. The last column, s^k, expresses the idle capacity corresponding to each solution z^k, i.e. $s^k = 4 - (z_1^k + 2z_2^k + z_3^k)$. The value of s^k is a measure of the distance of ^{k} from the efficient surface. In case of an efficient solution, $s^k = 0$.

It is clear from Table 1 that the convergence, measured in terms of the improvements $U(x^{k+1}) - U(x^k)$, is very fast at the beginning but decreases very quickly as x^k approaches x^*. (See also Table 3.) Nevertheless, a nearly optimal solution is reached after just 4 iterations.

Note that even in such a simple problem the relationship between objective function U and optimal solution is far from trivial. One cannot intuitively relate the optimal solution to the constrained problem. Hence, as a rule, an objective function does not have a meaning intuitively. Decision-makers do not think in terms of overall objective functions, but in terms of the desirability of a solution or of a change. The interactive procedure exactly interprets such desirability information to help the decision-maker recognize the best feasible alternative. Note, for example, that the overall objective function does not contain x_3 as an argument although we stated $x_3 \rightarrow \max$ as a goal. Such a case can take place when, because of special structure of the problem, a goal variable (here x_3) consistently takes values that the decision-maker considers to be optimal relative to the values of the other variables.

Table 2 illustrates what can happen when the decision-maker is unable to express exactly the weights w_i^k corresponding to his preferences. The values of x^k in this table were obtained by stochastic simulation using the value $w_i^k = (1 + \varepsilon_i^k)(\partial U / \partial x_i^k) / (\partial U / \partial x_1^k)$ for w_i^k, with ε_i^k an equally distributed random variable on $[-0.10, +0.10]$ and $U(x) = 2x_1 + x_2 + x_4$ as before. In other words, we simulated a decision-maker who expresses the w_i^k's with an error factor up to 10% from their true values. The values presented in Table 2 are, of course, the result of one particular simulation; they are not, however, atypical. As can be seen, the introduction of uncertainty does not seriously impair the quality of the results.

Iteration k	x_1^k	x_2^k	x_3^k	x_4^k	Optimal step-size t^k	$U(x^k)$	s^k
1	1	1	1	3.667	.82	6.667	0
2	.854	.595	1.755	4.788	.38	7.091	.201
3	.877	.619	1.779	4.795	.54	7.168	.106
4	.872	.606	1.770	4.786	.92	7.136	.146
5	.881	.628	1.786	4.799	.19	7.189	.077
6	.890	.650	1.801	4.809	.47	7.239	.009
7	.883	.634	1.790	4.803	.77	7.203	.059
Optimal values	.875	.625	1.875	4.875		7.25	0

Table 2

Finally, Table 3 illustrates the importance of the choice of x^o by showing the working of the algorithm for U as above, but $x^o = (0, 0, 0, 0)$. The convergence becomes very slow after the 5th iteration, and the current solution is still quite distant from the optimal solution at the 10th iteration. In fact, over 30 iterations are needed in order for the current solution to agree up to two decimals with the optimal one.

Iteration k	x_1^k	x_2^k	x_3^k	x_4^k	Optimal step-size t^k	$U(x^k)$	s^k
0	0	0	0	0	.25	0	4
1	1	0	0	1	.48	3	3
2	.52	0	1.92	3.88	.12	4.92	1.56
3	.920	0	1.699	3.677	.26	5.417	1.381
4	.677	.529	1.250	4.248	.06	6.222	1.015
5	.871	.498	1.177	4.098	.16	6.338	1.056
6	.730	.418	1.633	4.602	.04	6.480	.901
7	.811	.501	1.843	4.461	.07	6.584	.394
8	.753	.524	1.645	4.602	.02	6.632	.545
9	.792	.463	1.772	4.616	.05	6.668	.500
10	.763	.484	1.670	4.697	.03	6.717	.594
Optimal values	.875	.625	1.875	4.875		7.25	0

Table 3

The choice of x^o is important for a second reason, which is independent of the formal working of the algorithm. It may be very difficult for the decision-maker to determine the weights w_i^k in a meaningful way if he considers the current point x^k a completely unreasonable solution. In this example, for instance, the question "What loss in x_i compensates exactly for a one-unit increase in x_1?" is bound to be considered by the decision-maker as meaningless when $x_1 = x_i = 0$.

III - COMPARATIVE EVALUATION OF THE METHODS

A - Experimental Results

Knowledge of the theoretical properties of the different man-machine procedures is insufficient for purposes of practical application or further development of the methods. It is at least as important to know how well they perform in actual situations. However, only a small number of experimental results have been published to date. (See, for example, Agarwal (1973), Dyer (1973b), Feinberg (1972), Geoffrion et al. (1972), Wallenius and Zionts (1975), Zionts (1967). They are all almost exclusively concerned with the interactive FRANK-WOLFE agorithm. Since the decision-making situation, the experimental framework and the interactive routing vary considerably from study to study, the partially contradictory findings are difficult to interpret in general terms.

Nevertheless, a most interesting experiment was conducted by Wallenius with the purpose of comparing from a decision-maker's point of view the relative performance of (a) an unstructured approach, (b) the STEM method and (c) the interactive FRANK-WOLFE algorithm. The ensuing results presented in Wallenius (1975) are summarized in the following sub-sections. [9)] The experiment itself, important for the interpretation of the results and interesting as an application example, is presented in some detail.

1. Decision problem. The framework for the decision-making situation consisted of a fictitious, but realistic, dynamic model of a company manufacturing a seasonal product. The model contained 19 linear constraints and 25 decision variables defining inventory balances, production capacity, labor and overtime for each of the seven periods of the planning horizon. Three conflicting goals related to production, inventory and work-force planning were to be taken into consideration.

1st goal: minimize cumulated cost due to regular payroll and overtime and cost of holding inventory over the seven periods of the planning horizon,

2nd goal: minimize average stockouts over the planning horizon;

3rd goal: minimize cumulated number of employees temporarily laid off over the planning horizon.

2. Methods. The unstructured method used was of the simplest kind. The decision-maker was instructed at each iteration to enter a vector of values for the goal variables into the computer. The only information provided by the computer program was whether or not the choice was feasible. The subjects did not receive information about the values of the non-goal variables corresponding to their choice.

The STEM method was applied according to the schema described above with the exception that the decision-maker was not shown the results of parametric variations of the goal variables (sensitivity analysis).

Within the interactive FRANK-WOLFE algorithm, the determination of the trade-offs was carried out with the help of DYER's indirect procedure.

3. Experimental design. Several pilot studies were made first to assure a satisfactory experimental design. The main experiment was then conducted with 18 undergraduate students of business administration and 18 top managers with formal training in engineering or business administration. All of the students, but only a few of the managers, had basic knowledge of mathematical programming.

The subjects were introduced one by one into the decision-making framework with the help of training sessions and a 9-page booklet describing the problem, the plant and its environment. Each subject was subsequently asked to play the role of plant manager. He was informed of the mechanical aspects of operating the terminal before being given instructions for using the first method. The instructions were accompanied by an introduction to the logic of the method to be tested and an example. The subjects were allowed to iterate as long as they wanted, except, of course, in the case of the STEM method. After they had finished, they were presented with instructions for the next method and the procedure was repeated. (The average length of the session was 2 hours and 40 minutes for the students and 3 hours for the managers.) The order in which the methods were presented was changed from subject to subject in order to compensate for eventual systematic learning effects. For the same reason, the parameters of the decision problem were changed in a random manner with each method. The feasible points found during the use of any one method were not feasible for any other method. Afterwards each subject was interviewed about the method and the experimental design. The responses were statistically tested.

4. Measures of performance. Seven measures of performance were used to evaluate the methods:

(a) Decision-maker's confidence in the solution obtained (ordinal ranking);
(b) Ease of use of the method (ordinal ranking);
(c) Ease of understanding the logic of the method on the basis of the instructions (ordinal ranking);
(d) Usefulness of information provided by the decision-maker (ordinal ranking);

(e) Rapidity of convergence, measured by the number of iterations and the total time for solving the problem;
(f) CPU-time on UNIVAC 1108;
(g) Distance of the solution from the efficient surface.

5. Results. Both managers and students considered the importance of the information obtained during the interactive procedure to be the factor playing the main role in their evaluation of the methods. This factor was followed closely by confidence in the solution obtained. In third and fourth place came the ease of use and understanding of the method, respectively. Decision-making time (time spent on the computer terminal and for preparation) was ranked last.

No statistically significant ranking of confidence in the results obtained could be determined for either group. This reflects the fact that the evaluation of the goodness of a solution in a fictitious setting, i. e. without recourse to past experience or to "intuition", is a very precarious task. An analysis of the subjects' answers leads, moreover, to the conclusion that their confidence in the results of the GEOFFRION method was weakened by the difficulties they experienced in determining the trade-off weights. On the other hand, they thought the STEM method left them too little freedom in their search for a desirable solution ("built-in" stopping criterion; impossibility of "undoing" a previous relaxation).

Both groups considered the GEOFFRION method the most difficult to use, followed by the STEM method. The main difficulty in the use of the GEOFFRION method lay in the determination of the trade-offs. The step-size problem was considered relatively easy to solve. In the case of the STEM method, the subjects had some difficulty in specifying a value for the relaxation $\Delta \bar{x}_i^k$. Finally, Wallenius came to the conclusion that with the help of the unstructured approach, it was relatively easy to find feasible solutions, but difficult to find good feasible solutions.

Managers and students varied in the way they judged ease of understanding. Both groups considered the GEOFFRION method more difficult to understand than the other approaches, but the managers more so. The students considered the unstructured approach easier to understand than the STEM method. The managers, however, considered both methods equally difficult.

Divergence between the two groups was also evident in their evaluation of the usefulness of the information provided. Both groups considered the unstructured approach the least informative. However, the managers ranked the GEOFFRION method below the STEM method in terms of information provided, whereas the students considered both methods equally informative.

The rapidity of convergence is shown in the following Table 4, which is for the most part self-explanatory.

	Students		Managers		Students and Managers		
	Iter-ations	Total time (min)	Iter-ations	Total time (min)	CPU-time pro problem (sec)	CPU-time pro iteration (sec)	CPU-time pro min. of total time(sec)
GEOFFRION Approach	3	31.5	3	38	4.6	1.53	0.13
STEM Method	4.5	14.5	4	13.5	5.8	1.39	0.42
Unstructured Approach	13.5	19.5	10	19.5	8.1	0.69	0.42

Table 4 - Median number of iterations, median total time (decision-making time + time for operating the terminal) and median CPU-time for solving the problem on a UNIVAC 1108 time-sharing system.

On the average, the distance of the solutions from the efficient surface was small in both the GEOFFRION and the unstructured approaches. (As stated earlier, the STEM method always leads to an efficient point.) However, single results showed large deviations from the efficient surface. It seems that the students were able to find slightly more efficient solutions than the managers.

Finally, managers and students were asked which method they preferred on the whole in terms of implementation willingness. The students' answers were randomly distributed. The managers considered the GEOFFRION and STEM methods the same but clearly preferred the unstructured method.

B - Conclusions

At first glance, Wallenius's findings may be interpreted as a clear rejection of sophisticated methods. Both the GEOFFRION and STEM methods performed less well than the unstructured approach in nearly every respect, with the exception of the information they provided.

Yet, a more thorough analysis shows that the validity of the rankings obtained by Wallenius is restricted to the particular experiment he conducted. On one hand, this experiment was characterized by a very simple structure of the feasible set and by a small number of goal variables (three). There is strong evidence, however, that, due to the unsystematic way in which the search is conducted, the efficiency of the unstructured method decreases rapidly with increasing complexity of the efficient set and, above all, with increasing number of variables. In particular, the number of iterations needed becomes unacceptably large. Therefore, 4 to 5 goal variables may be the upper limit for practical use of the unstructured approach.

In comparison, the experiments mentioned at the beginning of section IV, A, have shown that the STEM and GEOFFRION methods are practically applicable even with as many as 7 to 10 goal variables. Even in particularly complicated problems the number of iterations needed remains within reasonable limits. In the case of STEM it is seldom larger than twice the number of goals. With the GEOFFRION method, the number of iterations rarely exceeds ten, including "fine tuning" in the final iterations.

On the other hand, the relatively poor performance of the STEM and GEOFFRION methods in the Wallenius experiment is partly due to the fact that students and managers did not have enough training in the use of the methods. Success with these two methods crucially depends on the decision-maker's ability at correctly interpreting the information provided by the computer and at stating exactly the information input corresponding to his preferences. A priori, his ability will be insufficient because the information exchange is based on data that the decision-maker usually does not quantify. However, the quality of the information exchange can be greatly improved by practice.[10)]

The main contribution of Wallenius's study is that it highlights the weak points in the use of the STEM and GEOFFRION methods. In both cases, the critical factor is the man-machine collaboration - in the STEM method the determination of the relaxations, in the GEOFFRION method the determination of the trade-off weights. The logical direction for further research would, therefore, seem to be the attempt to improve this collaboration, both by adjusting the information exchange in order to more adequately correspond to the characteristics of a human decision-maker, and by devising training programs to improve the information processing by the decision-maker.

We note that the STEM and GEOFFRION methods are not applicable in the very important case of discrete decision problems. There is a need here for more powerful methods. In this context, an apparently promising research field could be the investigation of interactive branch and bound algorithms.

In summarizing, it can be said that the STEM and GEOFFRION methods

- are expensive methods in the sense that they place high demands on the decision-maker, both in terms of time and intellectual effort. Their programmation is also rather complicated;
- are restricted to continuous problems;
- permit a more efficient search of the "best solution" to complex problems. Their relative advantage as compared to the unstructured method increases rapidly with the complexity of the problem;
- provide the decision-maker with significantly more decision-relevant information than the unstructured method.

As for the GEOFFRION method, it offers important advantages as compared to the STEM method.

- It is not restricted to the linear programming framework;

- It is more efficient than the STEM method, both in terms of number of iterations and of quality of the solution, when the number of goal variables is large;
- It does not restrict the decision-maker in his search;
- It provides the decision-maker with more information than the STEM method;
- Generally, it is a more powerful and versatile decision-making tool.

However, it places many more demands on the decision-maker in terms of training required and of intellectual effort than STEM. In other words, no one method is superior to the others in all respects. In a practical situation, the choice of the method will depend both on technical factors (structure of the problem) and on the preferences and needs of the decision-maker relative to information, costs, etc. The above presentation should offer preliminary guide-lines for making such a choice.

FOOTNOTES

1) When a goal variable is supposed to be minimized, it is assumed to be transformed to maximization by an appropriate sign change. We use in the following the notation $x := (x_1, \ldots, x_n)$, $z^k := (z_1^k, \ldots, z_m^k)$, etc. A' (x') designates the transposition of the matrix A (the vector x).

2) See, for example, Baumol (1959), Johnsen (1968).

3) $\nabla z(z^k) := (\partial U/\partial z_1, \ldots, \partial U/\partial z_m)$, $z = z^k$ is the vector of partial derivatives $\partial U/\partial z_i$, $i = 1, \ldots, m$, evaluated at $z = z^k$. We use the notation $\partial U/\partial z_i^k = \partial U/\partial z_i$, $z_i = z_i^k$. $\nabla z(z^k)$ represents a local linear approximation for the "direction of greatest increase" of U at $z = z^k$. The main difference between the different large-step algorithms lies in the definition of the "best direction" y^k. As a rule, however, y^k will be derived from the solution of a standard LP formulated on the basis of both $\nabla_z U$ and (a linear approximation of) the constraints defining the feasible set D. (See, for example, Simmons (1975).)

4) The term "large-step method" expresses the fact that the improved point z^{k+1} is not restricted to a neighborhood of the current point z^k, but may lie at some distance from it.

5) The FRANK-WOLFE algorithm was used as the basis for most of the studies of GEOFFRION's approach. It is more specifically designed for problems in which the objective function U is concave on $\{z\}$. However, it converges even when U is not concave.

6) The problem $U\,[(1-t^k)\,z^k + t^k \bar{z}^k] \rightarrow$ max is formally equivalent to the problem $U\,[z^k + t_1^k\, y^k] \rightarrow$ max, z^{k+1} feasible, stated under "General Remarks".

7) This problem is atypical in so far as x is of a higher order than z.

8) Note that the w_i's are only marginally valid, i.e. express the preference of the decision-maker only with regard to a relatively small change from the current solution. In order to grasp the intuitive contents of this requirement, each z unit can be thought of in terms of thousands of physical units.

9) A new comparative study, Tell (1976), was not available in time to be considered in this paper.

10) In an experiment with 7 goals conducted by the author, graduate students needed for an example 6 to 7 hours practice with the GEOFFRION method before considering themselves able to correctly solve trade-off and step-size problems. In comparison, Wallenius's students had on the average less than 1 hour console time to familiarize themselves with GEOFFRION's method.

REFERENCES

AGARWAL, S.K. 1973: Optimizing techniques for the interactive design of transportation networks under multiple objectives, PhD Dissertation, Northwestern University, Evanston, Illinois 1973.

AUBIN, J.P.; NÄSLUND, B.: An Exterior Branching Algorithm. Working paper, European Institute for Advanced Studies in Management, Brussels, 1972.

BAUMOL, J. 1959: Business Behavior, Value and Growth, New York 1959.

BELENSON, S.; KAPUR, K. 1973: An Algorithm for Solving Multicriterion Linear Programming Problems with Examples, in: Operational Research Quarterly, Vol. 24, No. 1, p. 65 - 77.

BENAYOUN, R.; TERGNY, J. 1969: Critères multiples en programmation mathématique: une solution dans le cas linéaire. In: Revue Francaise d'Informatique et de Recherche Operationelle, 3, V-2, p. 31 - 56, 1969.

BLUM, E.; OETTLI, W. 1975: Mathematische Optimierung. Berlin/Heidelberg/New York: Springer 1975.

CHARNES, A.; COOPER, W. 1961: Management Models and Industrial Applications of Linear Programming. Vol. 1, New York: Wiley 1961.

CONTINI, B.; ZIONTS, S. 1968: Restricted Bargaining for Organizations with Multiple Objectives. In: Econometrica, 16, 1, p. 397 - 414, 1968.

DEISSENBERG, Ch. 1976: A general characterization on interactive methods for solving the multiple-criteria problem. To be published in: H.W. Gottinger: Decision Theory and Social Ethics, Reidel, Dordrecht 1977.

DIKIN, I.I. 1967: Iterative solutions to problems of linear and quadratic programming (in Russian). In: Dokl. Akad. Nauk SSSR 174, 1967.

DYER, J. 1972 : Interactive Goal Programming, in: Management Science, Vol. 19, No. 1, p. 397 - 414.

DYER, J. 1973a: A Time-Sharing Computer Program for the Solution of the Multiple Criteria Problem, in: Management Science, Vol. 19, No. 12

DYER, J. 1973b: An Empirical Investigation of a Man-Machine Interactive Approach to the Solution of the Multiple Criteria Problem. In: J. Cochrane and M. Zeleny (eds.): Multiple Criteria Decision-Making. Columbia, S.C.: University of South Carolina Press 1973.

DYER, J. 1974: The Effects of Errors in the Estimation of the Gradient on the Frank-Wolfe Algorithm with Implications for Interactive Programming. In: Operations Research, 22, 1. p. 160 - 174, 1974.

FEINBERG, A. 1972: An Experimental Investigation of an Interactive Approach for Multi-Criterion Optimization, with an Application to Academic Resource Allocation, Ph. D. Dissertation, University of California, Los Angeles 1972.

GEOFFRION, A,M. 1970: Vector Maximal Decomposition Programming. Paper presented at the seventh International Symposium on Mathematical Programming, The Hague, Holland, September 14 - 18, 1970.

GEOFFRION, A.M.; DYER, J.S.; FEINBERG, A. 1972: An Interactive Approach for Multi-Criterion Optimization, with an Application to the Operation of an Academic Department, in: Management Science, Vol. 19, No. 4, December, Part I, p. 357 - 368.

GEOFFRION, A. M.; HOGAN, W. W. 1972: Coordination of Two-Level Organizations with Multiple Objectives, in: A. V. Balakrishnan (ed.), Proceedings of the Fourth IFIP Colloquium on Optimization Techniques, New York, Academic Press 1972.

JOHNSEN, E. 1968: Studies in Multiobjective Decision Models, Lund 1968.

ROY, B. 1971: Problems and Methods with Multiple Objective Functions. In: Mathematical Programming 1, 239 - 266.

SASKA, S. 1968: Linear multiprogramming. In: Economike Matematiky Obzor 4, p. 359 - 373, 1968.

SIMMONS, D. M. 1975: Nonlinear Programming for Operations Research Englewood Cliffs, N. J.: Prentice Hall 1975.

TELL, B. 1976: A Comparative Study of Some Multiple-Criteria Methods, Lund 1976.

WALLENIUS, J.; ZIONTS, St. 1975: Some Tests of an Interactive Programming Method for Multicriterion Optimization and an Attempt at Implementation. In: European Institute for Advanced Studies in Management. Working Paper 75-3, Brussels.

WALLENIUS, J. 1975: Comparative Evaluation of Some Interactive Approaches to Multicriterion Optimization. In: Management Science Vol. 21, No. 12.

WOLFE, P. 1970: Convergence Theory in Nonlinear Programming. In: J. Abadie, Integer and Nonlinear Programming, New York: Elsevier 1970.

ZIONTS, S. 1967: A bargaining model for allocating steel production. In: CORSI Bulletin, p. 69 - 78, 1967.

INDEX

AFFILIATIONS OF AUTHORS

Patrick Bond, Political Science Department, Case Western Reserve University, Cleveland, Ohio, U.S.A.

Hartmut Bossel, Institut für Systemtechnik und Innovationsforschung (ISI), Fraunhofer Gesellschaft, Karlsruhe, F. R. Germany.

Christophe Deissenberg, FB Wirtschaftswissenschaften und Statistik, Universität, Konstanz, F. R. Germany.

Edelgard Gruber, Institut für Systemtechnik und Innovationsforschung (ISI), Fraunhofer Gesellschaft, Karlsruhe, F. R. Germany.

Pieter van der Hijden, Social Science Research Group, Department of Psychology, University, Nijmegen, The Netherlands.

Walter Hudetz, Institut für Systemtechnik und Innovationsforschung (ISI), Fraunhofer Gesellschaft, Karlsruhe, F.R. Germany.

Karl-Friedrich Müller-Reissmann, Institut für Systemtechnik und Innovationsforschung, Fraunhofer Gesellschaft, Karlsruhe, F.R. Germany.

Eduard Pestel, Deutsche Forschungsgemeinschaft (DFG), Bonn, und Institut für Mechanik, Technische Universität, Hannover, F.R. Germany.

Francois Rechenmann, Ecole Nationale Supérieure d'Informatique et de Mathématiques Appliquées, Grenoble, France, and European Nuclear Research Center, Ispra, Italy.

Hermann Schwember, Industrial Sociology Unit, Imperial College of Science and Technology, London, U.K.

Karl-Heinz Simon, FB Philosophie, Universität, Erlangen-Nürnberg, F. R. Germany.

Michael G. Strobel, Psychology Department, Université de Montréal, Montreal, Canada.